SECRETS OF
THE SECRET
SERVICE

Also by Gary J. Byrne

CRISIS OF CHARACTER: A White House Secret Service Officer Discloses His Firsthand Experience with Hillary, Bill, and How They Operate

SECRETS OF THE SECRET SERVICE

The History and Uncertain Future of the US Secret Service

GARY J. BYRNE
with GRANT M. SCHMIDT

CENTER
STREET®

NEW YORK   NASHVILLE

Center Street
Hachette Book Group
1290 Avenue of the Americas, New York, NY 10104
centerstreet.com
twitter.com/centerstreet

First Edition: January 2018

Center Street is a division of Hachette Book Group, Inc. The Center Street name and logo are trademarks of Hachette Book Group, Inc.

The publisher is not responsible for websites (or their content) that are not owned by the publisher.

The Hachette Speakers Bureau provides a wide range of authors for speaking events. To find out more, go to www.HachetteSpeakersBureau.com or call (866) 376-6591.

Print book interior design by Timothy J. Shaner, NightandDayDesign.biz

Library of Congress Cataloging-in-Publication Data has been applied for.

ISBNs: 978-1-5460-8247-7 (hardcover), 978-1-5460-8248-4 (ebook)

Printed in the United States of America

LSC-H

10 9 8 7 6 5 4 3 2 1

CONTENTS

This book was written with pride, albeit with a heavy heart. It is my hope that through this book, things can be made right, but, as Albert Einstein said, "We cannot solve our problems with the same thinking we used when we created them."

DEDICATION.

A former colleague in the Federal Air Marshal Service, in his memoir, *Unsecure Skies*, made mention of the "Secret Service mentality" toward its workforce, which he learned was "Ride the horse until it dies, then eat it and get a new horse." That quote was made famous through the Service after one rightfully disgruntled agent sent a fax citing it to every Secret Service fax machine across the nation. As it still rings true today, this book is dedicated to all the unsung workhorses who have carried this nation and especially to those who made the ultimate sacrifice.

TO GENNY . . .

For reminding me that my service to the country was not the end but the means—the means to serve what's most important: "God, family, country"—and that you can't succeed in serving one without the others.

TO ELIZABETH AND ETHAN . . .

"If you're doing something and you have to look over your shoulder, you probably shouldn't be doing it." Your grandfather told me this often. My whole life, I've heard his voice over my shoulder. It's a constant reminder that has always kept me on the right path leading me to what's most important, the path that leads me back home to you.

INTRODUCTION.

DISTRUST AND NO CONFIDENCE

Worthy of Trust and Confidence
—Official motto, US Secret Service

Every Secret Service story begins with "All seemed quiet." The events of March 4, 2015, were no different, except that three years later the *Washington Post* found out about what had transpired. Then came the ensuing cover-up and media storm.

All did seem quiet at 10:25 p.m. for the Uniformed Division officers standing their posts outside the White House. No matter how many years they had on the job, it still took a bit of discipline not to turn and breathe in the incredible sight of the White House, all lit up at night. The air was breezy and cool. And although every Secret Service story begins the same way, the Uniformed Division's unofficial motto always rang true: "There's always something going on at the White House."

Life as a Secret Service Uniformed Division officer would have been a dream job if not for the nightmare the Secret Service bureaucrats had made it. The trouble was staying awake and alert and not having a complete mental breakdown, heart attack, or really ugly divorce. There were officers who couldn't avoid all three happening at once, and then there were the suicides. Seven days of twelve-hour shifts, plus management threatening punishment for taking scheduled days off, can have that impact. But some Secret Service officers made hundreds of thousands of dollars in overtime. Though management seemed to be in denial about the new practice, the plan of so many new recruits was to survive, serve, make a mountain of cash, and then quit after just two or five years of service. Their spouses had to agree to the plan, and they were immune to the immensely powerful lure that had enthralled the old-timers who had stayed on. This, after all, was the White House, the most recognizable building around the globe, and it was there that its most powerful leaders shaped the world.

This Uniformed Division officer manning one of the security gates around the White House, scanned, watched, and waited. As an owl snaps to at the sight of its prey, he saw a woman park her sedan in the no-parking zone, as dozens of lost tourists did each day. Enforcing the no-parking zone usually meant giving directions, but the zone was still an integral puzzle piece in detecting attacks launched at the White House.

She leapt out of the car.

"Ma'am, you can't park here," the officer called out.

"I have something for you," she said, full of anger.

That, too, wasn't unusual. People often naively tried to deliver letters or gifts to the White House.

"I have something for you. It's a book," she said, excited.

"Ma'am, we can't take packages. We can't—we can't do this. You have to mail it." That's when she said the magic words.

"Actually, it's a fucking bomb!" she yelled.

That's when all the routineness left. This wasn't a normal night; it was one of *those* nights.

"Back up! Back up!" the officer yelled at her, clutching his firearm as she dropped the package onto the sidewalk, jumped back into her car, and sped off. The officer radioed in her vehicle description. He couldn't make out the license plate, as his brain was flooded with training videos that demonstrated the explosive power a book-sized bomb could have.

Meanwhile, across town, two hotshot Secret Service agents, types who had "been there and seen it all," had been out celebrating the retirement of a colleague. They figured it was about time to leave the party.

The two men prided themselves on being "the elite of the elite." The most powerful office of the world, held at the time by President Barack Obama, was protected by them—and that made them the "the best of the best."

They had protected President Obama, George W. Bush, and Bill Clinton. Vast amounts of trust were placed in their hands. And tonight they were drunk in their take-home government car, heading home from a retirement party.

Life in the Secret Service was good. Well, not for everyone. It was good only for the old boys' club, the high-up agents, the "made men" of the Secret Service, like those two. One was from the Presidential Protection Division (PPD), and the president's life rested in his hands each and every day. The other was the head of the Secret Service Washington Field Office. Men like them set the tone and culture of much of the Secret Service.

The Secret Service couldn't pay them any more due to congressional pay restrictions, but the agency found ways to up the ante and keep the agents' whistles wet, such as take-home cars and prestige. The prestige was the best.

The prestige led them, despite being drunk in a government vehicle, to approach the White House as though they owned the place. But they could tell that something was off. It was quiet; too quiet. They cursed their fellow Secret Service men, the Uniformed Division officers. They thought to themselves that they must have abdicated their post. The entry gate was wide open. There were police tape and vehicle barricades set up.

Where the hell were the Uniformed Division officers?

No matter, they thought, and they pushed slowly through the barricades, picking up a bit of speed. That's when Uniformed Division officers sprinted to them yelling something but the agents didn't care. Near them was a Secret Service bomb tech all suited up, dressed like something out of *The Hurt Locker.*

Someone yelled, "You're next to a bomb!"

The agents stumbled out drunk and immediately doubled down berating the officers. Meanwhile, the bomb was still considered active. But calling out those top agents, even to keep them safe, came at a price. That's when the intimidation and cover-up began. The agents demanded that the officers on the scene not breathalyze them and that they keep the incident quiet. It almost worked—but the director caught wind of it from an internal agency message board five days later.

Despite the multiple Secret Service and Department of Homeland Security investigations, the congressional investigations, and more, the two agents, months later, were able to retire with full benefits—not so much as a parking ticket. Some would try to minimize the incident as anecdotal, that they were just two knuckleheads—but those "knuckleheads" were two of the highest-ranking members of the Secret Service. The example they set filtered downward. And soon after, as word spread far and wide throughout the ranks of the Secret Service, all of the new recruits learned what the old-timers knew: nothing in the Secret Service changes, and you never cross the made men of the Secret Service. The officers who had run up to the agents' car had found that out the hard way—even if they had been trying to save their lives. The Department of Homeland Security and congressional investigations outed a culture that makes the lives of whistle-blowers miserable, shields those who lie to investigators and Congress, and carries on protecting the president as if this were normal behavior.

None of that mattered at the top ranks of the Secret Service, because nothing ever happened to them. They were elite, after all, and the prestige kept them safe.

Strong-arming, intimidation, and covering up from the top down—those were not unusual procedures for the Secret Service. What was unusual was that the American public would eventually find out about the incident and the congressional investigation that followed and failed to instill change. But there have been many such incidents of incompetence followed by cover-ups in the Secret Service, and this goes back decades—more than a century, to the very beginnings of presidential protection in the United States. The patterns keep repeating, and the lessons have not been learned. If we don't break this cycle soon, tragedy is going to strike once again.

This is a book that can save the president's life.

For more than 116 years the brave and loyal men and women of the United States Secret Service (USSS) have put their lives on the line, day in and day out, to protect our nation's leaders. Some of their missions are well known—the officer who gave his life and took his final shot to protect President Harry Truman when two armed gunmen sought to murder him outside the White House in 1950; the agent who jumped into the line of fire when another assassin very nearly took the life of President Ronald Reagan in 1981.

But today we must accept a difficult truth: the Secret Service isn't failing—it has failed. That's not hyperbolic or alarmist. The frontline men and women of the modern Secret Service not only face threats that multiply by the day, but they have to deal with vindictive mismanagement, political correctness, and a deep-seeded old boys' network that is more interested in empire building than protecting our presidents. In a downward spiral that has lasted decades, the inner leadership circle refuses to see the relationship between the wellness of the agency's employees and the service's mission performance. Behind the agency's "tacti-cool" veneer, it has come to represent everything wrong with big government. Fortunately, the cure for the Secret Service might just be the cure for what has plagued our far out of control, underperforming, over-budget government.

Right now the security of our presidents is a matter of alignment: the failed Secret Service is hoping that its glaring gaps won't align with the plans of an opportunistic assassin who is willing to take the chance of his or her own success and the agency's failure—which is exactly what occurred before each assassination of past US presidents. With each Secret Service scandal that goes unpunished and unsolved, it is clear that the gaps are getting worse. The Secret Service's malfeasance is encouraging more attacks because attackers see increasing chances for success.

The best predictor of future behavior is past behavior, and the Secret Service is repeating a tired and destructive pattern.

President Donald Trump will be lucky to survive his presidency, just as it was only luck and coincidence that so often saved President Obama's life. Many of those incidents and the state of the agency were kept secret from President Obama, and they are surely being kept from President Trump.

Should President Trump survive under the Secret Service's plan of theatrics, hope, and chance, the next president will be at risk. This will continue until we change, either by choice or by catastrophe. Up until now it's been difficult for the public to imagine, but the president, Congress, and the public need to know what has happened and what is to come.

This book will share the secrets of the Secret Service with the American people—untold stories of remarkable heroism and shocking misconduct. It will provide an inside view into Secret Service exploits, some well known and some swept under the rug. But it also describes the agency's leadership style, culture, and strategic thinking that have lead to the scandals and failure of today. Many of these secrets have even been kept from the Secret Service—until now.

As much as I wish I could, there is not enough room in this

book to address in depth the war on counterfeiting, the agency's founding mission, and the other areas the Secret Service
has expanded into. The general public knows little about how
the Secret Service is involved in many areas, but the results are
consistent: it is failing. The Secret Service is responsible for
and is failing at combating the state-sponsored efforts of Iran
and North Korea and criminal enterprises in countries such as
Nigeria that victimize individual Americans and our economy,
while also bankrolling our enemies in the War on Terror. It cannot operate in Iran or North Korea and has not found any creative ways to stem the tide of their counterfeiting. In Nigeria,
the government the USSS is supposed to be helping fight counterfeiters and other criminals was found to be complicit in some
of the crimes. Still, the Secret Service is so stagnant that it cannot figure out new and innovative ways to fulfill those missions.

Even more newly developed Secret Service missions are
already failing. Most of them stemmed from large power grabs
in the 1990s and after the attacks of September 11, 2001, in a desperate attempt to compete against the FBI. Though it may seem
difficult to believe, one serious abdication is school shootings.
The agency has long argued that the dual missions of executive
protection and fighting counterfeiting aid each other. Unfortunately, it is failing across the board as it prioritizes presidential
protection—and still comes up far short.

Let's be clear: many of the agents and officers who surround
and protect President Trump are the most loyal and dedicated
men and women ever to serve their country. For me, it was the
biggest honor to serve for twelve years as a Secret Service officer and be shoulder to shoulder with those patriots. Every day,

the Secret Service seeks to fulfill its core mission to protect the president.

But the "secret" side of the Secret Service, the internal culture that the public doesn't see, has been rotting from the inside out and is working against the dedicated patriots who want only to see the mission succeed. That internal rot has prioritized the agency's "brand" over our president. As a former insider, I feel compelled by my oath to let the public know; it is vital that they be informed. Failure in presidential protection significantly impacts us all.

Unlike any DC or New York pundit giving you a trickle-down version rife with outsider commentary, in this book you will read about the true past, present, and future of the Secret Service, directly from frontline sources. I detail how real security works, how it fails, and how politicized corruption has infected every mission of the agency.

In *Crisis of Character*, I told the story of what it was like to be one of the first Secret Service employees to be subjected to and subpoenaed in a criminal investigation of a sitting president. It was miserable to live through and at first to write about. When I regained my First Amendment rights after retiring from federal law enforcement, I wrote my story. With each chapter written, I felt as though an enormous weight had been lifted off me. Keeping silent was a far greater burden on my soul than I had ever realized. When Hillary Clinton's campaign surrogates and smear machine failed in their attempts to blackball me, I was comforted. When they chose their brand over their truth, they fell into the trap of two simple lessons: history never ceases to be relevant, and secrets are like ticking time bombs.

But the Secret Service's problems didn't begin with the Clintons and surely didn't end with them either. Of the twenty-five presidents protected by the Secret Service, the problems involved in protecting Bill Clinton were not unique. Each officer and agent charged with protecting our president, and the agency's leaders up to the highest level, know the Secret Service motto: "Worthy of Trust and Confidence." But they must also ask themselves, of whom are they "worthy of trust and confidence"? During the Clinton years, the agency's inner circle landed on a shocking answer: to itself. From then on, the agency has been turned against itself.

Like so many of those who joined the Secret Service, I joined because I wanted to see the Secret Service win—and winning meant enabling the president to live and lead without fear. Keeping the president safe keeps the country together. Can you imagine the grief, the anger, and the fallout if any future president—or any member of the first family or a foreign dignitary—were assassinated?

It seems impossible, even unthinkable, but four US presidents have been murdered. Four presidential candidates have been shot: two killed, one paralyzed. Especially in recent years, there have been far too many "near misses" in which the deciding factor between a living protectee and another assassination was luck. Since 1951, when the Secret Service was officially tasked with permanent presidential protection, the agency has had a 91.7 percent success rate, but it drops down to less than 66.7 percent when also considering the nearly catastrophic failures on the attempts of Presidents Gerald Ford, Ronald Reagan, and George W. Bush in which the deciding factor was largely luck. That's unacceptable.

After each near miss, the Secret Service puts on a "shake-up," a big show in which it promises the nation that it really is the "elite" protection force it claims to be. "You can trust us," its spokespeople say. "The president is safe in our hands."

But can we believe it? Through all the failures, can we trust it this time?

The Secret Service will say whatever it needs to to achieve its goals—but so will I. Answer the question yourself: If the Secret Service were focused on its main priority, would it have allowed so many serious breaches in just the last few years?

In 2011, a man fired several shots from a rifle at the White House, but responding officers were told to "stand down" and that their eyes and ears had deceived them; the shooter even initially got away.

In 2012, more than a dozen agents and their management planned to use President Obama's trip to Colombia to party and hire prostitutes. They went ahead with their plan and nearly got arrested for refusing to pay the prostitutes—and in the investigation that followed, the director even misled and deceived Congress.

In 2014, advance agents screened everyone at the Centers for Disease Control and Prevention ahead of a visit by President Obama—everyone, that is, except the private armed security guards. A guard with a criminal history managed to get onto an elevator with the president—he simply walked past all of the Secret Service's security. He caught the Secret Service's attention only when he started snapping pictures inches away from the president's face. Afterward, the director misled, deceived, and failed to inform Congress and the president, who had to find out about the breach from the news media. Once again, the only thing that protected the president that day was hope and that the unscreened man, *who was armed with a handgun*, wanted merely to snap a picture and not to shoot the president. If he had wanted to shoot Obama, the Secret Service would have been responsible.

Then there's the 2015 incident in which two intoxicated agents—one of whom was part of the president's protective detail—drove drunk in a government car into an active bomb investigation at the White House. The agents intimidated those on duty to not breathalyze or arrest them, to falsify reports, and even to withhold the incident from the director, who found out about the incident through an internal message board five days later. But the cover-up afterward really took the cake!

We are led to believe that each incident is isolated and not indicative of the rest of the Secret Service. We can judge the US Secret Service only by the standards it sets for itself. Each recent director has testified, "We are only as strong as our weakest link," and "The bad guys only have to be right once, while we have to be right one hundred percent of the time." Then there's the official motto, emblazoned on the back of every Secret Service commission book: "Worthy of Trust and Confidence."

So what's the truth? Is the Secret Service elite? Is its primary enemy an assassin, or is it transparency and change?

The 2016 "Best Places to Work In the Federal Government" report, which was created by the Partnership for Public Service on the basis of employee responses, named the Secret Service as the worst place to work. Out of 305 federal agencies, the Secret Service came in dead last. Even Transportation Security Administration (TSA) employees had better morale and more confidence in their agency than Secret Service employees did.

Just to give you an idea of how bad morale is and how the old adage "The beating will continue until morale improves" plays out within the Secret Service, after the 2016 "Best Places to Work in the Federal Government" rankings came out, an officer bought a cake and took it into the break room for the other Uniformed Division officers to share. The icing said, "Congrats on making 305 out of 305." The officer who had bought the cake was given two days off, unpaid, as punishment for insubordination. Compare that to the two high-ranking agents who received no punishment after driving drunk, armed, in a government car into an active bomb investigation at the White House, intimidated officers to falsify reports, and more.

The rankings were based on employees' responses to three simple prompts: "I recommend my organization as a good place to work"; "Considering everything, how satisfied are you with your job?"; and "Considering everything, how satisfied are you with your organization?"

The 305 participating agencies averaged 59.4 points out of 100, but the Secret Service scored a mere 32.8. The numbers have been going down since 2011. This is especially incredible considering that the most downtrodden agents, officers, and technicians continue to leave in droves, which means that each year the most disgruntled are no longer participating in the surveys. The House Oversight Committee has called this an "exodus." How long can it go on?

Meanwhile, the agency seems to have as a good a handle on its finances as it does on its employees. In 2017, the director of the Secret Service surprised Congress by reporting that he was out of money and hadn't seen it coming—as the agency has done numerous times in the past. The current director, Randolph

Alles, told the press, "The Secret Service estimates that roughly 1,100 employees will work overtime hours in excess of statutory pay caps during calendar year 2017. To remedy this ongoing and serious problem, the agency has worked closely with the Department of Homeland Security, the Administration, and the Congress over the past several months to find a legislative solution."

Is it a legislative solution that's needed, or maybe one brought about by changing the agency's internal culture?

The legislative branch has certainly expressed its concern about the direction the Secret Service is going in. The 2015 bipartisan House of Representatives Committee on Oversight and Government Reform report entitled "United States Secret Service: An Agency in Crisis" said this about the agency's ballooning $2.8 billion budget: "One of the major problems with USSS's current budget system is that there *is* no system. . . . In fact, the Panel [in meetings with the director] could not even determine who at USSS should be responsible for answering budgetary questions." In other words, the agency in charge of fighting counterfeiters, which has made history by "following the money," has no clue how it spends its own? So is the problem "legislative," purely in the hands of Congress not to be stingy, or is the problem the Secret Service leadership ?

A panel of independent experts organized by the Department of Homeland Security had something to say about that. The United States Secret Service Protective Mission Panel (USSS-PMP) released its findings in 2014. They wrote, "Of the many concerns the Panel encountered, the question of leadership is, in our view, the most important. The Panel found an organization starved for leadership that rewards innovation and excellence and demands accountability. . . . We heard a common desire: More resources would help, but what we really need is leadership."

According to that same report, "The Panel found that, due in large part to limitations on personnel, the Service's training regimen has diminished far below acceptable levels. The Presidential Protective Division's (PPD) so-called 'Fourth Shift' had once ensured that for two weeks out of every eight, the President's detail was maintaining its strength, practicing, and getting better. But Secret Service reports show that in FY 2013, apart from firearms re-qualifications and basic career development technical requirements, the average special agent received only forty-two hours of training."

That's an abysmal forty-two hours of training a year for the people who protect the president of the United States! The supposedly "elite" Secret Service agents who protect the most powerful man in the world train for less than three leisurely weekends. The report went on to note that "In FY 2013, Service data shows that the [Secret Service] Uniformed Division *as a whole* received 576 hours of training, or about 25 minutes for each of over 1,300 Uniformed Division officers."

This means that a private citizen in Washington, DC, who has a concealed-carry handgun permit has more annual firearms training than a Secret Service officer or PPD agent. By law, to receive a concealed-carry handgun permit and requalify every two years, a private citizen must prove that he or she has received at least sixteen hours of firearms training, including two hours of range time. It should frighten every American that a concealed-carry permit holder in our nation's capital has more annual firearms training than the average officer or PPD agent employed by the Secret Service!

The culture has deteriorated so much that agents' reports, such as requalifications and performance evaluations for physical training and tactical proficiency with a firearm, are "self-reported." As one agent reported to Ronald Kessler, "Standards are so lax that agents are actually handed blank evaluations for possible promotions and fitness ratings and asked to fill them in themselves!" During my time in the Secret Service as a firearms instructor, I saw this firsthand. Today the practice is far more rampant.

That's not all that's swept aside by "self-reporting." According to the 2015 House Oversight Committee report, "USSS senior supervisors believed fellow senior supervisors would self-report their own misconduct," and therefore various types of 'misconduct' such as drinking, hiring prostitutes, and driving a government car drunk over an active bomb investigation at the White House, were not reported because other supervisors expected that the criminal behavior would be 'self-reported.'"

What happens if an upstanding agent or officer has finally had enough and decides such incidents shouldn't be swept under the rug? The same report found that "USSS utilized non-disclosure agreements [for its employees] that do not comply with whistle-blower protections." In layman's terms, this means that the Secret Service coerced its employees to sign nondisclosure agreements that were against the law in an effort to shield the agency from bad PR and transparency even to Congress! According to a Department of Homeland Security report, less than half of employees felt they could report to Congress without unlawful retaliation from the agency.

So the answer is clear: the Secret Service cares more about protecting itself from transparency and change than about stopping assassins.

That's why I felt a moral obligation to "speak out of school," as the Secret Service calls it. Between interviewing officers and agents outside the White House, I stood on Pennsylvania Avenue observing my former colleagues. It was just as I remembered, only worse, just as so many other agents and officers told me. This has to stop.

What does this all add up to? As the House committee report put it: "The UDLC [Uniformed Division Labor Committee] leadership described a workforce on the verge of collapsing due to understaffing and pending attrition."

"Collapsing" was its word, not mine.

The panel of independent experts stated clearly that mismanagement and poor leadership were to blame—not the budget or pay caps.

But let's dig deeper to the roots of how and why the Secret Service is failing.

The House committee report continued, "[The Labor Committee] cited the exhaustive nature of the job, constant overtime, and lack of respect from Presidential Protective Division leadership as a major factor in UD attrition. . . . Approximately 1,100 of 1,300 UD officers were eligible for retirement, and USSS personnel estimated over 1,000 officers accepted the offer." Instead of fixing the systemic problems causing this exodus, the Secret Service leadership made it far worse by forcing agents away from counterfeiting and financial fraud investigations around the world and the country to fill the gaps in the

White House's protection, for which they lacked training and understanding. As a result, the agents' morale plummeted and their performance tanked.

The committee wrote, "As with the UD, many factors may contribute to high attrition and low morale among special agents," noting that "At the end of fiscal year 2015, USSS was [net] down 285 special agents from 2011 levels."

The agents and officers of the Secret Service are at their breaking point. It is not sustainable to work Uniformed Division (UD) officers at the White House twelve hours a day, six to seven days a week. Though the agents have pay caps, the Secret Service had to get rid of the pay cap on officers' wages more than a decade ago.

Right now, there are officers standing post around the White House who have a base pay of about $70,000 per year, who are working so much overtime, both voluntary and involuntary, that they are making more than the director of the Secret Service and even more than the director of the Department of Homeland Security. Some accrue near a quarter of a million dollars each year.

But money doesn't matter when they hardly ever see their families. They're exhausted and at the point of snapping. Many plan to make insane salaries for a few years, then quit. This is not a sustainable practice for any workforce. The service's workforce is aging rapidly. An experience vacuum is approaching. But soon, as new recruits quit and old-timers retire, the agency will collapse.

The president needs to be protected by agents and officers who are well rested, well trained, and supported by their leadership. We need an agency management and culture that value individual rest, good mental health, training, morale, and family. Instead, the divorce rate is the highest of any agency. Suicide, dangerous sexual behavior, drug and alcohol use, and other reckless behaviors are serious problems at rates far higher than in any other federal law enforcement agency. Agents are having sordid affairs with presidential staffers; directors are lying to Congress and our presidents; DUIs are rampant; there is a reason the Secret Service doesn't track or make public its statistics on suicides, depression, or dangerous sexual habits among its employees. One officer serially clubbed squirrels to death just to stay awake on the White House lawn, and agents have exchanged gunfire among themselves in anger.

After two moles brought the FBI to its knees, the agency began polygraphing its agents five times a year to prevent another lethal traitor within its own ranks. But the Secret Service wouldn't dare to implement such measures, because corruption, coercion, incompetence, and waste can be found at all levels.

These are not the actions of well-cared-for employees, and the agency's current environment is dangerous to everyone.

So my service isn't really over, not when the state of the Secret Service is worse than ever—worse even the day we last lost a president, November 22, 1963. Our current president is not safe.

This book digs deeper and answers two questions: How the hell did things spiral so hard and so far out of control? And how can we save our current and future presidents from the Secret Service's impending systematic collapse?

This book is not meant to critique the men and women "in the arena," who, despite everything, are standing post and putting their lives on the line as best they can. I, too, was once in that arena, and through this book I still am. My hope is that this book can spur the change that will save them. If our president and the frontline men and women of the Secret Service weren't at high risk due to the Secret Service's systemic failings and ignored history, I wouldn't have written this book.

This is still my fight. The good men and women of the US Secret Service, long undermined, deserve to have their stories told; they deserve to win; and they deserve to work for an agency that won't abuse them, lie to them, and sacrifice them at the altar of indulgence, corpulent ineffective government, or brand management.

The Secret Service needs to start winning again. If we start the fight to drain the "Secret Service swamp" now, we still have a chance to make that happen.

ONE.

CLINTON CHARACTERS

It should come as no surprise that President William Jefferson Clinton and First Lady Hillary Rodham Clinton's time in the White House had a pivotal and irreversibly negative impact on the Secret Service. This has nothing to do with their politics. It's an obvious fact.

If a frog is dropped into boiling water, it will jump out and avoid being cooked. But if it is dropped into placid waters that are then slowly brought to a boil, it will remain unsuspecting and meet a horrific end. This metaphor applies to the Secret Service as it arrogantly readied for major external threats throughout the Clinton era but never for the internal threats a protectee would and did present. It simply was not prepared for the kind of president who would crash it headlong into one of the most divisive moments in American political history.

Though it was the initial investigation into bribery, sexual assaults, and subsequent obstruction that got Clinton into hot water, it was his continued dogged obstruction, lying under oath, and asking other federal employees to lie for him (one being a mistress he lied about being "alone in the same room with") that led to impeachment proceedings and the unfortunate involvement of the Secret Service.

Even before the investigation that led to his impeachment, the Clinton presidency would turn the Secret Service inside out in a number of ways. The Clintons' media relations demands, as well as their demands for professional and personal conveniences, suddenly took priority over standard event and transportation security procedures. The executive branch was flooded with a cult of staffers who were less than trustworthy or even criminal. The Secret Service was forced to be more "user friendly" in every aspect of its mission by turning a blind eye to criminality and double standards in law enforcement. This eventually pitted it against the president and the Department of Justice. Meanwhile, the long-standing divide between the Uniformed Division and the Special Agent Division grew worse and untenable.

The problems began even before President Clinton took office. As the Secret Service replaced the Arkansas State Police detail that had protected the Arkansas governor's mansion, the Clintons anticipated that the Secret Service personnel would operate very much like their state troopers. The small, almost unnoticeable state trooper presence was a badge of honor for the affluent neighborhood in Little Rock. But serenity left when the Secret Service arrived.

Newly installed floodlights flooded the governor's mansion at night. Large black Secret Service cars came and went night and day, blocking the streets. Doors slammed. Hard-looking uniformed and nonuniformed men and women patrolled at all hours. The agents and officers posted on the street talked and laughed to stay awake and alert. The upscale neighbors were spooked by the agent's scary looks and the officers uniformed presence.

The Secret Service personnel were just as surprised. Many Clinton friends and acquaintances seemed accustomed to waltzing up to the governor's mansion at all hours and expected hospitality at their own convenience, even when the candidate and his family were away. They were appalled to be questioned and by the fact that everyone, even staff, was required to pass through Uniformed Division magnetometers and have their bags searched, despite the countermeasures being the answer to the assassination attempt on President Reagan. The Secret Service had no exceptions. The arrogant staffers and self-styled VIPs complained to the Clintons, and the Secret Service soon found itself having to defend its policies at every turn.

At first this was chalked up to the normal adjustment period. But the problems quickly followed the Clintons from the Arkansas governor's mansion to the White House. In the past, presidents would learn to work with their protectors, even if it took a near miss to convince them. But the Clinton team was especially stubborn, and the Secret Service decided to be soft with no contingencies in case the protectee pushed things too far. Previous campaigns had, of course, made their candidates into celebrities. But Hollywood producers Linda Bloodworth-Thomason and her husband, Harry Thomason, and political strategists George Stephanopoulos, Rahm Emanuel, Paul Begala, and James Carville, along with Democratic Party National Committee leaders and Hillary Clinton, rewrote the script. In 1991, they created not just an effective candidate but a pop culture icon and highly marketable brand rivaling President John F. Kennedy's but supercharged by 1990s communications. The Clinton brand was effectively deployed and depended on the idea that here was someone the public could really relate to, who played the saxophone, and who could, as he liked to point out enthusiastically, "Make America great again." And many people believed him. That was because they *liked* him. He was cool.

The Secret Service was used to doing things a certain way, because if done correctly, it worked. The agency believed its tried-and-tested strategy based on case studies and emerging intelligence would fit every protectee. It was a one-size-fits-all approach that needed little tailoring. Yet for the first time since President Jimmy Carter, here was a candidate and an operation that warranted much greater resources than candidates before him. The Clintons regularly coordinated massive events that rivaled celebrity music concerts. The Secret Service had failed to plan for this eventuality and repeatedly turned to Congress, President George H. W. Bush, and anyone else they could for supplements to its budget, but the demands on the agency only increased with the candidate's rise in "political currency." Because of its limited resources, instead of preempting issues before they occurred, the Secret Service had to rely on threats being immediate and urgent before it could even attempt serious change.

One urgent problem emerged early in the 1992 campaign when a deputy sheriff entered a Clinton event with a concealed handgun. He was a Clinton supporter and posed no threat, but when he informed the detail that he had not been screened, the

Secret Service gained the "political capital" it needed to act. Additional Uniformed Division teams were deployed with magnetometers to screen the increasingly massive crowds at Clinton events within hours. Despite the attempts on the lives of Presidents Ford and Reagan, the service had not yet applied those hard-learned lessons. Instead of diligent, advanced strategic planning, it was playing catch-up, and its overworked agents and officers answered each call for more: more work hours, more security details, more gear, and greater sacrifices from its employees. But the gaps in its strategy and the culture that was willing to overlook those gaps remained.

As Clinton fandom ballooned, events were scheduled at an increasing pace, and the Secret Service had to manage its finite resources in an ever-changing campaign schedule. The campaign's always low estimates of attendees were frequently wildly off. The Clinton campaign continually wanted to cram events to or beyond capacity, providing one estimate of participants to staffers and another to fire marshals and the Secret Service. Cable news stations, which were becoming the primary news medium for voters, would broadcast filled events to show how popular the Clintons were becoming. The Secret Service was regularly notified at the last minute of event requirements and changes. I was assigned to one such event where an entire magnetometer detail was deployed to Kansas City, Missouri, but the event had been canceled two months prior. The Clinton campaign had neglected to notify the Secret Service. The advance agents involved were nearly despondent to have put so much work into something, only to have it be a complete waste.

Meanwhile, other events were hamstrung because Uniformed Division officers were spread so thin to cover the campaign.

The Clinton campaign felt there was no point in security if it was going to compromise the goal of the event. The Secret Service, on the other hand, felt that there was no point in doing an event if the protectee was going to get killed. The staff considered the Secret Service to be a hindrance and burden as opposed to a partner in protection. They couldn't understand simple security protocols, such as the fact that in winter, screening for concealed weapons takes much longer, as patrons are dressed in more layers. One event in Ohio was beyond capacity and the magnetometer detail was ordered to "shut it down"— and it wouldn't be the last time.

The campaign's insistence on drawing capacity crowds created plenty of logistical headaches. The Secret Service, the local fire marshal, and the event and campaign planners are supposed to work together to plan for the Secret Service's unique policy on exits. Two exit routes are always locked down exclusively for the protectee's exit. For example, if a 10,000-person capacity room had ten emergency exits and the Secret Service appropriates two exits for its needs, the number of participants admitted to the room should be reduced accordingly. But the campaign staff never heeded this, as the goal was continually to broadcast Clinton's popularity to the world. Fire marshals even tried to shut down some events. Though in theory they had the authority, with the candidate under Secret Service protection and the agency running the show, the fire marshals had no clear way of actually exerting that authority; they were forced to hope that things would play out fine without a fire or stampede.

As the campaign ended and Clinton became the forty-second president, the Secret Service anticipated a return to calm, as had occurred with past presidencies. But the Clinton campaigners had won the White House, and they were convinced that their successful campaigning strategies and tactics could be applied to governing.

Sometime in 1992, as Clinton neared the presidency, FBI agents who were "in the know" met with their Secret Service counterparts for off-the-record discussions. The IRS, the FBI, and the Federal Election Commission (FEC) had investigated both associates of the Clintons and the Clintons themselves. The FBI alerted the Secret Service as a courtesy, warning it of the kind of people who were in the Clintons' orbit. Some of those were clear-cut criminal connections, such as Jim McDougal, who went to jail following investigations of money laundering and insider deals with Arkansas government officials. As the Clintons formed their presidential staff, they surrounded themselves with such people, creating a greater risk of subversives, moles, criminals, and even spies within the Clinton camp. The FBI and Secret Service faced a choice—and the start of a long succession of dilemmas.

The FBI's primary investigations, known as "Whitewater" and "cattlegate" (or the "cattle futures controversy"), explored whether the Clintons had accepted bribes through shell companies and from various shady corporate arrangements and favors to pay back their political debts and more. Though the media and TV viewers became bored with the continued obsession with Whitewater and cattlegate, FBI investigations operated on evidence, not entertainment value. The leaders of the Secret Service ignored much of this and failed to see the incoming avalanche.

In January 1993, any hope of normalcy on the part of the new administration vanished. Immediately the former campaign staff began taking apart the security system for screening prospective employees. Instead of being required to pass investigations by the FBI followed by approval by the Secret Service, prospective hires simply began showing up at the White House northwest employee gate. They were then given visitors' passes—which was unprecedented and virtually negated the security measures that were in place. Frontline Secret Service employees quickly got wind of the plan, and Secret Service leadership put an end to that specific practice. The practice was discovered only because of bizarre behavior by the new staff, including brazen vandalism of the White House. One potential employee even brought in a concealed firearm and handed it to a UD officer.

The Clintons wanted to hire anyone they pleased without reporting to Congress or having to explain things such as prior drug use, arrests, medications, or anything else to anyone. They believed that as they had won the White House, they could staff it without hindrance from pesky security measures.

The Secret Service gave in to the Clintons' plans to give prospective employees "temporary passes," much like the standard for a visitor's pass, provided they made it through a provisional National Crime Information Center (NCIC) check. But many would-be hires were not cleared by the process, which was not as thorough as a full background check. The FBI was unable to build full reports to then hand to the Secret Service for decisions. Under pressure, the Secret Service issued the temporary passes while simultaneously issuing memos putting officers, agents, and technicians on alert.

The president and first lady should have pressured new hires to cooperate fully with the FBI investigators. Instead they complained the process was politically corrupt and took too long, just more bureaucratic red tape. Those investigations had extremely high standards, as the presidential staff work in the highest office in one of the most secure intelligence locations on the planet. Yet the president and especially the first lady pressured the FBI and Secret Service to approve whomever they wanted.

The staff even complained that the "T" for "temporary" on the badges was too prominent; apparently it hurt their feelings. But the whole point of the blue passes and the "T" was to signal to Secret Service personnel that such pass holders were temporary, were not trustworthy, and should be more heavily scrutinized for area denial and behavioral analysis. The compromise had a very negative effect on relationships among the various people doing their jobs in the White House. Secret Service personnel and presidential staff had more run-ins when officers had to question or hold up staffers. The most routine conflicts were with staffers who expected to be able to enter secured areas without their passes but who were stopped and issued visitor passes. Many key staff members from the campaign, who should have known better, were notorious for this. After the T-passes became so cumbersome and annoying to the staffers, who continually had to get them reissued, the Secret Service compromised again and stopped putting an expiration date on them.

The process was constantly screwed up, and the FBI agents who were assigned to the White House and their Secret Service counterparts had to pick and choose their battles. Dee Dee Myers, as an example, had a very hard time securing a "hard" or permanent, pass. As White House press secretary for almost the first two years of the administration, Myers was certainly senior staff. However, the Secret Service was also aware of issues uncovered during her background check, which made granting her a permanent pass unlikely.

When White House staff without proper passes ran up against Secret Service personnel charged with keeping people out of secure areas and confrontations resulted, the Secret Service leadership had a choice to make. They could have held firm and stood by their own agents and officers who were trying to do their jobs, letting the staffers know that they wouldn't be able to sneak into places without proper clearance. But that didn't happen.

Speaking of drugs—the Secret Service cross-trains its Belgian Malinois dogs to sniff out both bombs and narcotics. This was known to the Clinton staffers. Normally they were known for their open-door policies, and "straphangers" hung about, endlessly debating policy and filling the halls with youthful energy—until the dogs came through. And it wasn't bombs the staffers were worried about hiding. The first time the K-9 units came through the east and west wings and other areas, many of the offices immediately became suspiciously light-staffed. One Clinton official had none of those concerns, however: Betty Currie, the president's secretary, loved the dogs and kept treats for them. The officers knew that treats would signal a job well done, so they made sure to visit Betty last. She even asked the K-9s to swing by more often, which might not have been appreciated by some of her colleagues.

Also causing tension was the firing of the FBI director of six years, the fourth ever director to lead the bureau, William S. Sessions. Attorney General Janet Reno, appointed by President

Clinton, cited reasons why Sessions could not lead the bureau, including charges of ethical violations such as a government-funded fence built around his DC home and a personal trip taken at taxpayers' expense. To Louis Freeh, Sessions's appointed successor, the Clintons made it clear that they expected their hires to be approved without regard to protective measures. They expected a "user-friendly" FBI. They simply did not understand how the FBI is structured. The Bureau was not required to notify appointees of open investigations targeting the Clintons and their people—a measure that kept political intrusions out of law enforcement work.

Congress even attempted to investigate the matter of staff approvals but was assuaged by George Stephanopoulos who testified before Congress and persuaded them not to. But by that point the standards had been diluted so much that they hardly mattered.

The Clinton White House attorneys felt that prospective employees should be treated as hired until proven guilty. Much like the Clintons' regard for the Secret Service's protection of a candidate as solely that agency's responsibility, the Clintons simply did not feel the need to have their prospective hires cooperate with investigations. The stalemate continued until the Clintons started escalating the situation.

A former FBI agent, Gary Aldrich, made it very clear in *Unlimited Access: An FBI Agent Inside the Clinton White House* that the friends of the Clintons were problematic, to say the least:

> One only had to look at Clinton associates like Little
> Rock businessman Dan Lasater, who was convicted

of cocaine distribution (and later pardoned by then-Governor Clinton) and whose former business partner is current Clinton director of White House Management and Administration Patsy Thomasson (responsible for drug testing at the White House), or at the cocaine distribution convictions of Clinton's half brother or of Surgeon General Joycelyn Elders's son to get a hint of possible murky depths.

While the Secret Service was struggling to protect the White House from its own would-be staffers, another official scandal arose in May. "Travelgate" or "the White House Travel Office controversy" is the name given by the media for a situation in which the Clintons allegedly illegally fired nonpolitical employees who handled White House travel so their positions could be filled with those loyal to the Clintons and the actual work of the office could be outsourced to other Clinton friends outside government. Again, this was only *alleged*.

The Secret Service was involved in several ways.

When Billy Dale, the long-serving nonpolitical head of the travel office, was accused of misconduct, it should have been the Secret Service's job to investigate. But the case was thin, and the service declined. The Clintons needed evidence, as they could not simply fire the seven travel office employees so they could outsource millions of dollars of work privately to their friends the Thomasons. The Clinton lawyers hoped they could drum up evidence of wrongdoing at the travel office under the previous administration and therefore at least arouse enough suspicion to warrant firing Dale. So the White House attorneys pressured the FBI to take up the investigation of Dale, who was prosecuted but found not guilty in 1995.

The Clintons were not happy with the Secret Service for turning down the investigation. Agency leaders, however, were concerned about the character of the people who would replace the previous employees and wondered about the character of those who would destroy such a venerable tenured employee as Dale, who had worked at the office side by side with the Secret Service since 1961 and led it since 1982. Nonetheless, "Travelgate" backfired on the Clintons as the FBI's investigation quickly turned against them and specifically implicated White House employees and even the first lady in the conspiracy.

The Clintons and their staff simply never learned, and neither did the Secret Service.

One illustrative run-in was with a staffer known as "the Rabbi," so called by his colleagues because of his beard and demeanor. Late one evening, the president received word that he had accomplished one of his campaign promises. The Rabbi wanted to make the most of the milestone by staging a regal presidential address before the press, immediately.

The Rabbi was exceedingly noncooperative with the Secret Service and developed a nasty habit of informing them of his plans at the last minute. As he prepared to set up this presidential address outside, in front of the media on the North Portico, he was unaware of one important fact: the Uniformed Division Counter Sniper Team had already been told to go home. The Uniformed Division rooftop patrols had taken their places, but they were mostly only visual overwatch. As a UD officer permanently posted outside the Oval Office, I was aware of this, but, not wanting to insert myself directly and have any back-lash fall on my shoulders (already the on-the-job politics had taken hold), I headed to "Staircase," the agents' radio room, to inform the agents there. They thought I was joking, but when they realized I was serious, they sprung into action. The Rabbi did not realize that he was about to place the president on the North Portico in an area that had minimal tree cover from the surrounding neighborhood and nearby hotels. Lights from TV cameras would highlight him perfectly for any sniper.

The agents were furious.

"Why not put a giant billboard and flare on him, for Christ's sake?" one demanded as he ran to find the Rabbi.

When he was located and confronted, the conversation grew heated. At one point, the Rabbi actually stepped into the personal space of one of the PPD agents, as if to intimidate him.

"I think you are having unrealistic expectations as to your authority here at the White House," one PPD agent calmly pointed out.

We Secret Service personnel were careful in picking and choosing our battles. Noncooperation and arrogance could be stomached to some degree, but we were ready to draw the line when we felt someone was willfully placing the president in danger. The line was up to each officer and agent to draw.

The Rabbi was soon let go, but the problem of staffers with the same problem of prioritizing ego or popularity over security remained. In another incident, Dee Dee Myers once held up the departure of Marine One, which was waiting to take off with President Clinton aboard—a sitting duck in the middle of the South Lawn—while she took a phone call she thought was more important.

We always had to be aware that this White House was just different. But there were exceptions. President Clinton's secretary, Betty Currie—who was very nice—gave me the nickname "Mayor of the West Wing." I didn't like it, but I recognized in many ways that I was one of the last layers of defense before the president's office.

But mostly, a double standard was readily apparent between the staffers let in with minimal security checking and the officers charged with protecting them. Therefore, the officers' morale continued to plummet. At times it seemed as if the Secret Service were just a big show, an elaborate theatrical security effort still in denial of its history and failures. The Clintons, their staff, and service higher-ups seemed fine with watching those past failures play out again.

Of all the Clinton employees who caused the Secret Service so much frustration, Craig Livingstone was the poster child. He was at the center of it all. He was a boorish, cartoonish child of a man. He would name-drop and throw supposed protection terminology into conversations. It felt as though he were trying to pry information out of each person he talked with. He was a DC bouncer who had somehow latched onto the Clinton campaign. He later testified that Mrs. Clinton had personally hired him. She flatly denied it. FBI attachés and Secret Service personnel who had such information were never involved to verify this. But Livingstone was indeed the "Head of the White House Office of Personnel Security." This had previously been a clerk's position, a simple document filer. Working out of an office in the Old Executive Office Building but coordinating with the East Wing staff under the first lady, Livingstone tried to morph the position into something in senior management.

He even bragged to me that he had gained his status within the Clinton administration and with First Lady Hillary by being the head of the off-the-record "opposition force," green-lighted by the campaign. He boasted that he had chased the campaign bus of then-president George H. W. Bush and then put on a chicken suit to heckle Bush with shouts of "Chicken George" for not debating candidate Clinton. Livingstone even bragged to me that Hillary had hired him directly for his position and implied that they were personal friends. The Secret Service aims to be nonpartisan and nonpolitical, but that kind of conduct is not something that was good form to brag about to any Secret Service employee. It was especially maddening to hear such things from a coward whose target, President Bush, had been a torpedo bomber who had fought the Japanese, been shot down in the Pacific Ocean, and been saved only because a friendly submarine happened to spot him adrift.

On another occasion, Livingstone offended the PPD agents when they got word of his newly made business cards. The cards read "Craig Livingstone: Head of Presidential Security." With those business cards, he implied that he ran the president's security and that PPD or all of the Secret Service worked for him. This was nuts. When PPD Agent "Dave," who was nicknamed "The Look-Alike" for sometimes being mistaken for President Clinton, caught up with Livingstone and demanded that he destroy the cards, Livingstone retorted, "Well, it doesn't *say* Secret Service." He was exactly the kind of person who was not supposed to be permitted to work at the White House, and he was involved in the hiring process! It was another reminder of the Secret Service's inability to protect the Clintons from themselves.

After the White House complex was flooded with hangers-on and those with less-than-desirable character (to put it mildly), the Secret Service still viewed itself as being at arm's length from the Clinton administration. But as former Secret Service PPD and Counter Assault Team (CAT) agent Dan Emmett noted in his book *Within Arm's Length*, a memoir of his service, strategically the Clintons had already compromised far more than the Secret Service's secure area. After compromising event and hotel security (as I describe in my own book *Crisis of Character*), it did not take long for the Clintons to compromise transportation security as well. Transporting the president is one of the more dangerous and serious tasks of the Secret Service.

Emmett wrote of one such shocking instance in which the Clinton staff forced the Secret Service to back down so the president, for a mere photo op, could be placed in an ambush zone and a tactically untenable situation. Clinton strolled across a bridge between North and South Korea in full view of North Korean guards armed with AK-47s, small arms, and even worse. The president was yards away from his motorcade and isolated. If the America-hating North Koreans started shooting, the president would have immediately been killed and the United States would certainly have been thrust back into the Korean War. Emmett wrote:

"As we sat in our vehicle, we stared at the North Koreans and scanned the surrounding area while the Communists stared back. Meanwhile, President Clinton leisurely strolled along the bridge as if he were at Camp David, with the satisfied, relaxed look of a man with no concerns. After walking a little farther onto the bridge than he probably should have, practically into

North Korea, President Clinton looked around the area for a few minutes and then returned to his vehicle, and we got the hell out of the zone."

Such instances happened regularly enough to reveal to all of the Secret Service a clear pattern of reckless behavior by the Clinton staff and a "hear no evil, see no evil" attitude on the part of the service's leaders. It was a cavalier disconnect that could lead to disaster—again.

Another tale that was kept from the public would have surely been called "Ringgate" had the media caught wind of it. The president was in a major metropolitan airport, en route to Air Force One, when he realized he had left his wedding ring at his hotel. He ordered the motorcade to turn around so he could retrieve it. He was especially concerned about being seen arriving or boarding without his wedding ring as he had been traveling without the first lady. But that was an unforeseen circumstance in the highly coordinated logistical ballet among the Air Force, local police, Secret Service, FAA, and other agencies, not to mention the airport itself. The compromise was that a group of agents at the hotel where the Secret Service was maintaining a skeleton safe room and control center would somehow quickly locate the ring and then rush to return it before detection.

That was a break from the plans in place to ensure that the president remained protected at all times. Unscheduled delays were not accounted for and could have been exploited by potential adversaries. For a nail-biting thirty minutes, the president was exposed on his own orders, violating the security procedures in place for his own safety as Air Force One, PPD, CAT,

Secret Service, military, and other security agents waited for the ring. They should have left without it, but once again presidential security was subservient to the wants and desires of convenience and PR.

In another instance, which was picked up by the media and dubbed "Hairgate," President Clinton held up air traffic at Los Angeles International Airport for thirty minutes so he could get his hair cut by a celebrity stylist named Christophe. Again, the Clintons created a double standard. Passengers on flights that were delayed and forced to use the one other set of runways available due to Air Force One's presence were delayed further by congested air traffic.

This mentality was also evident in President Clinton's jogging habit. Every president has one thing that the Secret Service, and specifically the PPD, has to just "figure out." President Reagan liked to use a chain saw at his ranch. President Eisenhower golfed on difficult-to-secure courses. President Clinton jogged around the National Mall area.

"Taking the president running at peak rush hour down Pennsylvania Avenue, around the Reflecting Pool at the Lincoln Memorial, or through Rock Creek Park, bordered on insanity," Dan Emmett pointed out in his book, *Within Arm's Length*.

Agent Emmett detailed how a domestic wannabe assassin had actually traveled to DC from Florida and waited in various parks with a handgun, hoping to ambush the president if circumstance ever brought the president jogging past him. The man was caught only after he disclosed his premeditated attempt to a confidant who then informed the Secret Service. The man was prosecuted.

President Clinton was even caught sneaking off the White House complex on more than one occasion. His personal lawyer, Bruce Lindsey, tried to hide the president in his car and leave the complex. They were stopped only by the good work of a Uniformed Division officer working the northwest vehicle exit gate on West Executive Avenue. On a hunch the officer inspected the vehicle and, much to his alarm, spotted the president trying to hide under a raincoat in the back seat. Despite Lindsey's pleading, the officer stood his post and would not open the gate. He immediately took to his post phone, saying "You better get me some help up here. I just caught Bruce Lindsey trying to drive out West Exec. with the president with a raincoat over his head."

PPD agents, alarmed to hear that the president had willfully sneaked past them, were past fury. They were dejected, disappointed, bewildered, and shocked. They tried to remain diplomatic, but they had to be adamant with Bruce Lindsey that this must never happen again. Other officers confirmed this report, and although this was the first and only time I had heard of it, Gary Aldrich wrote of another similar instance. Word circulated that "sneaking off" was something to look out for.

If the president could not completely duck his detail, he would at least take them "off the record," or OTR. Sometimes this was done for highly honorable reasons, such as when President Clinton, without fanfare, along with many other top military leadership, visited the grieving widow of a fallen high-ranking military official. But the freedom of OTRs under this president was soon to be abused and, in one instance, nearly cost an officer his life.

President Clinton used the OTRs to visit the well-known and lesser-known mistresses he frequented outside the complex, meaning the ones who did not have access to the White House. Standard motorcade procedures utilized a multitude of preplanned routes and UD and local law enforcement uniformed officers, particularly from the DC Metropolitan Police Department, to block intersections ahead of the motorcade, so that it could move through at accelerated speed without stopping. For events and long drives, sewer and drain ports were welded shut. Even sections of highways were shut down just in case the president might use them on a route. All the vehicles in the motorcade kept close to one another, speed limits were obviously ignored, and lights and sirens were always used. All of that was designed to keep the president safe from ambush, what some called the "kill zone."

President Clinton wanted all that changed at the last minute. The Secret Service again capitulated. Convoys of big black SUVs moving far above the speed limit with flashing red and blue lights with sirens are not uncommon around the nation's capital. Without indicator flags, the protectees of those convoys could be our own government officials or even foreign dignitaries. But anonymity, mystery, and being off the public record were not enough for what the president had in mind. He wanted to move even more secretly, but the Secret Service could not invent a new plan and retrain its agents and officers simply because President Clinton didn't like the procedure. Instead it eliminated layers of protection altogether. As the remaining layers became disjointed and nonconcentric, both the service's own personnel and the public were put at extreme risk. Half of the Secret Service's protective measures are for the protectees, but the other half are to safeguard agents and officers as well as the public from our operations.

Several late-night OTRs were mysteriously ordered to not use sirens, lights, or exceed the speed limit. The number of cars was reduced to bare bones, but it was still about twelve, more than could push through an intersection without running a red light. Many of those diminished OTRs did not notify DC Metro PD of their movements—which created a snake pit of problems. Without the sirens, the motorcades could not alert other vehicles that they were on-duty police vehicles and to steer clear. Without the red and blue lights, the vehicles looked just like any other civilian car on the road. Without the consistent accelerated speed, the vehicles could not keep consistent distances between one another as they constantly stopped, slowed, and accelerated again. Civilian cars kept trying to cut into the convoy. As intersections were not blocked off ahead of the motorcade, red lights and regular traffic prevented the motorcades from pushing through intersections unimpeded. Agents and officers held their breath as the motorcades got caught in the middle of civilian traffic, engines humming idle in potential kill zones, exactly what their Secret Service training had engrained in them not to do. On one occasion, the motorcade became entirely split and had to wait for lights to change to try and reconnect. That left the president's vehicle vulnerable, as each vehicle had a separate and important function. In case of an ambush, the agents would have nowhere to go and would have to ram or shoot their way out through the clogged and unaware DC traffic. No one had trained for such a compromised scenario; everyone was improvising. And what was all the danger and sacrifice for—an uncontrollable president's late-night dalliance?

On one occasion, a Metro PD car spotted the convoy and called over to the Secret Service Foreign Missions Branch, asking something to the effect of "Hey, do you Secret Service guys have a convoy operating tonight? This looks like you guys." The Foreign Missions Branch responded, "No, that's not us." As far as they knew, that was true—they had not been notified of the clandestine OTR. It appeared to Metro PD that there was a mystery twelve-car convoy breaking numerous laws while traversing DC. They naturally considered trying to pull one of the vehicles over but figured there must have been some kind of interagency miscommunication. However, they had to figure it out on the fly because they recognized the motorcade's movements as illegal, suspicious, and extremely dangerous to everyone else—which it absolutely was.

"Reverend," a Uniformed Division officer, was driving the tail car, a marked police car. Another officer sat next to him in the front seat. Due to the haphazard, improvised, and extremely dangerous way the motorcade was operating, the tail car was T-boned by a civilian car correctly crossing the intersection at a green light. It wasn't that Reverend's car *just* missed the red light. But many of the cars in front of him had missed the light as well, and he had simply followed through. The car that hit him had not been stopped and waiting at the intersection; the civilian driving it had accelerated to full speed from a significant distance away. For the civilians, the light had long been green.

Reverend was severely injured, as were another officer and two civilians. The convoy continued on. Metro PD was alerted, and that's when it learned that the Secret Service had been operating throughout DC in such a dangerous fashion. Still, things could have been much worse.

Reverend was hospitalized with a severe traumatic brain injury. It was significant enough that he was pulled from duty pending his recovery and even then would return only on "light duty" status. In an unfortunate mix-up and evidence of the Secret Service's horrible management, as Reverend recovered, the service tried to deny him benefits, saying that he had "operated outside the operational envelope" by running a red light against protocol without lights and sirens! The service made him burn up all of his sick leave even before he could physically advocate on his own behalf. Once Reverend's lawyer rattled the cage of going to trial and hashing out the issues— and the evidence—in court, the service immediately backed off and settled handsomely, including fast-tracking a transfer for Reverend to another government agency in Colorado. Word of what had happened to Reverend spread like wildfire through the Uniformed Division because any UD officer could have been in Reverend's place. And although many would take a bullet for the president, what was the risk for? Were Clinton's sordid personal affairs worth an officer's life? Was that the duty we had signed up for, the reason we spent so much time away from our families?

Despite the payout, Reverend knew and quietly disclosed to others that his injury had permanently changed his personality. He didn't feel much like himself anymore. As for the civilians, all anyone had heard was that they had been handsomely compensated for their injuries, losses, and silence.

Still, the Clintons' attitude toward their protectors and their security never changed.

The service's run-ins with staff worsened. As strange as it seems, despite all the other scandals and the special committees of the House and Senate investigating so much about the president's administration, it was the run-ins between the president's staff and the Secret Service that ultimately and directly threw the service under the president's bus.

The Secret Service, and especially the PPD, grew more capitulating with the first couple and presidential staff. Yet from the staff's perspective, the Secret Service would never be "user friendly" and docile enough. The Secret Service leadership went along with the staff's demand that the Treasury Department (the service's parent agency) hire a private-sector human resources company to instruct the Uniformed Division how to be nicer, kinder, gentler, and "less abrasive." Secret Service higher-ups assumed that that would be of no consequence. Morale was not much of a consideration. The UD officers were insulted and distanced. Through middle management they tried to explain that they were always diplomatic with the staff. Management chalked it up to a gesture, a harmless placation. But the staff didn't realize that their seemingly simple requests would actually jeopardize the Secret Service protection measures, even ones mandated by Congress. When management did learn of the course curriculum that encouraged making those measures flexible, they finally looked into the program and ended it.

Issues related to White House tours caused constant conflicts with the Uniformed Division. The Clintons used the tours as political currency to pay back donors and various political pals. Lots of presidents had done the same thing in the past with standard tours, but the Clintons were constantly trying to take tours into restricted areas to convey to groups how "special" they were—that they were so valued they deserved to see what nobody else could. And the Clinton staffers' seemingly innocent request (from their perspective) to skirt protocol was a key factor in the October 29, 1994, attack on the White House. Today we would call this an "active shooter" incident.

The attacker was hovering by the fence line in an overcoat. Officers had cued in on him. They analyzed his suspicious behavior from a distance so as not to spook him, biding their time to confront him without endangering the public. Meanwhile, a Clinton staffer had insisted and pressured her way past an officer with a tour group in tow. Despite the warnings from the officer of protocol and security considerations, she knowingly took the tour group through to see the lawn from the perspective of the staircase of the White House. The officer did not want to embarrass the obstinate staffer by escalating the issue—by this point, the Secret Service culture had devolved to a mixed bag and some officers were unsure whether their agency would back them if they enforced the rules against a staffer's wishes. One tall gray-haired man on the tour resembled President Clinton. A woman at the fence line shouted and pointed at the gray-haired man as he emerged with the group, believing him to be the president. That's when the shooter initiated his attack and began firing his SKS rifle through the fence.

The Uniformed Division Emergency Response Team (ERT) ran in the face of the gunfire as other UD officers at the fence line charged in from the sides. A handful of civilians rushed the shooter and tackled him. Since the shooter believed he was shooting at the commander in chief, he was charged with attempting to assassinate the president. But had that Clinton staffer simply heeded the warning of the officer citing protocol, the shooting might never have happened. Instead of recognizing that the common denominator with each run-in with officers was the Clinton staff's "what-harm-could-it-do?" mentality, the Uniformed Division officers themselves were actually sent to further "sensitivity training."

Despite all the reasons to change, the Clinton administration never relented in the behaviors that continually put the president and Secret Service officers into jeopardy.

Examples abound. One such incident nearly placed President Clinton at grave risk at the hands of his protectors. The president and Mrs. Clinton requested that aside from the Uniformed Division Counter Sniper posting on the White House roof by their private residence balcony, the Secret Service abdicate the rest of the Uniformed Division rooftop postings. It was openly discussed that the Clintons had made this request because of the rumors of their domestic disputes leaking out to the press. There was a sense in the Clinton White House that the leaks had come from Secret Service conspirators working on behalf of the previous administration. Vice President Al Gore even pulled the alarms out of the ceiling of his residence, fearing that the Secret Service had bugged him. The Clintons did not realize that their screaming could be heard by all executive residence staff such as electricians and ushers, as well as agents and officers posted around the residence. One such tale that infuriated First Lady Clinton was of a lamp being broken in the residence—in fact, it was a vase—but in any event there was a grand effort to dispute it in the press. In the first couple's eyes, the problem was not that their marital problems interfered with their public service; it was that people knew about them.

Yet no explanation justifying removing the important rooftop protection seemed reasonable. The post was not there to snoop, only protect. The Secret Service again capitulated, and when the Counter Sniper Team members retired one evening, no one replaced them. Many officers didn't like the posting anyway as it required standing on a high, narrow catwalk. It was removed later in the Clinton administration anyway, after a small propeller plane was hijacked and flown into the White House (causing minimal damage) on September 12, 1994.

Soon after that, Counter Assault Team (CAT) agents were posted inside the complex during a particularly tense period when there was a high threat level. The president and first lady were in the residence, their private living quarters. Unlike the rest of the complex, no agents are posted in the private living quarters, and therefore no one reported on their movements. Suddenly the balcony alarm sounded. It seemed to the agents that someone was breaking in through the balcony, and without the officer posted on the catwalk to confirm or deny, the CAT agents responded with guns drawn, ready for anything. As one agent turned the corner, he aimed the red laser of his MP5 submachine gun, putting the little red dot on the man in the room.

"Whoa, fellas!" the president exclaimed with his typical charm, and the exasperated agent took his aim off the president's chest.

There was no break-in. But the Secret Service had again removed another layer from an established defensive plan without reevaluating: Does the plan still work with that layer removed? Clearly the roof was not secure enough, so the service reinstated the rooftop posting. Amazingly, one of the suggested solutions after the plane crash attack that was in the direct field of view of the rooftop posting was to give the officer posted on the roof a flare gun. The idea was that the rooftop officer would use the flare gun to signal the plane and officers would be able to discern between friendly and nonfriendly aircraft before shooting with small arms. Many jokes followed, of course. The small instructional material kept with the flare read, regarding firing flares, "If necessary, repeat." Whereas once .50-caliber machine guns on the roof had protected the White House from low-flying aircraft, the defenses had now devolved to a "please don't" flare gun.

But that near miss, like all the others, never caused the president, nor his staff, to consider how their patterns of behavior and inattention to security were pushing the Secret Service into disarray and dysfunction. Much of the service was so overworked and bogged down in the day-to-day stress of the Clinton craziness that the long-term issues were never addressed with sustainable long-term solutions. The biggest reason for this was seemingly a small but constant issue: the run-ins between the service and the arrogant Clinton staff, which increased tensions throughout the White House.

At one point, I walked up to Lewis Merletti, then the Secret Service director, and asked, "Everything all right, Lew? Seems a bit more tense than usual." He turned to me and said, "Oh, you know, Gary. The president has a higher threat level than Abraham Lincoln. And we all know how that went." Good humor was a must to keep the stresses at bay. But Director Merletti had no idea how much stress was heading his way.

In Washington, a new Starr was about to rise, as larger, darker issues were immediately ahead for the Clinton White House and for the Secret Service.

TWO.

KENNETH STARR TARGETS THE SECRET SERVICE

In 1998, for the first time in the agency's existence, the men and women of the Secret Service found themselves pitted *against* their protectee. In many ways, it seemed that the Secret Service could hold the key to determining whether President Bill Clinton would be impeached.

The chain of events that led to the agency's torturous involvement in Clinton's impeachment investigations began in tragedy. On July 20, 1993, Vince Foster, one of the loyal members of the "Arkansas mafia," Hillary Clinton's personal lawyer and longtime close confidant, was found dead by an apparent self-inflicted gunshot in Fort Marcy Park in McLean, Virginia, just across the Potomac River from Washington. A passerby found his body on July 20 at 7:40 p.m.

After finding White House credentials on the body, US Park Police immediately contacted the FBI, which joined the investigation. Simultaneously, the Park Police notified the Secret Service that "one of your guys," a White House pass holder, had died and the service should be on alert. Whenever a pass holder was in jeopardy or the victim of a crime, there was the concern that the crime might be part of a larger threat against the executive branch.

Foster's office was located on the second floor of the West Wing, just down the hall from Hillary Clinton's West Wing office. Though a first lady typically has only an office in the East Wing, the Clintons were famous for mixing personal and professional matters. The night of Foster's suicide, the FBI requested that the Secret Service post a sentry, an officer, on his office door until their arrival.

Uniformed Division officer Hank O'Neill was posted to make sure no one went in or out. FBI investigators needed the office to be as Foster had left it, so they could investigate the space and ascertain if there was evidence relevant to their investigation into Foster's death. Because of attorney-client privilege, the FBI could not look at any files deemed personal. This was another example of the Clintons' mixing personal and professional records and communications. Foster was involved in the Whitewater case, which the FBI was investigating, and now the Park Police and FBI were investigating his death. That also presented a constitutional conflict, as Foster's files were confidential to the Clintons under attorney-client privilege.

Maggie Williams, the first lady's chief of staff, along with White House aide Patsy Thomasson, approached UD officer O'Neill, trying to gain access to the office. Williams, in an account she gave in July 1995, two years after the suicide, testified that she had been distraught and was merely searching for a suicide note. She said she remained in Foster's office for several minutes, wallowing irrationally in grief.

According to O'Neill's testimony in the same hearings, Williams threatened his job, his career, and more. The officer succumbed to the pressure and allowed her access but kept a log of anything she removed from the office, which turned out to be several files. He logged the removal and notified the UD Control Center. Williams accused O'Neill of lying to Congress. The Uniformed Division officer tried to remain steadfast in his version of the story, while not speculating why Williams was providing a completely different account. The senators grilled O'Neill but went easy on Williams. That was the first time a Secret Service employee had been compelled by subpoena to testify against a member of a president's administration in an open hearing.

Though Williams testified that she had not removed the files, she admitted that they did exist and had somehow ended up in the White House's private residence with Hillary Clinton. What has never before been revealed, garnered from exclusive interviews during research for this book, is that after Maggie Williams first took files out of the office, against every crime scene investigation protocol, Officer O'Neill's post was not manned by another officer after he went off duty. On the morning after the suicide, Secret Service officials contacted the agency's Uniformed Division Control Center. At the behest of the Clinton administration, those officials ordered that the alarms to Foster's office in the West Wing be temporarily turned off and that no logs be kept of the doors opening and closing. During that window of time, the office was plundered of additional unknown documents, according to Secret Service sources stationed in the control center.

One former Secret Service employee involved in the incident reported to me that he had informed the FBI investigators about it when they had interviewed him. Despite their stricken faces, nothing had come of it. As the source put it, "I always figured I'd get questioned about the alarms or get subpoenaed later, but nothing came. It was weird. I don't think they knew what to do with the information I had given them. They were shocked. I supposed they didn't have anything else to go on but what I told them. At least that's what I hoped. I certainly wasn't going to make my own federal case out of it."

Everybody had questions about the incident. In 1994, Attorney General Janet Reno named a special prosecutor, Robert Fiske, to investigate Foster's death, a continuance of the initial alleged bribery scandal that came to be called "Whitewater." The special prosecutor law was soon changed by Congress, resulting in the creation of the Office of Independent Counsel (OIC), headed by a circuit judge named Kenneth Starr.

And so began a battle of wills among the presidency, the Supreme Court, the FBI, the Justice Department, and the Secret Service. It was a struggle that nearly tore the Secret Service apart all at once but instead is integral to the slow collapse happening today.

By this point in the Clinton administration, the Secret Service had jumped into normalizing the Clintons' inappropriate—perhaps even criminal—behavior with both feet. The unofficial rationale for this was that it was the agency's job to protect the president and his staff and secure the area but not to police the administration—even as it policed all other suspected criminals throughout the nation. But that presented two paradoxes: First, how can a security agency protect its protectees from themselves, especially when the protectees continually seek to systematically destroy the protocols that ensure protection? The agency had decided to err on the side of blind loyalty— and that was nearly its undoing. The second paradox: How can a law enforcement agency maintain its integrity, say in policing counterfeiting, while admittedly having compromised integrity in the area of protection?

At times the Secret Service leadership seemed to believe that the Clintons were invincible. The view from the front lines, however, was that something, somehow was bound to ensnare them. It was simply a matter of the right scandal. But the Secret Service, thus far, had done a good job of keeping itself out of the various investigations into the Clintons. It had even managed to escape implication in "Chinagate," the 1996 US campaign finance controversy in which campaign contributions to the Democratic Party from Chinese shell companies had allegedly been used to buy access for Chinese goods to be imported into the United States. The Secret Service knowingly allowed Chinese generals, disguised in civilian clothes, to meet administration personnel at the White House and logged them as "business guests" at the administration's request so as to avoid transparency. The Secret Service also willfully ignored the contents of the generals' paper bags brought to those meetings. The administration would later be accused by journalists of accepting bribes, though investigators never discovered a specific enough foothold to subpoena any Secret Service or White House personnel about the case. Then, when attorneys for Paula Jones, who alleged that she had been sexually assaulted by Bill Clinton when he was governor of Arkansas, tried to subpoena Secret Service personnel, the judge refused. As with President Richard Nixon and Watergate, it looked as though the Secret Service might pull through unimplicated.

If the Secret Service leadership felt that the Clintons were invincible, the Clintons themselves felt that they were, too. Secret Service Director John Magaw (seventeenth director, 1992–93) and his successor, Eljay Bowron (1993–97), never anticipated that the service would become involved in those investigations, so they had no contingencies in place. Directors Magaw and Bowron's cult mentality, which enforced the belief that the Secret Service was invincible, blinded them from anticipating the strategy of the wily OIC investigator Ken Starr.

The US capital has always been a close-knit network, and somehow a claim reached Starr's office that President Clinton was having an affair with a twenty-one-year-old White House intern turned employed mistress. OIC staffers set a trap for President Clinton. They strategized that if they challenged the arrogant president, got him to sign an affidavit, and then proved that he had committed perjury, they could put his entire defense in peril as his integrity would be destroyed. The fallout could endanger his presidency politically and could potentially lead to impeachment and even jail.

The trap sprung when the president swore on a legal affidavit that he was not having an affair with an intern. But he could not help but double down, and he claimed he had never even been alone in the same room with her. Clinton, a lawyer himself, fell right into the trap.

*   *   *

On June 6, 1997, the Secret Service welcomed Lewis Merletti as its nineteenth director. Merletti had been raised old-school Catholic. He had served as a Green Beret in the Vietnam War and earned a Bronze Star. He had joined the Philadelphia field office of the Secret Service before moving to DC. He had soon become part of the service's Counter Assault Team (CAT) and later a CAT team leader. From CAT, he had joined the PPD. He had gone on to become the special agent in charge (SAIC) of President Clinton's PPD, the position that usually leads to the directorship of the Secret Service. As lead agent of the president's detail while the president visited Manila, Philippines, Director Merletti saved the president's life by exerting the override authority and rerouting the motorcade based on some sudden intelligence reports. The hunch was confirmed when a special forces group did indeed discover that a major terrorist organization intended to assassinate the president and had planted a large bomb under a bridge on the initial motorcade route. Director Merletti was an incredible agent and a hero.

Director Merletti was the kind of guy the American people and everyone in the Secret Service would want with them in a firefight. He was damn good at what he did: soldiering, fighting, leading soldiers into battle, and protecting the president's life. President Clinton seemed intimidated by, almost standoffish with, most military personnel, especially those in uniform. Many in the administration who had been carried over from the presidential campaign more or less shared the president and first lady's aloof attitude toward military and law enforcement uniforms. Vice President Gore once gave a pep talk to one of his children saying something to the effect that the child had better do well in school lest the child end up like "one of those guys," referring to the agents on the vice president's protection detail. Despite the release of the young Bill Clinton's correspondence with his draft board outing him as a Vietnam War draft dodger, Clinton and Merletti, the Vietnam War veteran, connected well.

The reasons behind the departure of Bowron, Merletti's predecessor, were clear only to Bowron himself. Theories emerged among Secret Service personnel that Bowron had known of the impending crisis and had not wanted to lead the agency through the fight that was bound to happen. What is known is that Bowron had withheld key information about the exposure of the Secret Service, revealing it to Merletti only after Merletti decided how to defend the agency from the investigations that later consumed it.

On January 17, 1998, less than seven months after Merletti became director, the Drudge Report website broke its now infamous story headlined in all capitals: "NEWSWEEK KILLS STORY ON WHITE HOUSE INTERN. BLOCKBUSTER REPORT: 23-YEAR OLD, FORMER WHITE HOUSE INTERN, SEX RELATIONSHIP WITH PRESIDENT." It was a few days before anyone from the Secret Service would look at the revelations and realize that the agency had been deeply involved throughout. The Drudge Report's exclusive story implicated the Secret Service directly. The choice was immediately clear: either the service could absolve the president of wrongdoing, or it could seal his fate.

The Drudge Report revealed that the president had begun his affair with the woman when she was merely twenty-one years old. The Secret Service had issued her an Old Executive Office Building pass while she was an intern, which she had used for her liaisons with the president. Her every visitation had been screened and logged by the Secret Service. The Secret Service had logged her into its system as a visitor when she came to see President Clinton late at night. The haste with which the Secret Service issued her a permanent pass was especially suspicious when she suddenly became an employee in the West Wing.

The Secret Service had cleared her to access anywhere in the complex except the private living quarters, and she could see what the president and chief of staff Leon Panetta saw in the West Wing, even operational intelligence. It didn't take Ken Starr long to lock onto the Secret Service as a potential font of evidence.

The second wallop for Director Merletti and the Secret Service came just over a week later. At midnight on Monday, January 26, 1998, the *Dallas Morning News* dropped its exclusive story—using a single, uncorroborated "close" source—that said a Secret Service agent was with Starr and "ready to testify." The story was picked up by the *New York Post*, whose headline read "Sexgate Stunner, Secret Service Agent to Testify: I Saw Them Do It." But only two days later, the story was dead. As the *Washington Post* headlined a story by its media reporter Howard Kurtz: "Dallas Paper's Story Traveled Far Before Being Shot Down."

Kurtz wrote that although the Dallas paper had reported "that investigators had spoken with a Secret Service agent who was prepared to testify that he saw President Clinton and the former White House intern in a compromising situation," which was, "to put it mildly, explosive stuff," it hadn't lasted long. "Hours later," Kurtz reported, "sometime after midnight, the *Morning News* retracted the story. The piece, published in the paper's first edition and posted on its World Wide Web site, was declared inoperative in a subsequent Web announcement."

Inside the Secret Service at the time, the view was that a mystery agent had indeed volunteered information; what's more, Merletti thought so, too. Starr was already probing at the agency.

Merletti, however, was determined that all Secret Service employees, both those still employed and those who had retired, stand fast and tow the "secret" line. Those of us on the ground felt his thinking was that patriotic Americans would see it that way, too—that protecting the presidency (and by extension the Secret Service brand) was essential. This was the mentality of the Counter Assault Teams and the PPD, where Merletti had cut his teeth.

As the Secret Service's leaders realized that their legacy was threatened by the developing "Sexgate" scandal, Director Merletti put his plan into action without strategic pause or objective reflection on the service's history. His advisers never entertained contrarian ideas or developed alternative methods of handling the situation. Merletti hadn't even had time in his career or his directorship to fully learn his agency's history. Had he done so, things might have been different. He should have known what Starr knew: that there was no basis for "secrecy" in the "Secret Service" grounded in legal statute or precedent. The Secret Service was no more secret than the FBI or DEA. Furthermore, he had never discussed the scandals with frontline officers or agents who had direct knowledge of the events. He simply forged ahead, unaware of the extent of the agency's exposure.

On top of this, the Secret Service's chief legal counsel gave Merletti bad advice, pointing out that Starr was a former colleague and as such would probably be friendly and amenable to keeping the service out of it. That was a grave error and led Merletti to misjudge Starr's intentions badly.

Merletti sat down with Attorney General Janet Reno, along with others including Deputy Attorney General—and future AG—Eric Holder. He made the case that the Secret Service faced serious threats every day, and in order to protect the president from them, they needed his trust that it would remain silent. His message was clear: if Secret Service personnel are forced to testify, the president will be forced to push them away, resulting in more danger to him. Under Director Merletti's direction, the Secret Service made the case that if the agency had an obligation to testify against the president, the president would be incentivized to push away the Secret Service, and the resulting distance could endanger the president; it even referenced President Kennedy's assassination. Despite being historically inaccurate, that deeply emotional view was shared widely throughout the Department of Justice.

The Secret Service legal counsel, with input from senior Secret Service and Treasury officials, created a legal notion that was pure extrapolation with no basis in actual law, calling it "the executive protective function privilege." It was based on the legal privileges given to spouses to avoid testifying against each other.

When Merletti made the case to Starr, Starr rushed him through his presentation and then came to what was apparently his true purpose for the meeting: questioning Merletti about the president's relationship with the young intern. Merletti felt frustrated, and Deputy AG Holder suggested that he try again. Merletti made the pitch again, and Starr once again brought the discussion back to his target.

At that point, Merletti realized that he needed backup. He called all living former Secret Service directors into his office and included a special guest, former First Lady Detail Agent Clint Hill, who had jumped onto the back of President Kennedy's limousine in Dallas all those years ago. Merletti still felt that invoking the Kennedy assassination would help his case. With that audience, it worked. Every former director backed Merletti's play. Each corroborated the director's view that the Secret Service had been, would be, and should be invisible to investigations into the president.

In that meeting, former director Bowron informed Merletti for the first time of a serious problem: Bowron had established a conflicting precedent during his tenure. During the Rose Law Firm investigation into the first lady and other investigations, Bowron had agreed to let agents volunteer to speak with Ken Starr if they had direct knowledge related to Starr's query. Bowron declared before his successor and all the predecessors present that the only regret he had in his entire time as director is that he had not resigned right then. Starr had not disclosed that fact to Merletti, either.

Hill, in the meeting and then again afterward, made sure Merletti understood the terms: if Secret Service employees testified, future presidents would die.

Agent Clint Hill was a hero for his actions in trying to save President Kennedy's life. He had not hesitated to try to save the president and first lady that day in Dallas. But he had been helpless, not because of a lack of protective privilege but because of a series of strategic failures by Secret Service leaders, the PPD, and President Kennedy. Agent Hill suffered from "survivor's guilt." But he also suffered from something largely unexplained and never before studied in the academic psychological community: "protector's guilt," a consequence of losing a protectee with whom you spent more time than your own family. Merletti took advantage of that to make an emotional and personal argument to shield the Secret Service from Starr's investigation.

In Ken Gormley's book *The Death of American Virtue: Clinton vs. Starr*, Merletti was quoted as saying "If there's a crime, you're not going to have to ask us about it. We're going to come forward and *tell* you about it. But if you have an investigation, then you're going to have to investigate it otherwise. Because it's compromising Secret Service trust and confidence, which then compromises proximity, and it's all over."

But that view meant that the Secret Service was not "worthy of trust and confidence" to all Americans but to only one American: the president. When Merletti made the decision to oppose allowing Secret Service employees to testify regarding anything they witnessed that could hurt the president, I believe he sacrificed the Secret Service's soul.

That pivotal choice of allegiance was crucial for the Secret Service. The president it sought to protect did not return the favor. When President Clinton doubled down on his perjury, the director and the entire Secret Service were forced into an untenable position.

Cracks soon appeared in the Secret Service's stonewalling efforts. In February 1998, a retired Uniformed Division officer named Lewis C. Fox, known as the "Silver Fox" to colleagues, watched a television broadcast about the investigation at a Pennsylvania diner. He made several comments about his knowledge of the case to other patrons, and they found their way to the news media. Soon it was reported that a "Secret Service guard" knew firsthand that the Drudge story was true, that he knew that the president had indeed been alone in the Oval Office with the intern in question, and that the president had lied. Starr now had another potential source—and unfortunately for Merletti, since Fox was retired, the Secret Service counsel had no leverage to use on him.

Then things got worse. Starr subpoenaed a former PPD agent from President Clinton's protective detail whom I will call "Bud." Bud was already internally famous for the way he'd left the Secret Service. After he had martial problems that spilled over into his work and caused disturbances, the Secret Service cut him a deal, probably trying to make the story go away. He had resigned and ended up with a higher-paying job in the private sector, presumably while he collected a retirement settlement negotiated with the service that included a positive recommendation letter. The Secret Service had swept Bud's story under the rug to protect its own name, but now he was in Starr's sights and could reveal a story that was a lot more embarrassing than his own adultery and corruption.

And with the "Silver Fox" in hand, it was only a matter of time before Starr discovered the full value of the Uniformed Division. UD officers manned the personnel and vehicle entry and exit gates on the fence line. There was always something going on at the White House, and though the agents protected individuals, the security of the White House hummed because of the committed work of the Uniformed Division. Among their postings throughout the entire White House, the UD officers saw everything that was going on. Starr soon discovered that he had stumbled into a gold mine.

Secret Service counsel advised everyone to "hold tight" as the subpoenas for specific UD officers and their physical materials started flying out of Secret Service headquarters fax machines.

Starr first subpoenaed the UD post logbooks and Workers and Visitors Entry System (WAVES) records. Getting nervous, Merletti offered Starr a deal: He asked Starr not to probe Secret Service leadership or any agents on the Presidential Protective Division, convincing him that they would be too loyal to their protectee and would go to jail to avoid testifying. If Starr would leave them alone, Merletti would provide Starr with access to UD officers stationed at the White House and any others who had had "run-ins" and "incidents" with the intern in question.

Starr had been duped and missed an opportunity to gather key evidence. The PPD agents were the ones who were with the president at all times and could have given him what he needed. What's more, Merletti had been bluffing when he had said they would fight to avoid testifying—though some might, there were many who would not have done so. As for Bud, the former PPD agent, he was brought back under the Secret Service's legal protection as part of the deal.

Several Uniformed Division officers—including me—were aware that they were likely to be targeted because of what they knew. Those officers notified their supervisors and managers in anticipation of the firestorm to come. The middle managers at first dismissed their concerns, but within two hours, we were taken off our posts and told to report to Secret Service headquarters for a legal debriefing the following morning. Everyone's minds and stomachs turned over as we thought about what would come next. Where would our loyalties lie? At first there was a collective sense of denial, dread, anger, and frustration. After everything we had witnessed on the job, we wondered: Is this *the* scandal that will either prove the Clintons invincible, as many believed, or could it be the one that will finally lead to their downfall?

When my fellow officers and I sat down with the Secret Service attorneys, the lawyers tried to gain our trust, but it soon became clear that their goal was simply to get us to sign on to the agency's plan. To complicate things, none of the officers there could afford private lawyers, so the Secret Service legal counsel would represent us, as long as we "cooperated." As for the alternative, if any officer decided to contact the OIC individually, it was heavily insinuated that his security clearances (necessary to keep our job) would be revoked.

Agreeing to play ball and accept Secret Service representation carried another important benefit: under the deal worked out among the Secret Service, OIC, and DOJ, Starr agreed that any subpoenas served to officers being represented by Secret Service lawyers would have to be faxed to the agency. That was important to the officers themselves, who didn't want to be served at work or at home.

The officers in the meeting began pushing back, and the lawyers only made things worse with a critical misunderstanding. In what they apparently viewed as a favor, the attorneys told us we were being pulled from all overtime duty, effective immediately. Many of us depended on the overtime pay to support our families, so of course we objected—but the lawyers were unmoved.

It was clear that the lawyers assumed President Clinton's professions of innocence to be true, while the officers in the room did not. When the lawyers implied that the officers might be placing the agency in legal risk if they suggested in testimony that the president was not being truthful, the room erupted in grunts and gasps. I saw many fellow officers shift their body language at the suggestion, and the lawyers were clearly on their toes. The officers also recognized something the lawyers did not: that their own security clearances were actually higher than those of the attorneys, meaning that what the officers could share with their supposed "representatives" was limited.

The lawyers clearly were not expecting the barrage of questions we threw at them. What was our personal risk if we refused to answer the OIC's questions? How wide would the scope of the investigation go? Would Starr's net catch other instances of fraternization, including the affairs between Secret Service personnel and Clinton staffers? The lawyers were taken aback; they'd had no idea of the Pandora's box the UD officers would open for the president, Starr, and the agency. But we had been on the front lines and knew what had been going on in Clinton world for years.

From the first meeting, it was clear to the Uniformed Division officers that we were being set up. Our choice was stark: we were either going to be accused of criminally withholding information from a federal investigation by the DOJ and FBI or be accused of criminally divulging sensitive information that was proprietary to the president and Secret Service. Saying the wrong thing could result in any of us losing his job or even going to federal prison for a very long time.

The UD officers were already locked in a prison of silence. In the meetings it was made clear that we could not discuss their situations with anyone, including coworkers, superiors, and family members, and, of course, the press. Furthermore, the Secret Service lawyers were federal employees themselves and therefore no attorney-client privilege existed between the officers and the agency's legal counsel. If we officers decided to cooperate with the Secret Service legal counsel and their legal agenda, we would have to decide for ourselves what was relevant to both the OIC and FBI and whether any bit of information could still be classified by the Secret Service. Police officers are not trained to be their own lawyers, and such decisions are beyond their training—but one false move could mean big consequences.

On top of all that, we were required to work our posts while this was going on. Adding that stress to the natural stress of the job made the work unbearable, and morale plummeted—all because the president had not been truthful at the outset.

After the tense atmosphere of the group meetings, Secret Service attorneys decided to interview all the officers individually to assess their legal exposure and relevance to the case. Starr was conducting interviews of his own, sitting down with disgruntled former service employees. He needed to find agents and officers who remembered that they were law enforcement officers first and foremost and would cooperate with the criminal investigation.

The OIC lawyers studied a diagram of the West Wing. They

needed to learn: Who controls access to the West Wing lobby? Who secures the West Wing? Several Uniformed Division officers' names kept popping up. Among them were one officer I'll call "Musket," another I'll call "Brett," an officer named Sandy Verner—and me.

Soon enough, the fax machine in Secret Service headquarters in Washington began buzzing with subpoenas.

During President Clinton's time in office, Sandy and I filled different shifts on the E-6 post, the last stationary post before the Oval Office. Along with our partners, we secured the area until the president arrived, while he was in the Oval Office, and after he and his staff departed. It was the responsibility of the E-6 post to know who was in the West Wing and that they were permitted to be there.

When I stood that post, I had turned away the intern, Monica Lewinsky, on numerous occasions for having a pass that did not allow her to be there. She was clearly making a point of crossing paths with the president by befriending presidential and White House staff, as well as other officers and agents. She even went so far as to openly flirt with them, which was conduct unbecoming the grounds. She concocted seemingly innocuous errands and elaborate excuses, even so far as to say she had tried to enter the West Wing to use the restroom. She found that some Secret Service personnel were more easily swayed than others.

When I asked Nancy Hernreich in White House Operations about that suspicious behavior, she called it a "mentorship." But there was nothing about a mentorship that required the intern to talk with the president over a secure emergency military hotline, to flirt with him in the hallway (even once flashing her read end), or to spend an extended period of time alone with him during a government shutdown. I was witness to all of those incidents, and after one such episode I even helped dispose of a semen-stained hand towel for a frustrated Navy steward and, on another occasion, discussed throwing out equally sordid tissues. But one of those incidents had nothing to do with the one mistress in question but, in fact, with another.

At one point, I suggested to Evelyn Lieberman, the president's deputy chief of staff, that the intern be removed from the West Wing for good. Gone for a while, she soon returned as a permanent employee, through a suspiciously expedited process. The president was going to have it his way, no matter what. I soon transferred off of E-6 as a result of my discomfort in working so close to the president. I had realized that many people around the president seemed to care more for the president's responsibilities than he did.

Though Officer "Musket" spent most of his time as a Uniformed Division counter sniper, the one time he rotated in for some overtime work at E-6 was more trouble than even a counter sniper could handle. While trying to inform the president of an important phone call on hold, the officer and Harold Ickes, President Clinton's other deputy chief of staff, walked into the president's study to find him and his young female friend in a "compromising position."

Officer "Brett" held a fixed post over the West Wing lobby. On a number of instances he had to run interference to prevent Lewinsky from going to see the president on the directions of his secretary Betty Currie, because Clinton was busy with another mistress, Eleanor Mondale. Upon receiving this news, the one mistress would often become noticeably emotional at having to wait for another.

Currie called on me to attempt to fix another similar incident. In one instance the Uniformed Division officer at the White House northwest gate had told Lewinsky something to the effect of "You'll have to wait. He's with his other piece of ass." She then called the president using the pillar phone at the northwest gate, calling the president directly on the special coded dropline. The officers described her as "hostile," and recognized that this emotionally compromised person should be kept away from the president. Worse still, the president's secretary asked who was responsible for the mistress at the northwest gate finding out about the other and "wanted someone [an officer] fired over this."

That was the reality for the officers on the ground, yet the Secret Service leadership and attorneys still remained committed to their charade. They briefed the officers on the "executive function privilege." The officers were led to believe that they had to invoke that "privilege" when answering any OIC question that directly involved the president. As a result, the frustrated OIC lawyers asked about the incidents that indirectly involved the president.

Other Secret Service personnel floating into and out of those meetings turned out not to be lawyers at all. Officer "Brett" once sat down with the OIC investigators with someone he thought was his Secret Service lawyer, only for that person to inform "Brett" that he was just an agent assigned to the counsel's office, whose job it was to report on everything that was said, not to give "Brett" legal advice. Another mysterious figure, who would show up for meetings and take notes, was later spotted with a pass identifying her as someone who worked in the Old Executive Office Building. None of that made the officers under scrutiny any more comfortable.

As the officers began to be interviewed by OIC, they immediately ran into problems. Answering even the simplest questions about the layout of the West Wing based on a tourist map, and details of security procedures they used every day, proved to be impossible—doing so would have given away detailed protected information that the officers were not authorized to divulge. The tourist map was propaganda to thwart attackers.

The officers believed in being "worthy of trust and confidence," but they were stuck in a quagmire. They believed the motto referred to following the law and preventing disclosure of tactical information that attackers could use, known as Operational Security (OPSEC). But it also amounted to being "worthy of trust and confidence" to the American people. When the officers testified that indeed the president had lied, they wanted their word to be sufficient alone. They were willing to tell the truth, but OIC, DOJ, FBI, and Secret Service personnel were tearing them apart, wanting to know every detail of how the officers knew what they did—which couldn't be done without violating OPSEC.

FBI agents threatened to arrest and prosecute the officers for withholding evidence. But the officers faced the same threat from their own agency if they disclosed, deliberately or not, any protected tactical knowledge. The Secret Service maintained its authority as the issuing agency for whatever was considered tactical or strategic and any bit of knowledge that could be considered classified.

Meanwhile, within the Secret Service culture, in locker rooms, around water coolers, and on what little jobs the subpoenaed officers were reduced to working, coworkers heavily insinuated that the subpoenaed officers should feign amnesia. Though plausible deniability and feigning poor or faulty memory could have worked, the FBI was threatening arrests at a moment's notice for doing so; in any case, all each officer truly wanted to do was the right thing.

Starr expected the pressure to get us all to open up and spill the beans. Merletti expected the pressure to create a collective stonewall. There seemed no way out.

"Brett" was even subjected to a bizarre interaction with President Clinton immediately after giving his testimony. After searching for him, the president asked about his family, wife, and kids—one on one. That was so bizarre it could only have been a form of intimidation.

As officers were subjected to investigations and interrogations under immense pressure, the spigot slowly opened. Many repeated what they had rehearsed under the Secret Service–backed attorneys: "On the advice of my counsel, without revealing any privileged information . . . ," so as to dodge the question. Asked why a particular question was privileged, the officers couldn't say. All of the main players— Starr, Merletti, Reno, Holder, and President Clinton—believed their pressure tactics would put them on top, but they were gambling with the legal outcomes, the officers' careers, and the risk of an officer snapping under pressure.

Officers who received subpoenas found themselves spurned and their loyalty to their agency questioned. In one instance the FBI made a concerted effort to threaten Sandy and me with arrests. Gary Grindler, Reno's deputy attorney general, went to bat for the two officers against the OIC's Jackie Bennett. When the day ended early and abruptly and the frazzled officers were told to go home, Secret Service lawyers pleaded with the officers that should the FBI make good on its previous promise to arrive in the middle of the night and arrest them in front of their families, "please, whatever you do, don't resist." Because of the OIC's tactics of adding pressure by leaking information to the press, the Secret Service lawyers informed the officers to expect camera crews to be there to witness the high-profile arrests. The sleepless night passed and the FBI's threat turned out to be a bluff, if only a tactic to exhaust and break the officers. The Secret Service surely hadn't won much favor with any of the officers it had served up.

The rift between the Secret Service leadership and the frontline personnel grew wider, and many of us lost faith entirely. To make matters worse, the leadership sought to downplay our significance by dismissing us as "guards" in the press, which only served to drive a wedge further between the Uniformed Division and the Special Agent Division that has never fully healed.

On July 9, 1998, the *Baltimore Sun* ran a piece headlined "Secret Service Secrets: Are They Worth Telling? Judges Rule: Testimony from Agents Is Required No Matter the Merit of the Case in Question." The paper reported, "The ruling by a three-judge panel that Secret Service officers must testify before a grand jury . . . cries out for the quickest possible review by the Supreme Court next term. . . . It held that the Secret Service had not made a good enough argument that the personal safety of the president requires it not to snitch on him, especially since

Congress had not passed a law to that effect." It also noted that two officers, Brian Henderson and Gary Byrne, had "refused to answer 19 questions put to them by independent counsel Kenneth Starr's lawyers" before the grand jury. Henderson, who had been stationed in the East Wing, had information about liaisons conducted by the president in the White House movie theater.

The world waited. The fate of the Clinton presidency hung in the balance. The future and culmination of the agency's past all came down to the Supreme Court finally deciding the question over a hundred years in the making: How "secret" is the Secret Service?

On July 16, 1998, the Supreme Court made its decision and CBS News ran their story: "Rehnquist: Agents Must Testify": "It was high noon in Washington Friday when Chief Justice William Rehnquist refused to spare President Clinton's Secret Service protectors from testifying. . . . The ruling ends a bitter legal dispute and clears the way for prosecutors to question some of their last key witnesses. . . . President Clinton's Secret Service protectors were at the courthouse when the ruling was handed down and have been taken into the grand jury hearing room. They arrived in a van minutes before noon, when an earlier court ruling blocking their testimony was set to expire."

So the two agents and about a dozen officers—myself included—filed in and testified before the grand jury, answering questions directly. When the critical piece of evidence, the infamous semen-stained blue dress kept as insurance by the president's young female friend, arrived, the case became even stronger. The president was then forced to volunteer a blood sample before that, too, was subpoenaed. The DNA from the semen on the dress was indisputable proof that the officers were telling the truth and that the president was indeed an elaborate liar who could not be trusted.

On September 9, 1998, the OIC delivered its "Starr Report" to Congress. The House of Representatives held a historic vote and impeached the president. President Clinton was then tried in the Senate. He survived, as a two-thirds majority was required and not one senator from Clinton's own party voted guilty on either of the two charges, obstruction of justice and perjury. Clinton remained in office, but by that time, the damage to the Secret Service had been done.

The Secret Service director and agency counsel had chosen to place their own officers and their testimony under enormous and unprecedented duress, just to protect the agency's brand. The officers had testified to the grand jury under immense pressure, and the entire agency stared them down as they did so.

Officer "Brett" went back to work and retired from the Secret Service in 2017.

Officer Sandy Verner resigned from the Secret Service soon after the investigations ended to focus on her family.

Before the subpoenas, I had transferred to the Secret Service Training Center to distance myself from the president and first lady and to pursue my new dream of becoming a firearms instructor for new generations of Secret Service personnel. I was informed that my promotion, in no secret fashion, was delayed indefinitely as payback for my participation in answering the DOJ's subpoenas. But good Secret Service men backed me, and I became an instructor, serving there until soon after the September 11 attacks. Officer "Musket" and I then left for the Federal Air Marshal Service (FAMS), as part of the ensuing "exodus" of Uniformed Division personnel away from the over-burdening Secret Service. I retired in May 2016. Officer Musket retired from FAMS in 2017.

The working relationship between the Uniformed Division and Special Agent Division deteriorated, and the agency's performance has also deteriorated so much as to become defunct. Director Merletti, the right director at the wrong time, fought for the "protective function privilege." But the Supreme Court's ruling against it proved that his interpretation of "secret" was a fallacy, generated by the agency's cult mentality. Many Secret Service leaders proved to be so entrenched in their beliefs that they had lost integrity as law enforcement officers, going so far as to bring the good name of the entire agency down with them.

Furthermore, Director Merletti, in keeping with a scheme that had been hatched by his predecessors, began to implement what was known within the Uniformed Division as the "Beltsville Plan." It was never written down, only spoken of, and used the fallout from the Starr investigation to a specific end: Merletti and his predecessor "restructured" the Special Agent Division to swallow the Uniformed Division whole, take control at the middle-management level, and secure the service's funding, all at the expense of the Uniformed Division being able to conduct its vital mission of White House and executive-area protection.

In the future there would never be a question of whether or not Secret Service personnel would testify. They would have to, but their integrity and conduct would forever be in question.

The trauma of the Starr investigation brought the Secret Service nearly to the breaking point and accelerated its downward spiral. It put the agency's entire legacy in danger. But that legacy is hardly an unblemished one. Organizational problems within the Secret Service did not begin with the Clinton era. As the agency grew and developed into what it is today, its successes were balanced by systemic failures that can be recognized even in the agency of today.

THREE.

FIRST SUCCESSES, FIRST FAILURES

After Julius Caesar was betrayed and stabbed to death, the Roman government's answer was the Praetorian Guard, but it soon became far too powerful and a threat to Roman liberty. In 1998, Ken Starr said the Secret Service risked becoming a Praetorian Guard. History never ceases to be relevant.

Today's Secret Service serves a constitutional, democratic, republican society. It serves—or at least is supposed to serve— the American people by protecting the person they've elected to the presidency. It is sworn to protect not a king who claims to hold a throne by divine right but an individual charged with leading a free society. The US Secret Service, therefore, evolved in a unique way, and its early history contains many instances of heroism but also some disturbing foreshadowing of the bureaucratic and organizational problems that hinder presidential protectors today.

Before America had a president, General George Washington formed his own Life Guard, almost immediately after accepting Congress's request on June 15, 1775, to lead the Continental Army against the British in the fight for independence. The Life Guard was the forebear of today's Secret Service's Presidential Protection Division. But there were problems even in that early protection force—a member of the Life Guard was hanged for "mutiny, sedition, and treachery" on June 28, 1776, possibly due to involvement in a plot against Washington.

In 1783, at the end of the Revolutionary War, the Life Guard was disbanded. It was not even revived in 1789 when President Washington and his troops marched on Pennsylvania to quell the Whiskey Rebellion, thus setting an early precedent that presidents did not need special protection.

The United States' first election and Washington's presidency were both unprecedented achievements in human history. No longer led by a ruler claiming divine right, the constitutional framework of the United States might have made violent coups obsolete. No kings, no coups. And what need did the country have for cowardly assassinations, when many of its leaders could settle their differences legally with duels? But the new nation would soon learn the importance of security even for democratically elected chief executives.

In 1814, America was again at war with the British, and it was not going our way. British troops marched on the capital of the new nation, seeking to burn it to the ground. The local militia was mustered to protect First Lady Dolley Madison and the presidential mansion. The militia placed a cannon at the mansion's north gate and camped out on the lawns. After the British defeated US troops at Bladensburg, Maryland, they continued on to Washington. Chaos gripped the capital city. First Lady Madison stood atop the White House roof looking through a spyglass and received instructions from her husband, President James Madison, to abandon the mansion.

She hurriedly collected the most important items to take with her. Her servants, both free and enslaved, bravely fulfilled her orders as the British closed in. The first lady escaped with silver and other important items, hidden among the horde of citizens fleeing the British. A courageous doorkeeper and gardener saved a famed portrait of George Washington. We know many of these details thanks to Paul Jennings, a former slave who wrote the first book about working in the White House, *A Colored Man's Reminiscences of James Madison*, published in 1865. White House staff, servants, and laborers, including slaves, have proven their loyalty to every first family over the years. The force designated to protect the first lady fled; those men and women were the last to leave.

On August 24 and 25, 1814, British troops ransacked and burned the mansion and all other government buildings. They added fuel to the fires for more than twenty-four hours. After two days, the capital city was returned to American rule by a hurricane and tornado known as "the storm that saved Washington."

Over the next few decades, the country passed out of the "founding" era and came into its own. In 1835, Andrew Jackson's administration saw the first recorded assassination attempt on a sitting president. A man broke from the crowd as Jackson was giving a speech, drew two pistols, and pulled the triggers. But the weapons misfired, and President Jackson, appalled at what he considered an assault on his honor as well as his body, beat the would-be assassin with his cane before the crowd joined in.

Around the same time, in nineteenth-century France, there was a man named Eugène François Vidocq, an enthusiastic and prolific criminal informant and spy for the French police. His methodology was summed up in his motto, "Set a rogue to catch a rogue." He enjoyed his work so much that he even concocted grand criminal conspiracies just to solve them. Still, his methods inspired police worldwide. It was Vidocq who first coined the term "secret service," which literally means to be in service to someone, but in secret.

Though that term was not yet in use in the United States, the beginnings of the Secret Service's executive protection strategy of concentric protective layers emerged in the 1800s. Far exceeding a single layer of bodyguards, the strategy employed multiple protective layers. Like a Russian nesting doll, for an assassin to get to the centermost doll, he or she would first have to pull apart each outer layer. But each protective layer works in tandem so that if and when an assailant or assailants manage to slip past or fight through one layer of protection, they will be funneled to and caught in the next.

In 1842, Congress authorized the DC police to post a captain and three others as a permanent White House contingent to patrol and control access. Previously, local police had scheduled beat cops to patrol the area around the White House. Congressman John J. Crittenden warned that those three men "might eventually become a formidable army." History, in some ways, has proven him correct. The police contingent at the White House grew steadily along with the DC metropolitan area. In 1853, an officer was assigned to be president Franklin Pierce's permanent bodyguard.

The game changed significantly on April 12, 1861, when the first shots of what would become the Civil War were fired upon Fort Sumter, South Carolina. When Virginia seceded from the Union, Washington found itself across a river from enemy territory overnight.

The security of President Abraham Lincoln immediately became a priority for the country but not so much for the president. The White House was protected by the "Bucktail Brigade," Company K of the 150th Pennsylvania regiment of volunteers, famous for their hats made from their native state's white-tailed deer. At Lincoln's request, however, they switched uniforms for civilian clothes because Lincoln did not want to cause a panic if the people thought that the White House had become an armed camp. Yet the presence of the regiment in itself was intended to discourage a direct assault.

The volunteers concealed their rifles at various posts for easy access (much as the Uniformed Division does today). The Bucktails were accompanied by an increase in Metropolitan Washington Police Force officers around the White House. Those forces were the precursors of the modern Uniformed Division of the Secret Service.

Another unit, the Union Light Guard, formally known as the Seventh Independent Company of Ohio Volunteer Cavalry, protected President Lincoln on his travels. The guards were the earliest precursor of Secret Service agents and the PPD. In *Lincoln's Body Guard: The Union Light Guard*, one of its members, Robert W. McBride, wrote of the company members' feeling an enormous guilt for protecting the president while other units fought and died in combat. This was especially apparent as they accompanied President Lincoln on tours of battlefields. There they felt the adrenaline rush that comes from being ready for imminent attack after long stretches of boredom while standing post at the White House—an experience no different from that of Secret Service agents, officers, and technicians today. There is a psychological burden associated with living one's daily life in comfortable surroundings—a relative heaven—while standing ready to enter hell at a moment's notice.

Even so, President Lincoln was largely defenseless from lone assassins or independent assassination teams. In at least two incidents snipers nearly killed him. In August 1864, while he was on a pleasure horseback ride, his hat was knocked off as a bullet passed clean through it; the president believed it was an unexplainable accident. Then, while observing the Battle of Fort Stevens, the surgeon accompanying Lincoln was shot by a sniper as the president approved shelling houses used by Confederate troops.

Plainclothes units formed during the Civil War became some of the first government outfits to refer to themselves as "secret services." Brigadier General Lafayette C. Baker, a Union spymaster, ran the Domestic Secret Service out of the State Department under Secretary of State William Seward. After President Lincoln suspended habeas corpus, a constitutional right requiring that an arrested person be taken before a judge or magistrate to be notified of the reason for arrest, Baker's Secret Service imprisoned 38,000 people in internment camps with no right for them to see a judge or have a trial for years, on the premise that they had participated in "anti-war activities."

Other forerunners of today's Secret Service were found in the private sector but still served the government. Allan Pinkerton operated the Union Intelligence Service and National Detective Agency. Pinkerton was an expert detective and very successful spymaster. If he is considered the first unofficial chief of the Secret Service, the first unofficial black special agent would be John Scobell, hired in 1861; the first female Secret Service agent would be Kate Warne, hired in 1856; and the most famous unofficial female Secret Service operative would be Hattie Lawton, known by her aliases HLL or Hattie Lewis—all successful Pinkerton agents. Warne and Lewis pioneered Pinkerton's Female Detective Bureau, formed in 1860, and were extremely successful assets in the Union's Civil War victory. As part of the "Pinkerton Black Agents" and a "black dispatch," Scobell carried out undercover missions in the deep South—under the guise of being a slave, even at times owned by Warne and Lewis—returning to Pinkerton with vital intelligence.

On one undercover mission to Baltimore, Kate Warne uncovered the "Baltimore Plot," a plan to assassinate President-elect Lincoln while he was traveling to Washington for his first inauguration. Pinkerton headed the first president-elect detail, and President-elect Lincoln kept his travel schedule. Under Pinkerton's command, the soon-to-be president traveled in disguise, then changed into normal clothes on arrival; the papers later accused him of cowardice for doing so. The agents carried multiple concealed pistols. Preceding modern Secret Service strategy by more than a century, Warne went ahead of the detail to sniff out "sleepers," as Pinkerton called them. Through their concentric and comprehensive protection, far more than a due-diligence bodyguard, President Lincoln lived to be inaugurated.

But even at that early stage, bureaucratic squabbles emerged. General Baker and Allan Pinkerton each claimed to be the real head of Lincoln's Secret Service and refused to work together. On various occasions they even arrested each other's operatives. Following the war's end on April 9, 1865, Baker was put on trial for domestic war crimes and found guilty. He was fined one dollar. Meanwhile, Pinkerton continued the Pinkerton National Detective Agency after the Union Intelligence Service dissolved. Congress and President Lincoln left a void by not specifically delegating new responsibilities, such as fugitive hunting, investigation of land and bank fraud, and investigation of interstate white-collar crimes to existing law enforcement agencies. The existing agencies were unsure of how to operate beyond state lines. Banks, railroads, and other interstate businesses hired their own forces, often Pinkerton's, to shut down criminals (and strikers).

President Lincoln and Congress were responsible for the creation of a new division within the Treasury Department under a one-year congressional appropriation. It was called the Secret Service Division (SSD). Its sole mission was to rein in the out-of-control currency issues that threatened the nation's economy during the period following the Civil War. Presidential protection was not yet part of its mission, but it would soon be made tragically clear how important that mission was.

On April 14, 1865, five days after General Robert E. Lee's surrender of the Confederate Army of Northern Virginia at Appomattox, President Lincoln and First Lady Mary Todd Lincoln attended a play at Ford's Theatre in Washington. On his travels, President Lincoln was without Union Light Guard, Pinkerton's, or General Baker's men. The concentric-circles strategy was gone, and the president thought that some local detectives would be sufficient bodyguards. His White House protection detail had been reduced to just three detectives.

During the officers' search of the theater's balcony, they failed to notice the measures the assassin had set up; he had drilled a peephole, disabled a lock, and fabricated a hidden lock to barricade the door. One of Lincoln's protectors left the theater to drink at a nearby bar. The assassin, a well-known actor and outspoken anti-Lincoln zealot named John Wilkes Booth, eyed the president through the peephole. He schmoozed his way past an usher into the darkened balcony box. Once inside, he barricaded the door. He then turned and fired a .44-caliber ball into the president's skull, then slashed an army major accompanying the Lincolns with a long knife. Booth then leaped from the box down onto the stage and escaped. Simultaneously, another member of the actor's cabal attacked Secretary of State Seward, stabbing him multiple times as he rested in bed in his home across the street from the White House. The attacker inflicted horrific knife wounds but fled following a struggle as Seward's two sons and a soldier stationed at the house saved the cabinet member's life.

Baker dispatched agents to hunt down the cabal. Booth was eventually shot to death at a farm in Maryland; four other conspirators were tried and hanged. Baker personally accompanied agents to protect the new president, Andrew Johnson.

Baker and his men soon found themselves at odds with the sleazy pardon brokers who visited President Johnson night and day. After Baker removed Lucy Cobb, a favor seeker and alleged mistress to the new president, from the White House and restricted her access to the president, Johnson fired Baker, just as Cobb had wanted. Through the decades, numerous presidents have put their protectors at odds through their personal dalliances, and, as many chose poorly, have put themselves and the country at great risk. President Johnson was the first on record to jeopardize his security, not out of principle but for personal pleasure.

Lucy Cobb returned to the White House in 1866. That same year, the State Department's domestic Secret Service ended. President Lincoln's legacy lived on in the newly formed Secret Service Division (SSD) under the Treasury Department. Many of Baker's agents found employment there and brought their expertise with them.

The unit was devoted to stopping the rampant counterfeiting that had cropped up in the wake of the Civil War. At that point, nearly two-thirds of the nation's currency was estimated to be counterfeit. If SSD couldn't bring integrity back to the economy by eliminating counterfeiting, the nation would surely fall to anarchy. The agency's chief, William P. Wood, led the first "war" on white-collar crime. Wood was a Mexican-American War veteran and had arrested the violent abolitionist John Brown for horse thievery. Wood set his sights on the biggest bank owner and counterfeiter, William E. Brockway, called by newspapers "the counterfeit king." Following his arrest, Brockway struck a deal with the prosecutors: he revealed the hidden locations of the plates he had used to make hundreds of counterfeit bills, up to $1,000 notes, and provided information on many other operations. In the division's first year, the Secret Service shut down two hundred domestic counterfeiting operations.

In 1881, tragedy struck the presidency again. For weeks, a mentally ill stalker, Charles J. Guiteau, had been following the undefended president, James Garfield. He had twice aimed and cocked his single-action revolver at the president but had not pulled the trigger. Stalking the president and writing him increasingly threatening letters was the stalker's sole obsession. On July 2, 1881, he tracked Garfield by using the president's schedule, which was routinely published in the newspapers. He stood in the crowd, which included the president's two sons and secretary, at the Washington, DC, train station, waiting for the doors of the president's train to open. As they opened, the crazed man drew a pistol from concealment, fired a shot that grazed Garfield's shoulder, recocked, and fired again. The crowd wrestled the assassin to the ground. The president died two and a half months later after fighting an agonizing infection. A mere sixteen years after President Lincoln's murder, history was repeated. Even after the second assassination, Garfield's successor, President Chester Arthur, refused protection in any form. The lessons of history were ignored again as debates over solutions fell to the wayside.

In 1884, SSD became involved in executive protection by happenstance as Congress broadened the division's authority to fight illegal gambling, mail and land fraud, and other forms of white-collar crimes. SSD chief James Brooks designated two agents to search for suspicious activity at the White House after agents discovered an assassination plot. Ten years later, at the request of SSD chief William Hazen, the agents were still there. First Lady Frances Cleveland learned of another plot: to kidnap her children. In both plots, the conspirators' aim was to harm the president as punishment for the Secret Service's efforts to quash gambling.

Fearing that the first family's protective detail would become a political liability, President Grover Cleveland removed it as soon as he learned about it—the agents, at the first lady's request, had kept their protection a secret from even the president. But President Cleveland did request an SSD agent to accompany him when traveling to his summer retreat, and so SSD became directly involved in presidential protection.

In its founding and formative years, "Secret" in the agency's name meant undercover, and its agents called themselves "operatives" but were referred to as Treasury agents, "T-men," or detectives by the Treasury. In 1875, Chief Hiram Whitley issued permission for operatives to fabricate their badges at their own expense. Operatives worked alone without partners, undercover, and in plain clothes. The agency reimbursed little more than travel and the cost of telegrams to report back to field offices and headquarters. As a result, many operatives were labeled "fake cops" and were regularly accused of trespassing and overreaching their authority because they were from a "made-up" government division. Simply put, many Americans had never heard of the SSD. The "secret" was causing problems for operatives on remote missions. They pushed for standardization and further reimbursements, but to them "secret" simply meant deep undercover.

"Secret" was and still is little more than a carryover of a colloquialism used by Seward, Baker, Pinkerton, and others during the Civil War. However, throughout the history of the Secret Service, that colloquialism has been falsely interpreted to justify the withholding of information from Congress, the president, its own employees, and the people of the United States. But no legal backing for keeping information "secret" exists. Over time, that theory has been used by chiefs and directors to suggest that the Secret Service is essentially different from other law enforcement agencies. It is not. Yet Secret Service directors continually attempt to justify their actions of thwarting transparency and accountability based on the hollow vestige of "secret," doing so out of their ignorance of history.

During the Spanish-American War, the Secret Service protected President William McKinley, the twenty-fifth president, part-time. After the war, the detail was again reduced to an on-request service, at the president's discretion. On September 6, 1901, during a victory tour following his reelection, the president insisted on appearing at a ten-minute meet-and-greet at a music hall in Buffalo, New York. Secret Service operative George Foster, the president's frequently called upon protector, along with operatives Samuel Ireland and Albert Gallaher, scanned the crowd. Seventy-five Buffalo police, soldiers, and Pinkertons guarded the perimeter. More people arrived than expected, and an event coordinator panicked and demanded that the soldiers, who were there purely for decoration, form a gauntlet inside the hall. The operatives lost their buffer zone and field of view as the eager line of visitors pressed right up to the president. The operatives should have whisked the president away, but Foster surely knew that the president would have been furious and blamed the operatives and the agency for overreacting. He most likely then would have disbanded his protection altogether and thus become completely vulnerable at all future events.

In the heat, many visitors wiped their brows with handkerchiefs, and the soldiers, inexperienced with protection, did not enforce the rule to keep hands out and open. One man, Leon Czolgosz, was sweating more than the visitors around him. He stepped ahead in line, drew a pistol from a handkerchief, and fired two shots into the president's abdomen, killing him.

In thirty-six years, three American presidents had been assassinated. Two had not had Secret Service protection; the other had been protected only part-time. Agent Rufus Young-blood wrote of that era in his 1973 memoir: "The presidency had become a surer route to the cemetery than Russian roulette." Something had to change.

McKinley's vice president, Theodore Roosevelt, who succeeded him after the assassination, became the first president to receive congressional authorization for full-time Secret Service protection. But SSD had to find the new president first. When President McKinley died, Vice President Roosevelt was on vacation, hiking in the wilderness with his family.

At first, the fiercely independent "TR" considered SSD protection a personal tyranny and a waste. Of the five permanent Secret Service operatives protecting him night and day, he said, "they would not be the least use in preventing any assault upon my life. I do not believe there is any danger . . . and if there were it would be simple nonsense to try to prevent it." Then came a near miss: A man in a tuxedo maneuvered his way through every White House security layer of officers, operatives, and the White House usher. For minutes the overly obliging president found himself cornered and alone with the dangerous "crank," as he called the man. The president escaped, and agents searched the man's tuxedo and found a large revolver. From then on, the president accepted the protection. As he admitted in a letter to a friend, "The secret service men are a very small but very necessary thorn in the flesh." A person admitted to the president's presence without proper clearance would become known as a "gate-crasher," and though such people typically have benevolent intentions, their ability to schmooze past security measures leaves a president's protection at the mercy of the gate-crasher's whim.

But with increased protection duties came increased risk to the protectors. On September 3, 1902, in Lenox, Massachusetts, a railcar collided with President Roosevelt's carriage. The president was injured but survived. Secret Service operative William Craig, a British military veteran, died after being thrown from the carriage. The president felt humbled by the loss and sacrifice, the first death of a Secret Service employee while on the job.

Roosevelt's respect increased for those who risked everything to protect him. Well known and deeply meaningful to those inside the agency are photos of Roosevelt's children reporting to the morning briefings and roll calls on the White House grounds alongside the police contingent protecting the White House, another precursor of today's Uniformed Division. Those early images show the love and dedication crucial to the job of protecting the First Family and serving in the Secret Service in any era.

During Roosevelt's administration, as its role expanded, the Secret Service encountered a new rival. A new federal agency, the Bureau of Investigation (BOI), under the Department of Justice, was created in 1908 in response to the Secret Service's complaints to Congress that DOJ too often "borrowed" its operatives. Its wish was granted but the BOI was born as a "bureaucratic bastard" and manned by SSD operatives who quit to join the new agency. That was the Secret Service's first exodus of manpower to another government agency, but it would not be the last.

One of the early SSD agents to jump to the BOI was William Burns, who eventually headed the agency and became a mentor to a young Bureau staffer named J. Edgar Hoover. Burns taught Hoover how to lobby Congress effectively and create a base of support among members, which Burns had learned from his work in the SSD. Hoover would turn the BOI into the FBI, pioneering his "G-man vision" for FBI agents, inspired by Secret Service operatives and techniques. The bitter rivalry between the Secret Service and FBI for national, presidential, and congressional favor continues to this day.

In 1917, Congress made threatening the president a federal crime. As a result, the Secret Service expanded, creating "Room 98," the precursor of the Protective Research Section, hidden in the Treasury Annex. Inside, operatives investigated, analyzed, researched, and turned over information on threatening individuals to prosecutors or mental facilities. Room 98 held a library containing every threatening letter and a dossier on every threat. Once a file was created on an individual, it was never removed. Those with a "presidential complex," the term for a dangerous obsession with the president, were graded by their motivation and capacity to carry out any threat. Agents from field offices all over the country would put Treasury-related investigations on hold to investigate, monitor, or even follow the subjects of those dossiers, especially when the president was traveling nearby.

Yet for all those expansions, would the SSD be able to thwart the kinds of assassins who had killed Presidents Lincoln, Garfield, and McKinley and nearly killed others? The assassinations of Lincoln and McKinley had commonalities. Each assassin had made threats by letters and threatening speeches. Each had stalked his target on several occasions, and each had made use of a concealed firearm, as well as charm or false claims, to get close to the president before attempting their deadly acts. President Lincoln's murderer had even made secret modifications to the president's booth at the theater. For "stalkers," SSD made a serious commitment to diligently investigate those who threatened the president; thoroughly investigate security details in advance of presidential trips; and improve upon specialized training so operatives could think like "a rogue to catch a rogue." But what of the "approacher," the spontaneous type who had killed President Garfield and would later pose a threat to President Franklin Roosevelt?

In 1930, the White House Police Force, first formed in 1922, became part of the Secret Service. Congress funded the force's first White House alarm and pass holder system, its expansion of manpower, and its members' desire for combat marksmanship training. The White House Police Force had a simple, effective plan of protection: Balancing security and optics, in the event of attack the approachable-looking White House police officers at the perimeter, armed with .38-caliber special revolvers, would fight and fall back to the White House. As the attackers advanced on the North or South Lawn, additional officers, using gun boxes filled with shotguns, Thompson submachine guns, and other weapons hidden throughout the White House, would intercept them. The spirit of that plan remains today, and the White House Police Force eventually developed into today's Uniformed Division.

The election of President Franklin Roosevelt in 1932 brought about a major reorganization of the federal government, including the Secret Service.

In 1933, during his first year in office, President Roosevelt appointed his longtime friend Henry Morgenthau, Jr., to head the Treasury Department. Morgenthau, a young Jewish entrepreneur, had become friends with Roosevelt when each had run his own Christmas tree farm business in upstate New York. In Morgenthau, Roosevelt saw a strong and impartial ally impatient with government bureaucracy. Morgenthau was comfortable as an outsider who could enter a completely new organization and fix it. He had no prior law enforcement experience and might have seemed poorly qualified for the job, but indeed he was the most qualified because he gave no significance to politics or personal loyalties. Later described by one famous Secret Service agent as possessing freezing water in his veins, Morgenthau cared little for how hard men worked; his focus was on results. A ruthless administrator, he cut out anything and anyone who got into the way of measurable progress. Aside from being integral to Roosevelt's New Deal economic plan, he set his own mission to overhaul the lagging Treasury Department and its worst offender, the Secret Service.

Morgenthau recognized that presidential protection had long been increasing in difficulty and complexity, yet under Secret Service chief William Moran and White House detail chief Edmund Starling, he believed that the guard protecting the president still relied far too much on hope and chance.

Moran and Starling made advances but fell behind the biggest threats: vehicle bombs, poison or bombs sent through the mail, "approachers," and warnings of ground-based assaults on the White House. Chief Moran's greatest achievement was instituting badges and standardizing operatives' firearms, as they had previously had to purchase their own. Starling was a personal confidant of several presidents. He was very good at coordinating with White House staff and workers to find each president as he tried to sneak off—and he also left behind a detailed memoir of his life in the SSD.

Changing times called for swift solutions, and an incident with an approacher early in the Roosevelt presidency made that clear. On February 15, 1933, an approacher, Giuseppe Zangara, managed the first critical assassination attempt on a president under full-time Secret Service protection. In Miami, President Roosevelt gave a short speech sitting on the back seat of his limo before a crowd of 8,000, all unscreened. Zangara, who had previously plotted to ambush President Herbert Hoover, pushed his way to the front of the crowd to try for Roosevelt. To Zangara's dismay, the president's speech ended and Miami Mayor Anton Cermak began his own speech as Roosevelt sat down in his limo, shielded from view. The SSD's plan had been to move Roosevelt while the mayor was speaking, but against protocol, they had acquiesced to Roosevelt's demand for the limo to wait, engine off, so he could leisurely read a telegram.

Zangara fired six shots. Five hit flesh, but none struck the president. Cermak was grievously wounded. A woman standing next to the shooter hit his arm with her purse and spoiled his aim. Operatives from the follow-up car closed in. A twenty-three-year-old civilian, a New York City police officer, and a Secret Service operative were hit, but all survived. Cermak died three weeks later. The errant sixth bullet missed Roosevelt by inches. Had the president been standing just where the mayor was, he would have been shot at close range as Secret Service protectors watched. The assassin died in the electric chair, but presidents' continued use of slow open convertibles would continue to plague the Secret Service. One wonders why it inexplicably went along with it.

Even after the assassination attempt, the president's SSD operatives described Roosevelt as "fearless." He became close with them thanks to their help in pulling off what came to be called a "splendid deception," as SSD operatives shielded from the press and public as much as possible views of the president that revealed his dependence on his wheelchair. Agents hoisted the president up and helped him stand, and at times they even helped him dress.

Two full years after the Miami assassination attempt, Starling had increased the president's detail from five to only nine agents. One new addition was Michael Francis Reilly, who recognized that in near misses, the Secret Service had contributed to the president's survival, but the only thing separating its successes from its failures had been luck. And under Starling's leadership of the White House detail, that was not changing.

New Secret Service leadership came when Frank Wilson was made chief in 1936, replacing Moran. To the operatives, Chief Wilson was an outsider planted among them by Morgenthau, but Wilson prioritized the SSD's war on counterfeiting above all else, including even presidential protection. Chief Wilson had participated in finding the kidnapper and murderer of Charles and Anne Morrow Lindbergh's baby. When the BOI and the power-hungry Herbert Hoover couldn't crack the case, the SSD and the Treasury had solved the "crime of the century" by turning to the public for help. Eventually a gas station attendant noticed one of the ransom bills' serial numbers and the jig was up.

Chief Wilson's SSD again turned the public into a major asset by forcing it to educate Americans on how to spot fake bills—and Wilson did so against the wishes of many appalled

SSD veterans who coveted their believed secrecy. Despite more than seventy years of the Secret Service losing the war on counterfeiting since its creation, Chief Wilson, using innovative approaches and determined leadership, cut counterfeiting nationwide by 88 percent in two years. Newspapers gleefully reported how American "store keepers and children alike" detected and rejected fake money as amateur sleuths catching criminals alongside local police and the feds. By 1942, Frank Wilson's Secret Service had won the second counterfeiting war.

Chief Wilson would have sealed the fate on "secret" when he penned his memoir, *Special Agent: A Quarter-Century with the Treasury Department and the Secret Service,* if not for one catastrophe soon to follow. But with the war on counterfeiting won, Chief Wilson was all ears to Agent Reilly on how to turn presidential protection around.

That same year, an approacher in a crowd threw a dagger and missed President Roosevelt by inches (the dagger was found *afterward* to be rubber). That was one of several near misses that cemented a truth for Reilly: the president's detail could not protect against assassins such as the ones who had killed Presidents Garfield and McKinley and nearly killed Roosevelt in Miami. For the White House Police, the same mentality was recognized: from 1937 to 1940, twenty fence jumpers were caught around and *in* the White House. Though none committed any violence during those attempts, some were found with knives or guns. Still, those breaches spurred little to no change.

Everything changed dramatically on December 7, 1941. Mike Reilly had just been promoted to assistant supervising agent within White House Protective Operations. He was the highest-ranking Secret Service employee on site, as Wilson and

Starling were miles away, off duty. When Reilly heard about the attack on Pearl Harbor, he realized that it had been designed to cripple the US Navy. Therefore, he reasoned, a larger strategy to cripple the entire US command-and-control structure targeting the president and White House was likely and could be imminent. He wasted no time obtaining the permissions of his off-site superiors. He called in every agent he could find, issued more firearms, and started new patrols.

Wilson and Morgenthau each conducted midnight inspections of the White House defenses. They found the Oval Office officer on duty snoring. Secretary Morgenthau estimated that two dozen enemy agents with guns and bombs could plow into the White House with a heavy truck and, with little resistance, slaughter every Secret Service protector, with the president meeting the same fate. The White House was nearly as vulnerable as it had been during its sacking by the British in 1814.

Reilly was placed in charge of the White House detail and, out of respect, kept Starling on as "codirector" for another two years. But it was Reilly's show now, and he had his work cut out for him. On his first day on duty, President Roosevelt requested to be taken on a drive around Washington in a show of national resilience. Despite years of begging for them, the Secret Service had no armored cars, Reilly, unlike Starling, was willing to work outside the specific allocations from Congress. Two hours after the president requested the ride, Reilly and Wilson procured the first presidential armored car, a custom-built Cadillac limo that had been seized from the Al Capone crime network.

As war on Nazi Germany and the Japanese Empire was declared, the Treasury, Congress, and the president deluged the

Secret Service with emergency war funds that allowed Reilly to make a number of critical changes.

The permanent White House detail was expanded from eleven agents to seventy. The size of the White House Police Force doubled. Marksmanship training was increased and would soon save the life of another president. Temporary vehicle barricades were installed. An underground zigzag tunnel was built connecting the White House to the Treasury Building's vault, which was turned into the president's own bomb shelter and temporary underground command center.

In addition, the Secret Service established a bomb team with the help of local police and military units. A military police unit posted .50-caliber antiaircraft machine guns on the White House roof, and a .50-caliber-armed car patrolled the area. Gas attack filters were added to the White House. Agents and officers received Geiger counters, and all White House occupants were issued gas masks. The military's White House Signal Corps (WHSC) (the precursor of the modern, White House Communications Agency, or WHCA) was established at the White House and created the Secret Service's first secure White House radio system.

Thus the White House was transformed into a true "complex." Comprising 18.5 acres, it included the North and South Lawns, the State Department Building (now known as the Old Executive Office Building) to the west, the White House at the center, and the Treasury Building to the east, all under the Secret Service's protective jurisdiction.

President Roosevelt, not to be held back by the challenges of his paralysis or the obvious risks to his life during wartime, scheduled four major international trips. All were fraught with near catastrophes. After he returned safely from Mexico, one of the Mexican president's guards, who had protected him on the trip, made an attempt on the life of the Mexican president, Manuel Ávila Camacho, revealing himself to be a Nazi operative. In Casablanca, General George Patton frantically tried to get the president to leave when intelligence showed that the Nazis knew he was there.

On trips to the Middle East and the Soviet Union, Reilly and the president dodged Nazi magnetically guided torpedoes, German submarines (two were destroyed on one presidential trip), and sea mines, as well as one incident of friendly fire, when an escort ship accidentally fired a torpedo at the president's ship. It barely missed.

But the success of those trips only encouraged Roosevelt, who announced that he wanted to personally visit American troops fighting in Italy. At that point, Reilly drew the line and exercised his override authority, refusing to allow the president to place himself in such danger. He knew that the president was sure to demand that he be fired, but Reilly, seeing zero chance of success in keeping the president alive if he went to oversee the landings, was finally the first operative to exert the "override authority." Amazingly, the president backed down.

Roosevelt's declining health in the later years of World War II created an increased focus on his vice president, Harry Truman. Vice presidents had not historically been protected by the Secret Service, but Morgenthau eventually assigned three men to Truman, who initially assumed that the strangers in his office were visitors. That simple effort, which very nearly didn't happen, helped ensure continuity of government when Roosevelt died of a cerebral hemorrhage on April 12, 1945, while staying in Georgia of his mistress and having his portrait painted.

In just a few years, the Secret Service had gone from failing to winning. It was all due to Henry "The Morgue" Morgenthau, Frank "The Untouchable" Wilson, and Mike "The Irish Cop" Reilly. SSD evolved from a gentleman bodyguard to effective protectors of a wartime leader, as well as winning another war on counterfeiting—which was won through transparency. But with World War II's end, fatigue calling in its debts, and the death of President Roosevelt, who had continually requested the postponement of agent retirements, the job and its stresses finally took their toll. Protection is a marathon, not a sprint, and those three leaders, though incredible, had failed to ensure that their efforts would be maintained. They failed to adequately pass the torch to the next generation of leaders. That was the beginning of the service's degeneration.

On President Truman's first full day as president, he strode right past his exhausted White House detail and out the front door and headed for Pennsylvania Avenue. He had always enjoyed a long, fast walk before breakfast. Sunrise walks were the hallmark of his style. Foolishly, the SSD failed to see that he would not be able to hold the schedule his predecessor had over four terms. Only one agent noticed Truman leaving and caught up with him on the lawn. The Southeast Gate White House Police officer urgently phoned the detail, who, panicking, caught up to the new president a half mile away on 15th Street. The president said, "Well, now, it's very nice of you to join me."

Why had the first agent not exercised his override authority? The agent believed that if the detail had not known Truman was walking the streets unprotected, approachers and stalkers would not have known either. It was a gamble, a protection style yet again based more on hope and chance than on procedure.

Throughout World War II, the Secret Service employed only about three hundred agents in total. On Starling's White House detail, there were about twenty-five permanent agents rotating in three shifts. Under Reilly, that number had immediately increased to seventy. But the additional forty-five-plus were not new hires; they were transfers from field offices across the nation serving temporarily. Field agents were shipped in to guard the president as he traveled or stayed at the White House, an imperfect practice at best.

Meanwhile, the biggest threat to the president was the White House itself. First Lady Eleanor Roosevelt had not been comfortable utilizing any of the $50,000 annual federal allocation for upkeep of the executive mansion while the government rationed food and called upon Americans to scrounge scrap metals, and grow "victory gardens" in parks and their yards to aid the war effort. During the war, therefore, the White House had fallen into disrepair. Even the allocation was little match for the now structurally unsound building.

In 1948, as First Daughter Margaret Truman played the piano in the sitting room, a leg of the piano suddenly crashed through the floor and into the rotting support beam directly below. It was the last straw for President Truman. Through embarrassing meetings with congressmen and visiting dignitaries, he shamed Congress into funding an extensive renovation.

In 1950, the White House received congressional support for its long reconstruction. With strong input from the military, Secret Service, and security professionals, the entire structure was rebuilt from the inside. Steel beams were added, along with air-conditioning, a basement and subbasement, and a nuclear fallout shelter, ready for the Cold War.

The president had to move his family to Blair House, across the street from the White House at the corner of Jackson Place and Pennsylvania Avenue. They would stay there for most of the duration of the four-year project.

From Blair House, President Truman continued his morning walks, which had become increasingly popular. There was even a walking club set up, where unofficial tickets were handed out to those seeking to join the pack. His Secret Service protectors, of course, were terrified. Chief Urbanus Baughman later reflected that the walks "represented the kind of 'habit' that was hand-picked for the assassin. . . . [The daily walks] made Mr. Truman a slow moving target, the delight of a sharpshooter." Anxious agents walked close to the president and his entourage; Baughman implemented a follow car brimming with agents with submachine guns to follow the president, which they did in secret, in case of a drive-by attack or car ramming but admittedly useless in case of a sniper attack.

Only seven Secret Service men, a mixture of agents and White House Police, ensured Truman's protection day and night during his stay at Blair House during the renovation. When the president departed and arrived at Blair House, the detail would be bolstered by additional agents and White House Police.

Chief Baughman's much-needed and well-conceived presidential security plan, called "defense in depth," was hard to implement at Blair House. Pennsylvania Avenue in those years was open to both pedestrians and vehicles. The chief's three layers (inner, middle, outer) intertwined like chain mail with each man an interconnected link. Agents with agents and officers with officers, they worked in pairs and maintained line of sight with each other. Doors could be unlocked but were always manned, ideally from both sides, in case of a bomb threat, fire, firefight, or a combination of the three. Secret Service men at the outer layer, carrying sidearms only, would identify and engage approachers, gate-crashers, or any other kind of potential threat, while the inner circle evacuated the president. Agents or officers near those engaged would then communicate with the rear layers, aid in stopping the threat, and, equally important, aim to prevent any gaps. The philosophy behind "defense in depth" did not fit well with Blair House's physical shallowness. An attacker needed only to burst in from the public street and then race up two flights of stairs to arrive in the president's bedroom. Unlike today, pedestrians, cars, and buses rushed by all day long. Unscreened crowds often formed just outside the building. There was only a knee-high fence that guarded the bushes under the windows. All the protective measures considered "needs" at the White House, such as the fence, were disregarded as "wants" at Blair House.

On November 1, 1950, aside from the occasional construction noise, all was quiet at the White House western front. Local newspapers had published the president's provided schedule, just as they always did. President Truman arrived with his detail at the back entrance of Blair House so crowds could not close in. All upper-floor windows were open so air could circulate throughout the house. The Secret Service often worried about the street-level entrances and the ushers, chefs, and housemen going in and out. The main doors were open, their screen doors closed and manned by Secret Service employees.

President Truman had lunch with Mrs. Truman, and just before 2 p.m. he lay down to take a nap prior to a 2:30 cemetery commemoration with British officials.

The outer ring of perimeter security consisted of four Secret Service White House Police officers. Officer Leslie Coffelt manned the west side security booth. Officer Joseph Downs manned the west entrance. The east security booth was covered by Officer Joseph Davidson. Officer Donald Birdzell was covering the stone staircase to the east side front door. Agent Floyd Boring made his rounds to everyone at their posts. Agent Vincent Mroz, the new guy on the White House detail, hovered around Blair House's interior. Agent Stewart Stout guarded the president's bedroom on the second floor's east side. At the intersection of Pennsylvania Avenue and Jackson Place, Metro Police officer Marion Preston directed traffic.

Two men had been driven by Blair House in a taxicab earlier that morning. After canvassing the neighborhood, they returned to their hotel and inquired about a late checkout, confident that they would return. After lunch, dapperly dressed for the occasion, they took a bus filled with sightseers to the Treasury, east down Pennsylvania Avenue. They walked past Blair House again, made a final survey, and split up. At 2:20 p.m., the novice gunman, Oscar Collazo, approached from the east, as the trained gunfighter, Griselio Torresola, moved in from the west.

Collazo stood unnoticed at the east entrance steps, between Officer Birdzell, stationed atop the steps into Blair House, and the security booth, where Agent Boring and Officer Davidson conversed. Seeing Officer Birdzell, who was facing the door, he drew a Luger pistol from concealment and pulled his trigger on him. The officer heard a sharp quiet metallic click and turned to see Collazo slapping the back of his Walther P38 semiautomatic 9 mm pistol, which had failed to fire. Agent Boring and Officer Davidson took notice just as the assassin's gun discharged, sending the first bullet into Officer Birdzell's knee.

President Truman awoke. Mrs. Truman went to the president to confirm her suspicion that the noise had been a car's exhaust backfiring. Chief Baughman had just left his barbershop and was walking back to the Treasury Building. He, too, thought he heard the sound of a car backfiring. But the trained officers knew what the sound really was and turned to see Officer Birdzell descend and hobble into the street.

Reporters, photographers, and tourists wandering by dived over fences and hedges, fleeing in all directions. Metro Police officer Marion Preston ran toward the shooting, gun drawn, and a bullet passed through his jacket. Officer Birdzell, thinking fast and remembering his training, continued to shoot and move. That forced one of the assassins further from the protectee, and reduced the chance that the three officers' return fire would hit one another or any civilians.

After the first shot, Officer Coffelt, at the west security booth, turned east. Officer Downs was entering Blair House through the open west basement entrance. Downs climbed back up the stairs to address the first shot. That's when Torresola, utilizing his compatriot's shot as a distraction, stepped to Officer Coffelt's booth and fired three shots into Coffelt's back. Torresola then rapidly pivoted and turned his Luger toward Officer Downs, shooting him three times. One shot almost severed Downs's neck. Downs backed into the Blair House kitchen, drew, and fired one shot at Torresola but missed; then, clutching his neck, he collapsed, unconscious. The door into Blair House was now wide open for the second assassin to enter.

Agent Vincent Mroz headed to a second-story window to take aim at one of the assassins below. His first carefully aimed shot missed; a tree blocked his second. Agent Stewart Stout instructed the first lady and president to stay where they were and lie low. He grabbed a Thompson submachine gun and stood at the top of the staircase. For an assassin to reach the president, he would have to somehow make it past Stout's .45-caliber, fully automatic defense. Stout followed protocol exactly, but the housemen yelled at him, called him a coward, and urged him to join the fight. Agent Stout held fast, and the inner layer held.

At that moment, Torresola had a choice to make: he could either enter the building over Officer Downs's body and head upstairs to the president or aid his fallen compatriot, who was on the east side facing down four police guns. Had Torresola chosen to enter through the basement door; had Agent Mroz taken a different route than the assassin; and had Agent Stout buckled under the accusations of cowardice and likewise run outside to aide in the gunfight, he would have had an unfettered path to the president and first lady. Agent Stout kept his post. Agent Mroz decided to take the fight to the enemy outside and ran down the interior steps to the west doorway entrance. If he could rush out, he would outflank the two assassins.

The two White House officers fired five quick shots each. Agent Boring was calmer. His first shot missed. His second hit one of the assassins square in the chest, knocking him flat on his face.

President Truman, unattended, leaned out his window and stared bewilderedly at the gunfight below. A Metro officer in the street yelled at the president, "Get back!"

Had Torresola looked up, he might have seen the president and had a clear shot, but instead he fired his last round at the agents and officers at the east end, then moved to a new fighting position. The sidewalk trees, bushes, and knee-high fence offered him intermittent cover. The new position disrupted the clear line of sight and fire between him and the Secret Service trio, who turned their fire on Torresola, who knelt, reloaded, and returned fire.

At one point during my employment with the Secret Service, a colleague had the opportunity to take a look at some of the old evidence files describing that incident. One uncorroborated witness taking cover reported to authorities that a plainclothes man on the (then) State Department Building side of the street had drawn his own handgun from concealment, taken careful aim, and fired one shot before walking off, but no such mystery shooter was ever reported publicly.

At the exact moment that the "plainclothes man" took a shot at Torresola, a few feet away from Torresola, Officer Coffelt, bleeding to death and slouched in his booth, took careful aim with his .38 special Colt revolver, just as he had been drilled in all his years of White House Police marksmanship training. He fired one shot before falling unconsciousness. The shot struck its mark.

Torresola was dead, a clean hole on the right side of his head and a gaping mess on the left from the single bullet that had passed through it. Officer Preston sprinted to a nearby drug store and phoned police. The Battle of Blair House was over.

The president's limo arrived soon afterward, and President Truman decided to keep his 2:30 appointment. His detail was glad to have him leave so they could get things under control.

Due to the brave work of so many agents and officers, the president had lived and the nation had been spared an enormous trauma. But it had come at the cost of the life of Officer Leslie Coffelt. In his honor, President Truman wrote a letter to the chief of the Uniformed Division, establishing the White House Police Benefit Fund. With it, the Secret Service White House Police would hold the exclusive rights to sell White House memorabilia carrying the White House and presidential seal. The fund was to be used for scholarships and to boost the morale of the workforce and champion their values, marksmanship, and sacrifice. None of those values was more worthy of honor than those of Officer Coffelt, who, with his last breath and final shot, had saved the president's life.

Not long afterward, the White House Police Force used the fund to accomplish all of those goals. The fund started a scholarship for officers' children, helped officers' families in desperate need, and assisted families of officers who had died. The fund also aided the White House Police pistol, rifle, and shotgun teams, which competed in and won championships worldwide. It boosted morale and kept the Secret Service operating at the forefront of combat marksmanship. The teams also hosted their own national and international competition as a way of honoring Coffelt's memory and giving back to police units nationwide that so often aided in presidential protection when the president traveled.

As an emergency measure, President Truman's detail was bolstered with even more agents transferring in from field offices. The Battle of Blair House was the most violent and lethal in the history of the Secret Service's PPD. As of late 2017, Officer Leslie Coffelt remains the only employee of the Secret Service to have sacrificed his life in direct protection of the president.

The incident, for a time at least, curtailed President Truman's walks. Agents drove him to fenced areas whose area and perimeters were secured. That way he could enjoy his walks *and* be protected. His protectors and their families appreciated the change.

Truman's successor, President Dwight Eisenhower, had one of the most amiable relationships with his Secret Service protectors that a president has ever had. But that brought its own challenges. Throughout his two terms of office, the Secret Service's experience in protecting the overly agreeable Eisenhower lulled them into complacency. Chief Baughman and the White House detail summarized their troubles as "Three G's— Golf, Gettysburg, and Grandchildren." Agents had to clear golf courses—easy open ground for snipers—before the president could play through, requiring the creation of the agency's first countersniper program. As for the grandchildren, some agents even became "honorary Camp Fire Girls" while escorting the first granddaughters to summer camp. After a great debate with the president, SSD finally closed a visitors' observation tower at the Gettysburg battlefield site to secure the president's nearby farm from snipers.

At the beginning and end of President Eisenhower's two terms, he became stubborn and brash when it came to foreign travel, leading to several near misses. In secrecy, SSD agreed to President-elect Eisenhower's campaign promise: a hair-raising trip to the front lines during the Korean War, where, according to agent Rufus Youngblood, "more than once the areas he visited were overrun and taken hours later by the enemy."

Eisenhower nearly died when his heart couldn't handle the altitude of Kabul, Afghanistan, in 1959, only to be saved by a quick-thinking Secret Service agent who'd brought a spare oxygen tank. In India, his open convertible was nearly crushed when local police became unable to control the enormous torrent of onlookers.

But it was Vice President Richard Nixon who had the closest brush with death during the Eisenhower administration. On a trip to Caracas, Venezuela—another trip that the Secret Service had argued against from the start due to safety concerns—Nixon insisted that his car lead the motorcade. He led it into an ambush. However, the SSD had succeeded in one change; using closed cars instead of convertibles.

Two large trucks rushed in front of the motorcade, cutting it off. Crowds, seemingly unarmed, surrounded the vehicle. Nixon's change in that arrangement of the cars in the motorcade nearly doomed everyone as the crowd's weapons materialized. All of the layers of protection were cut through in seconds. Stones, mud, and wooden bats pulverized the vehicles' windows. Members of the crowd communicated to one another, identifying Nixon's location in the motorcade; then they focused on breaching the window closest to the vice president. Had the Venezuelan military not come to the SSD's rescue at the last minute, the crowd could have killed Nixon there—or when he reached his destination, where it was later learned that four hundred Molotov cocktails had been stockpiled for an even larger assault. For that, Chief Baughman called the vice president and later candidate Nixon "an assassin's dream boat" and urged the public not to elect him.

Nixon survived the trip and went on to run for president in 1960. He was defeated by a young senator from Massachusetts, John F. Kennedy. The Kennedy administration brought the promise of a new, youthful era in US politics. In practice, it also brought fresh new problems for the Secret Service and would end with one of the most tragic episodes in the agency's—and the nation's—history.

FOUR.
BULLETS FROM DALLAS TO WASHINGTON

The trip to Dallas, Texas, on November 22, 1963, and the Secret Service's protection of President John F. Kennedy were not unique. All that was unique was the number of negative factors that came together in this instance: an assassin had finally recognized the systemic security gaps, identified the right time and place, and committed completely to "violence of action."

But the story and its hard lessons have been completely lost in the nuances of what preceded that day and the petty arguments and excuses that followed. Its lessons are universal, whether you're in the Secret Service or not.

As the famed military strategist Sun Tzu pointed out two and a half millennia ago, battles are won *before* they're ever fought. The Secret Service had failed years before they lost their protectee and our nation's president.

When President John F. Kennedy became president in 1961, the SSD security gaps that had long existed began to open wider almost immediately. Before JFK was even inaugurated, an elderly stalker-type assassin, Richard Paul Pavlick, loaded his Buick 8 sedan with enough dynamite to level the Kennedys' vacation home in Palm Beach, Florida. The assassin headed there. At least three times in December 1960, Pavlick was about to make an attempt, but as he clutched his makeshift detonator in his hand, he spotted the president's wife and infant children. "Had he not had a change of heart, there was little we could have done," said Agent Gerald Blaine of the president's detail. After Pavlick shied away, the agents became suspicious of his car, but he concealed the explosives on his chest under his clothing and hid in the president's church. After a tip was called in by a mail clerk in Pavlick's hometown who had seen threatening postcards that Pavlick was sending to the president, the Secret Service nabbed him at a traffic stop. One unsuspecting advance agent led him away by the arm, never realizing that the elderly man was, as the papers called him, "a human bomb."

The near miss should have served as a moment of clarity, a spur for the Secret Service to reevaluate and institute a strategic pause to determine if they were on the right course Instead, it pressured the press to downplay the story, appealing to the media's morals by insisting that the story could inspire copycats. In truth, the agency was more concerned about its reputation than about facing the increasingly more sophisticated and more frequent threats that were knocking ever more loudly on its door.

Then came November 22, 1963, and just as in all previous cases, the assassination of President John F. Kennedy was extremely simple: the Secret Service did everything wrong; the assassin(s) did everything right. And although many, including numerous agencies of the federal government, have devolved into focusing on theories of the "who" and "why," for the sake of keeping future U.S. presidents alive, only two questions are important: How did the gap arise, and how can we make sure this never happens again?

For every crime, there are four primary factors: means, motive, opportunity, and intent. To understand how protection succeeds or fails, only the "opportunity" for an assassin to make an attempt and the "intent," the psychological commitment to extreme violence, are relevant.

Richard Pavlick, for example, could have killed the president, but his conscience had kept him from committing to the violence that would have overpowered the Secret Service—and that would have been as simple as a press on the accelerator and a flick of the detonator. As the Secret Service chose not to adapt, it was only a matter of time before another assassin would recognize that the same opportunity existed and fully commit to "violence of action," no matter the proximity of First Lady Kennedy or any other innocents.

Though the Secret Service has nabbed thousands of potential and extremely dangerous assassins, including as suicide bombers, the work of the Protective Research Section is only a helpful aid, a useful tool, and, at best, one layer of concentric and comprehensive protection, no matter how advanced profiling and forensic efforts become. The existence of the security gap, the "opportunity," is everything. Real protection is based on concentric circles that stand between an assassin and a protectee. For an assassin to reach the president, all layers must fail—or, as in this case, be nonexistent. The only barriers between President Kennedy and a sniper's bullet were air and the Secret Service's prayers.

When President John F. Kennedy took office in 1961, the Secret Service's main problem was still fatigue, which had been exacerbated by the demands of World War II and the Cold War. Secret Service chief Baughman retired suddenly in 1961 after visiting his doctor for tension and fatigue.

Chief Baughman had taken over in 1948 from James Maloney, who only served 2 years after taking over from Chief Frank Wilson who, citing fatigue, had made enough requests to retire to eventually have one accepted. Special Agent In Charge of Presidential Protection James J. Rowley took over from James Drescher, who said he lived "a gypsy life" for too long. The sense of exhaustion had carried over through all the ranks of the Secret Service into the Kennedy years. The pace the new president set only made matters worse.

Drinking, partying, and finding rest and relaxation in all the wrong places often happen when workers hardly see their families, the grounding wires of their souls. Plummeting morale, arrogance, bullheadedness, and tunnel vision ensued. Every agent had to ask himself: Were the sacrifices he was making to create the last line of defense or just an elaborate presidential decoration?

Numerous agents on President Kennedy's detail revealed years after his assassination that despite being in the throes of the Cold War, when Soviet operatives assassinated targets with sophisticated nerve agents and radioactive poisons, President

Kennedy refused to wind back on his frequent affairs with unscreened mistresses, extreme sports, and high-society social life.

President Kennedy had a fascination with the poem "Rendezvous with Death" and was even known to casually remark, "If anyone is crazy enough to want to kill a president of the United States, he can do it. All a man needs is a willingness to trade his life for mine." He expected the Secret Service to adapt with little regard for resources, human or otherwise—again, a trait not unique to himself.

The National Park Service agents were trained to ride horseback, ski, swim, and sail and how to make rescues in each sport, yet numerous agents admitted they hadn't even received basic training in the use of, let alone held, the submachine guns or rifles put into their hands the first time they were assigned to the president. That practice of "faking it," as one agent put it, had been going on for years, as revealed in the memoirs and exposés of other agents.

The agents knew that any one of President Kennedy's frivolous actions could make it easier for an assassin to kill him. The only precedent for agents' overriding the president had been Agent Reilly preventing President Roosevelt from visiting a World War II frontline near Naples. Lead agents and SSD chiefs after that time never answered the question that remains unanswered today: Where is the threshold for agents to override the president and his staff?

Every agent knew then, as every agent still knows, that if he countermands the president, the president has both the motivation and the ability to replace the head of the Secret Service until he or she is assured that the security detail will be most agreeable.

A culture shift ensued. In accordance with a theory known as the Peter Principle, most of the agents who stayed on and rose to higher ranks were the only ones who could stomach the capitulations. Agents who tried to buck the system, such as Agent Abraham Bolden, the first black Secret Service agent to officially be part of the president's detail, were rebuked and crushed by the agency to secure their silence. In the wake of the Kennedy assassination, Bolden, who had been personally picked by Kennedy for his detail, was ready to testify about agents' drinking in Dallas and other Secret Service secrets, only to end up in jail on trumped-up bribery charges.

By many agents' admissions, they simply prayed not to be the one without a chair when the music stopped, if and when it happened. They knew that if an attack were made, much in the same style as had killed presidents before—let alone a highly trained sniper's ambush—they would be little more than witnesses to the attack.

And so a fait accompli was established, in which everyone hoped, carried on, and gambled on an incredibly expensive, elaborate, and demanding protection plan—which, in practice, quickly devolved into theatrics.

November 21, 1963. The advance agents of the president's detail had stayed out well into the night before, some as late as 5 a.m. They had drunk and socialized in spite of the demands of their work. The following day, they were mentally, physically, and emotionally exhausted, and their reaction time was a casualty. The president's experienced driver, Agent Thomas Shipman, had died six weeks earlier during a temporary assignment at Camp David, of a heart attack most likely caused by stress. His replacement was less than capable, due to lack of experience, training, extreme fatigue, or a mixture of all three. It was not common practice to cross-train and make each agent readily replaceable.

President Kennedy's motorcade of open convertibles rolled at speeds of 10 to 12 miles per hour, slower than parents picking up their kids in a school zone. The president's limo had cost hundreds of thousands of dollars, but little had been spent on its protection capabilities, only to extend the president's exposure to the cheering public—and any potential assassin. The seats lifted the president even higher above the car so more onlookers could see him wave back. Even "the bubble," the transparent but not bulletproof rain cover, shielded Presidents Eisenhower and Kennedy from rain only after Eisenhower complained of being drenched by rain in similar slow-moving motorcade parades through crowded streets.

The security advance team knew the futility of any of their observations. The crowds were so massive and excited that often in Dallas they caused the motorcade to come to a complete halt as unscreened masses pushed local police officers into the street to get a few feet closer to the celebrity president. That was exactly the purpose of the trip: to increase his exposure and galvanize voters into a frenzy before the 1964 election.

The president's protection was so compromised by the Secret Service's culture that, as the crowds enveloped the motorcade, any assassin could have leapt into the president's lap and repeated history and the agents wouldn't have had the positioning or reaction time to make a difference.

As who is to blame: it is only the killer. But it was the Secret Service that had the final responsibility to protect the president against a threat it *knew* was out there and had known about for decades. It had been concerned about snipers' having a clear shot at President Eisenhower on the golf course. President Truman's protectors had been terrified that a sniper would take a shot at him on his frequent walks. Even Lincoln had been shot at on at least two occasions. It was hardly a new threat.

There is a rumor that deep within the Secret Service archives is a letter signed by President Kennedy to Chief James J. Rowley in which he acknowledges having been told that on the route set by the president's staff—such as passing through Dealey Plaza—the Secret Service could simply not guarantee protection. Numerous protectees had signed such letters or made such verbal agreements, including First Lady Jacqueline Kennedy, who publicly and often refused any protection for herself or her children. That was how much the situation had been allowed to deteriorate.

As the motorcade emerged from the crowded narrow streets, it approached Dealey Plaza. In the Dallas motorcade, numerous agents from different details rode in following vehicles. Per their training, they scanned for threats that might be tucked in among the thousands of onlookers packing the streets from the airport to the Dallas Trade Mart, where the president was scheduled to deliver a speech. Unlike the president's detail, the first lady's and vice president's details had been disciplined enough to be as well rested as their schedules allowed. Agent Clint Hill of the first lady's detail rode in a car directly behind that of the president's. His reaction time and athleticism were honed and ready. Agent Rufus Youngblood, the head of the vice president's detail, rode with Vice President Lyndon B. Johnson and Mrs. Johnson. He too was ready.

But they were sitting ducks for a trained sniper. When they reached Dealey Plaza, they slowed to a near stop to execute two ninety-degree turns; there were no alternate roads or cover; crowds were on all sides; the vehicles headed toward an overpass at the plaza's far end—which was supposed to have been closed to the public by Dallas authorities but had not. And still the Secret Service held its course.

As the motorcade made the last hard turn at low speed, the car passed right into Lee Harvey Oswald's field of fire, and luck ran out—for the president, the Secret Service, and the country. The first shot likely missed everything, depending on which account you believe, and ricocheted off the ground hitting a civilian. The second shot hit President Kennedy in the upper back, exiting from his throat. The president lurched in his seat. Just behind the limousine was Agent Clint Hill. Seeing that the president was in distress, Hill sprinted toward the president's car. In a car behind the president's, Agent Rufus Youngblood leaped onto Vice President and Mrs. Johnson. President Kennedy's driver, a replacement new to the job, hesitated, unsure of what was happening and what to do. He turned around to look, slowing to a near stop as he did so.

The president's detail was bewildered, wondering if the sound had been a car backfiring or a firecracker. The final shot did horrific damage, splitting the president's head in a shocking way that was immortalized in a motion picture shot by Abraham Zapruder. One agent on the president's detail grabbed a brand-new Secret Service–issued Colt M-16 but could not identify the source of the fire. Jacqueline Kennedy climbed onto the trunk of the accelerating car on all fours, panicked by what she had just witnessed. To some, she appeared to be reaching for a section of the president's skull that had landed on the trunk. That she did not tumble off into the street seemed a miracle. At nearly the same moment, Agent Hill leaped up onto the rear step, pulled himself atop the trunk, and pushed Mrs. Kennedy down to cover her with his body—a measure that might actually have been ineffective, as high-caliber shots are capable of tearing through several bodies. But his act was selfless and courageous. By the time Hill arrived on the trunk, the shooting had stopped. The motorcade accelerated toward the overpass and out of Dealey Plaza.

The bullets might have stopped flying, but the detail was hardly out of the woods.

In the first car, accompanying the Dallas chief of police and Dallas police driver, was Agent Winston Lawson, who had been in charge of the security arrangements for the Dallas trip. In the third car, Agent Emory Roberts radioed, "The president's been hit! Get us to a hospital, fast but safe!" Even as Agent Hill was shielding the first lady as President Kennedy lay slumped in his seat, he still wasn't sure the president was beyond saving. He yelled for the driver to get them to the hospital. The Secret Service agents had spent their careers readying for this one moment and had failed in an instant when it had come. Immediately afterward, they were faced with what they'd never fully prepared or trained for: what to do after an assassination.

The motorcade had three possible destinations in its southwest direction of travel: five minutes away was the original destination, the Dallas Trade Mart, where the president had intended to speak and which was therefore secured by Secret Service and local law enforcement; Parkland Hospital was only a mile past the Trade Mart; the third option was to drive past both locations to reach Love Field airport, ten minutes later, where Air Force One was secured and waiting to take off.

The location they chose, Parkland Hospital, was unsecured. The emergency room had not been prepped. But they sped toward the hospital in the hope of saving the president's life, attending to Texas governor John Connally, who had also been shot, and making sure nobody else was injured.

It was still unknown whether the attack had been perpetrated by a single shooter or a team, whether it was a lone madman or a highly sophisticated state-sponsored plot. At that point, the details should have split up. Agent Youngblood informed his protectee, Lyndon Johnson, that he might need to take over as acting president for the time being. Yet with both Johnson and Kennedy kept in the same place—at the hospital— the continuity of government was in jeopardy. Once it was confirmed that Kennedy was dead, that became even more clear.

Acting President Johnson, however, wouldn't leave without former first lady Kennedy, and she wouldn't leave without the former president's body, which couldn't be moved without the dignity of a casket, which would have to be ordered and delivered. Youngblood did finally manage to convince Johnson and his wife to slip off to Air Force One in two unmarked police cars, where they could be secured as they waited for Kennedy's body.

Youngblood's clear thinking and adaptive style were the standout performance among the Secret Service that day. Though the acting president was safe on Air Force One, nobody was sure who should be joining him there—or whether assassins were still after him.

Youngblood ordered Secret Service agents and air force guards to secure the runway as, in his words, "a stream of cars began converging on Love Field, some carrying people who would be indispensable to Lyndon Johnson in the crucial hours to come, some who came because everyone else seemed headed in that direction." The vice president's detail had to decide whom to allow on the plane and whom to keep away. Worse still, as they waited, nobody was sure how to formalize the passing of the torch from Kennedy to Johnson.

Agent Youngblood wanted to get the hell out of Dallas for security reasons and pleaded that "there were people aboard the plane who were empowered to administer [the oath]— among them, every Secret Service agent." But the Constitution clearly states that a judge must administer the oath of office. Through the White House operators and the secure communications system made possible by the White House Communications Agency, Acting President Johnson got President Kennedy's brother Robert F. Kennedy, the US attorney general, on the phone and made his condolences before asking him the appropriate course of action. Kennedy pointed out that "any judicial officer of the United States can officiate."

So before Air Force One could leave, everyone aboard had to wait for a judge to be found and brought to the plane, along with the first lady and the late president's body. Meanwhile, they were still unsure whether the attack was still on or off, and the world panicked. Stock traders panicked, and the stock exchange market dropped nearly 3 percent, in the hours after shooting as the country wondered if it had a president or not.

Finally an emergency inauguration was held in the crowded plane's cabin when Texas judge Sarah Hughes administered the oath of office to President Johnson, with former first lady Kennedy, still covered in blood, standing at his side.

November 22 was one of the nation's darkest days, a day of grief and fear. The Secret Service had lost a president, and it could only wonder what changes would result to their agency in the hours and days to come.

The psychological answer to explain the failure of protection in Dallas is groupthink, in which an organization's culture disincentivizes dissenting opinions. Most every honest Secret Service officer or agent can attest to one of the Secret Service's unofficial mottos: "Because that's the way we've always done it."

Under President Eisenhower, the Secret Service had abdicated its responsibility for the initial coordination of the president's itinerary for foreign trips. But under President Kennedy, the Secret Service had handed over coordination of the president's domestic travel itinerary to the president's overzealous staff. As Chief Baughman noted at the Kennedy administration's dawn, far too often many people who surround the president are willing to overlook security to achieve shortsighted political objectives. The reason for all the travel that political season had been to boost the president's ratings for the 1964 election. The White House staff's priority was to maximize his positive political exposure. But his exposure to danger was maximized instead.

Weeks into his unexpected presidency, Lyndon Johnson was furious with everyone in the Secret Service, save for Agent Youngblood. In his commendation of Agent Youngblood for his actions during the assassination, he wrote, "In that awful moment of confusion when all about him were losing their heads, Rufus Youngblood never lost his. Without hesitation, he volunteered his life to save mine." Now that Youngblood had taken over the presidential detail, the young agent had to restore the faith in the detail that had failed his predecessor. Now that Johnson was in the top spot himself, the target was on *his* back.

Agent Youngblood noted that at that point "the awards notwithstanding, the Secret Service was on shaky ground, and the FBI, the CIA, and the Defense Department were all reportedly looking into the business of presidential protection as a possible addition to their own jobs . . . the Secret Service was fighting for its very existence as a protective unit."

The service's internal problems were bubbling up to the top. One anonymous agent wrote a memo to the president alleging that "morale in the Secret Service is at an all-time low," and another "bellyached" to a major newspaper about Johnson not letting agents close enough to protect him at his Texas ranch.

Johnson turned to Youngblood, the agent to whom he was closest. "You know I can't have disloyalty," he railed, "and I can't talk in front of your people and have them repeat it. I told Chief Rowley that, to call 'em in and take their resignations of anybody who wanted out, and I'll be glad to have his or yours or anybody else's. If they don't want to handle it we can get the FBI to do it."

But J. Edgar Hoover, perhaps fearful of the gravity that came with protecting the president, stood down and dialed back his attempts to move in on Secret Service territory. For perhaps the only time in his long career, he blinked.

Several investigations took place in the months after President Kennedy's assassination. Americans and the world wanted to know what had gone so terribly wrong with the supposedly elite Secret Service and how one of the most important men in the world had been killed by a simple attack: a man with a cheap rifle shooting from an elevated position. Numerous details bewildered the public: the lack of motorcycle agents and agents on the rear bumper of the president's car, why the transparent bubble roof on the president's car hadn't been used, why the motorcade had passed through a sniper's paradise such as Dealey Plaza in the first place, why the area hadn't been secured, how the suspect had also been so unprotected while he was under police custody that he, too, had been assassinated— and the list went on. But despite the heroic efforts of Clint Hill and Rufus Youngblood, even those measures wouldn't have stopped most any high-caliber rifle bullet. Maybe they would have deflected its trajectory, but again, hoping a bullet's trajectory will be deflected enough to stop a kill is preposterous. As the next Secret Service systematic failure would prove again, deviated and ricocheting bullets are still just as deadly, and they should not be the focus of a plan to save the president's life.

As each investigation into the circumstances of the assassination failed to restore confidence in the official report and focused far too much on the shooter, many solutions eluded the Secret Service. Agents who had been present that day filed written reports that were passed up the chain of command, screened, and then passedf along to Congress. After that, they testified directly in front of Congress. Though the investigations found no fault on the part of the individual agents, they broadly found fault in the Secret Service and recommended improvements in reaction timing, positioning, and using armored vehicles. But the "solutions" were merely recommendations; the funding to carry them out was not contingent on their execution and achievement. Therefore the funds were used, but many of the changes were never implemented.

The Secret Service took its licks and then took the initiative to make changes. It became an agency within the Treasury, the US Secret Service (USSS) and was no longer the Secret Service Division (SSD) of the Treasury. Chief James J. Rowley was now Director James J. Rowley, and he had his work cut out for him. He implemented the changes he had always wanted but ignored most of the Warren Commission's findings—an error that continues to plague the agency today.

First of all, he standardized firearms training across the organization. Previously, firearms training for Secret Service agents had been held at the Treasury's training center, or agents had been brought into the Secret Service via a probationary period based on their previous employment. The Secret Service would blindly trust that new recruits had satisfactory firearms training from their previous employers—but if they hadn't, they could join the Secret Service without it. That's almost unthinkable by today's standards. Finally, the Secret Service adapted and created its own program and its own standard of firearms training. To lead this, it brought in some of the world champion marksmen from the old White House Police.

Despite the new funding and training program, the service still ignored the strategic failure that had left President Kennedy open to assassination. In 1964, the late president's brother Robert Kennedy was campaigning for a New York Senate seat accompanied by President Johnson. Just a year after the tragedy in Dallas, the two protectees stood on their seats in the back of their open limousine. They smiled and waved at the seemingly unarmed crowds cheering for them. The feverishly excited crowd yelled, cheered, and pushed the New York police officers and Secret Service agents against the limousine. The motorcade came to a near halt. The rooftops and windows were unsecure. How could the Secret Service have allowed this— the former president's brother? What lessons, if any, had really been learned?

The year 1968 was a year of tragedies that, although they did not involve the Secret Service directly, showed the great risks still faced by American public figures.

Dr. Martin Luther King, Jr., was not a government official or presidential candidate, but as the nation's most prominent civil rights leader, one wonders why he was not provided with some form of official protection. Perhaps that could have prevented his assassination by a sniper on April 4, 1968.

After his assassination, the country erupted in riots. Cities burned. National Guardsmen and armored troop carriers moved about the White House and surrounding areas in case the riots turned toward the White House. A haze of smoke from nearby fires floated over the White House lawns. The Secret Service canceled all scheduled leaves, and off-duty agents and officers were put on high alert to be ready to return to work at a moment's notice. The president's helicopter was kept at the White House as an alternative means of escape in case the entire complex was surrounded. Gas masks, helmets, and long guns were readied for all officers.

When Robert F. Kennedy announced his candidacy for president in 1968, he was initially protected by friends of the family who were paid to be bodyguards—or at least act like ones. Those individuals were certainly accomplished—they included a minister, an actor, and an Olympic gold medalist, but none of them had any formal training in law enforcement or protection.

The Ambassador Hotel in Los Angeles was swarmed with fans, reporters, hotel guests—all unscreened—and they surrounded and hounded the candidate. Senator Kennedy was in a rush, behind schedule, and had just finished his speech; he waded through the overcrowded hotel, trying to figure out the ideal route to get to the pressroom, to which his campaign was trying to move his press conference. After some confusion about how to get there, the candidate and his detail followed the maître d'hôtel through the narrow hotel kitchen, despite his detail wanting to go through the more open hotel ballroom. The Secret Service has used and continues to use kitchens as possible throughways for protectees, but they are screened and locked down in advance, and nonessential personnel are cleared out. All employees are screened and told in no uncertain terms to keep their hands out and open, not to make any sudden movements, and the consequences if those rules aren't followed.

None of that happened for Robert Kennedy. As soon as the candidate entered the kitchen, a man named Sirhan Sirhan approached, drew the handgun he had hidden in a campaign poster, and fired at the candidate from a foot away. Kennedy's bodyguards punched, grabbed, and tackled the murderer, who kept firing and hit five other bystanders.

After Robert Kennedy's death, President Johnson immediately assigned specially formed details of Secret Service agents to the other candidates, including two former vice presidents, Richard Nixon and Hubert Humphrey—which prompts the question: If a security measure can be added in an instant following a catastrophe, why can't it be added beforehand, when the need becomes clear?

Nixon won the 1968 election and took office as a less headstrong protectee than he had been as Eisenhower's vice president. He was friendly and amiable toward the Secret Service. One story that will always be famous to the men and women of the agency is that when one agent accidentally honked his car horn, Nixon humbly responded, "Okay, boys, I'll be out in just a minute."

But Nixon embroiled the Secret Service in other problems. One famous piece of Uniformed Division lore tells of a safe discovered in the basement of the Old Executive Office Building during the Nixon years. Though the officer responsible for securing the area did not know what the safe was for, he was responsible for checking that it was locked. It always was—until one day it wasn't. That day, the officer noted multiple passports and aliases inside, as well as a large amount of money that nearly filled the safe. He did as he had been trained and made a report about his find but was told by his superiors to forget what he had seen.

What he had stumbled upon was the bribe money from the Jimmy Hoffa pardon scandal, used to fund the president's left-hand men. The men were connected with the Committee to Re-elect the President (nicknamed "CREEP"), which would later perpetrate the Watergate scandal. Nixon came close to dragging the Secret Service into an impeachment proceeding—but that would have to wait until the forty-second president.

During the 1972 election, a third-party candidate, George Wallace, received Secret Service protection, as had been the practice since Robert Kennedy's assassination. But the protection was a complete joke, a bodyguard unit based on hope. It consisted of a few agents hovering in close proximity and one "whizbang"—Secret Service slang for "gadget"—a bulletproof podium that covered more than half of Wallace's body as he delivered a speech in Laurel, Maryland, on May 15, 1972.

During his appearance at a shopping center, the Secret Service relied on creating a buffer zone between the candidate making his speech and the unsecured crowd. What ensued was caught on film by ABC affiliate cameraman Stephen Geer. The unsecured crowd is shown engulfing candidate Wallace.

"Hey, George! Hey, George!" called out a young blond man from behind another man who was shaking Wallace's hand. The man, Arthur Bremer, was a would-be assassin who had been stalking President Nixon for weeks across many states and even into Canada. He had made one attempt on Nixon's motorcade but it had driven by too fast, and he had shied away from drawing his handgun and pulling the trigger. So he waited and observed and realized the disparity in candidate Wallace's protection.

The Secret Service detail protecting Wallace was little more than a feel-good measure. It was ad hoc, a knee-jerk response to the assassination of Robert Kennedy in the previous election. The detail was all that separated the protectee from the crowd. But as candidate Wallace descended the stage after his speech and deviated from the path, choosing instead to shake hands with the unscreened crowd, he was totally surrounded. There was nothing separating the candidate from any one of the dozens of strangers shouting his name. The agents accompanying Wallace didn't react quickly enough and simply watched the frenzy of dozens of people reaching for the candidate. It was hopeless. There was zero chance that any of the agents could do anything if something should go wrong. But they were hoping, like so many agents before, that this wouldn't be the day their theatrics aligned with the right assassin, at the right place, at the right time. But it was.

As the agents huddled around the protectee being squeezed by the frenzied crowd, a man approached Wallace, drew a pistol from concealment, and fired three shots directly into Wallace's stomach. The crowd and the agents pulled the assassin down, and it was over. Wallace would forever be paralyzed from the waist down, and the backing for his candidacy would fade in the coming weeks. Because he lived, his lack of protection is often not tallied among the agency's failures. But in the years since Presidents Lincoln, Garfield, and McKinley had been killed in almost exactly the same manner—by an approacher—attempts on numerous presidents had been so nearly successful, and there had been such a short time since the similar (but successful) attempt on Robert Kennedy, what had changed? What was the difference? The answer was clear: nothing, except that the Secret Service had spent a great deal of time and money simply to be little more than trained witnesses.

President Nixon was reelected in 1972, and the Secret Service was not spared the chaos of his abortive second term. The agency was caught up in the Nixon administration's scandals after Congress and the public learned of the president's eavesdropping and recording device he had installed in the White House. It was clear that two possibilities existed: that the Secret Service had been unaware of the listening device and was therefore incompetent or that it had known everything about the listening device, among other things. It was quickly revealed that the Secret Service Technical Services Division had installed and maintained the elaborate recording device per the president's request, even swapping out the old tapes for new ones and maintaining possession of them. When Congress and the investigation wanted to learn how a secretary could delete nearly twenty minutes of tape that *coincidentally* would supposedly have been the key evidence in Congress's investigation, Technical Services Division head Louis Sims and agent Alfred Wong were dragged in to testify before the judge.

Gerald Ford took office after Nixon resigned in 1974, offering to help heal the nation after the "long national nightmare" of Watergate. Though he was in office for only a little more than two years, his term saw two very critical near misses. Like Wallace before him and Reagan after him, he found himself stuck in the middle of a "fatal funnel"—a situation from which the Secret Service should be able to shield its protectee.

Imagine, for a moment, an open football field, you're a Secret Service agent at the fifty-yard line. Next to you are your teammates, spread out evenly along the fifty-yard line. In the center of the field is the protectee, and closely surrounding him are four agents in a diamond formation. In the end zone is an attacker. Even if one or two agents go down, the team will be able to return fire and save the day. But what if the attacker was on the fifty-yard line at your flank? And what if there were barricades or walls on both sides of you and your team, preventing an escape? Even once you identify where rapidly fired shots are coming from, you still have to clear your line of fire, as between you and the attacker are the protectee, your fellow agents, the public, and people screaming and running for their lives. This is a fatal funnel. This is the nature of the Secret Service's extremely difficult task.

In both instances when his life was threatened, President Ford was leaving a speaking engagement—and was in the midst of a fatal funnel as unscreened gatherers waved, shouted, and yelled. The first attempt was on September 5, 1975. President Ford left the California State Capitol building in Sacramento and moved alongside his motorcade on his walk to the California State House. He waved to an unscreened crowd of onlookers who had been allowed to gather, gawk, and cheer. The president decided to deviate so that he could shake hands with onlookers. The Secret Service allowed him to do so, knowing full well that at that moment the protection would become impractical, relying (again) almost purely on hope. A woman in the crowd, Lynette "Squeaky" Fromme, drew a .45-caliber Colt 1911 handgun from concealment and pulled the trigger. The only reason Ford survived was that the gunwoman—a member of the Charles Manson cult—didn't know the difference between a single-action-only handgun and a double-action handgun. If the hammer had been cocked, the president would have been dead. It was only through luck being with the Secret Service that agents managed to grab the gun and nab the woman before she managed to fix her problem by cocking the pistol.

In the days afterward, the news media clamored about the idea of the first female assassin to target the president—although there *was* the shadowy account of the possible female coconspirator in the alleged plot against George Washington.

Another woman, Sara Jane Moore, made an attempt on Ford's life just seventeen days later. This assassin waited in her car a block away from the president's location. The Secret Service had interviewed her previously for making threats against the president but had deemed the threats not credible. She

had practiced for the assassination with her .44-caliber mag-
num revolver and was an excellent shot. But just the day before,
police had arrested her on an illegal handgun charge and confiscated the revolver. Due to complications in the arrest, she was
released, though the revolver was confiscated. So she acquired
a .38-caliber Smith & Wesson handgun and planned to use that
instead. She drove to where President Ford was exiting the St.
Francis Hotel and at a distance of forty feet fired two shots
from her handgun. The first missed by a few feet, but nearby
was a marine veteran, Oliver Sipple, who reacted immediately,
dashing out to Moore and grabbing the gun as she fired again,
hitting a nearby civilian, who survived. The Secret Service covered and evacuated the president.

During the prosecution of the assassin, it was noted that
if she had used the original firearm she had practiced with,
the bullet would have reached its mark. It was just by happenstance that President Ford had again thwarted death. Chance
had been the deciding factor between a near miss and a catastrophic failure.

As the Secret Service rapidly continued to expand after
Director Rowley's overhaul of the agency, begun in the wake
of the Kennedy assassination, the same problems persisted.
Elected in 1976, President Jimmy Carter was as reckless a president as any. An unscreened gate-crasher slipped into a White
House function and was able to approach the president and
dump ashes on the ground in protest before he was appre-
hended. In another instance, President Carter took a multiweek
tour down the Mississippi River on an antique steamboat, stopping to shake hands with unscreened crowds along the way. It
was a security nightmare.

Two months later, after the new president, Ronald Reagan, took the oath of office, all the hope that had kept President Carter safe from an assassin, left him in the line of fire.

For Agent Jerry Parr, March 30, 1981, began as a typical day. He started off with an early-morning jog and then a trip to the gun range inside the Old Post Office Building to brush up on his Model 19 revolver skills. The trip to the Washington Hilton with President Reagan for a routine speech was supposed to be just that, routine—as it had been for every other president. But exhaustion, fatigue, arrogance, and complacency finally caught up with the Secret Service, *and* it aligned with a would-be assassin taking his chance. It wasn't the first time that a gap had existed in the Secret Service's protection; it just happened to be a moment when an assassin was there to exploit it.

Immediately surrounding the president that day were Agents Parr, Timothy McCarthy, Eric Littlejohn, James Varey, Dale McIntosh, and Raymond Shaddick. Agent Shaddick carried with him a messenger bag with collapsible bullet-resistant (what most people mistakenly call "bulletproof") steel plates to be used as deployable hard cover. A few Uzi submachine guns were contained in nearby briefcases and vehicles for the agents to access. But the agents were prepared to fight an attack outside of twenty feet, and the crowds surrounding them outside the hotel were unscreened and within ten feet. Agent Parr believed it was unnecessary to require the president and his agents to wear their body armor, as the trip was routine, the weather was muggy, and the vests were nontailored and uncomfortable to wear.

A psychotic stalker known to police, John Hinckley, had traveled across the state to make an attempt on Reagan's life.

But nothing unusual stuck out about him as far as the Secret Service was concerned as he waded from the unsecured crowd of onlookers to the supposedly screened press. Though agents and officers are trained in behavioral analysis, psychotics and zealots can be so mentally, emotionally, and intellectually wrecked that they seem unusually calm, instead of nervous.

Agent Mary Ann Gordon was the lead transportation agent and organized the motorcade. Agent William Green was the lead advance agent in charge of the security measures on-site.

As he exited the hotel after making his speech, President Reagan stopped for a brief moment on his walk to the limousine to wave to onlookers. A woman called out, "Mr. Reagan," and the president turned, gave his signature smile and waved heartily. The walk from the hotel to the limousine was only about twelve feet—*what could go wrong?*

That's when Hinckley broke out of the unsecured crowd. He pushed in front of a man in a yellow sweater, Alfred Antonucci, an Ohio labor official. Both Hinckley and Antonucci were pressed up against the stone wall of the hotel. In the three seconds during which the president waved, his left side faced toward them. That's when the assassin drew his .22-caliber rimfire revolver from concealment and fired as quickly as he could pull the trigger. The shots were shockingly loud—which meant they were close, not far away like the long-reverberating, echoing shots at Dealey Plaza. The bullets began to cut down the officers and agents who served as hindrances for the shots bound for the president. We used to refer to ourselves as "bullet sponges." On the first two shots, half the agents froze, the other half reeled— where were they coming from? James Brady, the president's press secretary, who had stuck close to the president, perhaps eager to share the limelight, caught the first bullet in the head and fell to the ground. His brain's blood poured from his skull. Metropolitan officer Thomas Delahanty took the second bullet in the neck and fell to the ground next to Brady. Agent Tim McCarthy turned toward the sound of the gunfire like a basketball player setting up for a block and caught the third bullet to his chest, leapt onto his toes, and dropped to the ground.

Agent Parr pushed the president into the limousine. Agent Shadduk scooped both their legs up into the car and slammed the door closed, sealing them inside. Unbeknown to both the president and Agent Parr, the next round had slipped through the gap between the open door and the limousine, ricocheted, and sliced into the president's lung, collapsing it. Agent Parr pushed the president to the floor and leapt on top of him shielding further incoming fire with his own body. Alfred Antonucci snapped to attention and tackled the shooter, who was rubbing shoulders with him. Local police officers piled on top of him and the assassin.

Then agents Dennis McCarthy and Daniel Spriggs leapt into action. In the time it had taken Hinckley to pull the trigger, they hadn't had time to draw their own guns. Instead they ran to the assassin and piled on top of the local officers. Agent Thomas Lightsey grabbed the assassin's revolver off the pavement. Agent Robert Wanko pressed his body up against the wall, drew his Uzi, and fumbled with the stock as he looked for additional shooters.

The gadgets, the whizbangs such as the bullet-resistant cover, had failed. There was no point in countermeasures against an attack from beyond twenty feet if the area immediately surrounding the president hadn't been secured. The same kind of attack that had been tried and proven before was, centuries later, still working against presidents of the United States.

The limousine sped off, and the president's detail was split in half, with more agents securing the assassin up against the wall, a result of new training following President Kennedy's assassination.

Then it was up to Agent Parr to assess the situation. Should they head back to the White House, where the area was secured and the White House physician could look over the president? The second option was George Washington University Hospital. President Reagan was winded, and Agent Parr checked his body for any sign of a wound or bleeding. There was nothing. But the president's shallow breathing only increased. Agent Parr noticed the bright red frothy blood on the president's lip and was deeply scared. He wondered if he had punctured the president's lung by breaking a rib when he had jumped on top of the president's body. Agent Parr harkened back to his training, the "ten-minute medicine" course, and changed his mind about their destination.

"We're going to GW Hospital," he announced.

If it had not been for the refresher course and the split-second clear thinking of Agent Parr, the president might have been returned to the White House, where he would have suffocated by the blood filling his lungs, which then would have been unable to inflate. In the limousine, the president's lips turned blue.

Meanwhile, Agent Mary Ann Gordon was another hero of the day. She told two other agents with Uzis to get into her car and accompany the president's limousine. Their vehicle pulled ahead of the "stagecoach," the service's code name for the president's limousine. As they sped to the hospital, if any car ran a stop sign or red light, they would hit her car and the president's car would be able to continue on. Her selfless act might well also have helped saved the president. She recognized in the heat of the moment that the president's protection detail had been split in half. While they had been grabbing and throwing themselves on the assassin, the president's detail had been thinned out. But no one knew if the attack was over, if another attacker was nearby, or if the hospital would provide another chance for an ambush.

Back at the chaotic scene in front of the Hilton Hotel, Agent Wanko was yelling for a police squad car to pull up and take Hinckley away. Suddenly, Carolyn Parr, his colleague Jerry Parr's wife, burst onto the scene. Carolyn looked at the officer presumed dead, his revolver lying by his head, and Brady's split skull. She looked for her husband's body and called out to Agent Wanko, who tried to make sense of why his colleague's wife would be there. As it turned out, she worked nearby and Agent Parr had called to invite her to come watch the president's exit and get a fun glimpse of her husband in action. It had gone horribly wrong.

But her husband had made the difference, albeit narrowly, that had saved the president's life. Had even the smallest of variables changed—the caliber of weapon Hinckley had used, Agent Parr's decision to head to GW Hospital, or Agent Mary Ann Gordon's decision to stick with the president and take the lead instead of hanging back to secure the assassin—the president might have not survived.

But still the Secret Service hadn't adequately prepared and was learning on the fly. Vice President George H. W. Bush, who was traveling on Air Force Two at the time, didn't have secure communications and the press intercepted the discussions in the immediate aftermath of the shooting. When the press asked who was in charge of the nation, neither the White House nor the Secret Service had an answer. Secretary of State Alexander Haig, in the vacuum of certainty, declared, "As of now, I am in control here, in the White House," and for a few hours, everyone believed he was. Once Vice President Bush returned to the White House from Texas, he was given the nuclear codes and took charge of the "crisis management" team, and the nation once again had a leader at the helm.

As President Reagan recuperated in George Washington University Hospital for thirteen days, the Secret Service made it into a makeshift White House. The presidential powers temporarily transferred to Bush were returned to Reagan, and the significance of a peaceful return to the elected president in the wake of a crisis cannot be understated.

An ironic happening in the immediate aftermath of the attack was that journalists, poring over the crystal-clear footage of the attack, all reported that the president had not been hit and had not been wounded. In those late days of the Cold War, when an attempt on the president's life could initially be seen as a Soviet plot, that was fortunate. The risk of creating a flash point and a war between nations was lessened when it became clear that a lone, mentally ill gunman had been responsible. But again, that was happenstance.

The ultimate consequence of the Reagan assassination attempt was that it not only proved that such an attack was possible but established a pattern of behavior for the Secret Service. The same kind of attack, an "approacher" with a concealed weapon, had happened in the past. "Approachers" had killed Presidents Lincoln, Garfield, and McKinley. They had killed presidential candidates Robert Kennedy and Louisiana governor Huey Long. They had nearly killed President Ford, candidate George Wallace, and former president Theodore Roosevelt. Now they had almost killed President Reagan.

Any assassin who watched the footage, just as the world watched, could see that if Hinckley had made small changes, such as using a slightly larger caliber bullet, taking better aim, or using an explosive, he could have succeeded. It was painfully clear that the Secret Service was not learning from its mistakes.

After the attack, the hope was that it would be the event that would finally spur the Secret Service to change.

That was the hope, anyway.

FIVE.

TRANSITION AND TRAGEDY

Politicians may run the town, but no one knows our nation's capital better than cab drivers and cops.

Sometime in 1993 or 1994, a man arrived at Dulles International Airport in Washington, DC, from a Middle Eastern country and hailed a cab from the international arrivals terminal. He told the driver to go straight to the White House. When he arrived, he got out, told the driver to wait, and walked around the White House complex, taking notes and seemingly making surveys. When he finished, he returned to the cab asked the driver to take him back to Dulles. Upon arriving, the man entered the Dulles international departures terminal and left the country.

Suspicious of his passenger's behavior, the cab driver drove straight back to the White House and informed the Secret Service of what he had seen.

Soon after, every Secret Service employee, or at least those working the White House, was informed by the same report that played in our ears via our radios. "Be advised," it began, "at approximately . . . at Dulles, a taxi driver drove a man of Middle Eastern origin, approximately 35, to the White House, asked the cab driver to wait, where the man appeared to make a survey, and then got back into the cab and returned to Dulles and departed the country."

I was working at the White House when the incident was reported. It was strange enough that I and several others remembered it years later, when the 9/11 Commission asked government employees to come forward with any information that might be related to the attacks. We contacted the commission to share our story, but, being unsolved, it never made it into the final version of the report. The identity of the mysterious White House visitor during the Clinton years remains unknown.

In the early 1990s, Al Qaeda killed scores of innocent people, though their prime targets were US military personnel in foreign countries. In 1993, a splinter faction infiltrated the United States, crafted a 1,200-pound bomb in New Jersey, and drove it into the parking garage of the World Trade Center. When detonated, it killed six people and injured more than a thousand. In 1996, the group targeted President Clinton on his trip to Manila, planting a bomb on a bridge. The fact that Agent Lewis Merletti exercised his override authority and changed the route at the last minute was all that saved the president. That attack was kept secret by the Secret Service until December 2009, when an interview with Merletti was published by author Ken

Gormley. In 1998, the terrorist group simultaneously bombed the US embassies in Kenya and Tanzania, killing more than two hundred people, including twelve Americans. Al Qaeda was steadily building its status as the world's deadliest terror organization, but the extent of its threat was yet to be realized.

But as the Clinton administration—and with it the 1990s—came to a close, the Secret Service was less worried about a foreign terrorist empire than it was about building its *own* empire. In 1999, Director Merletti retired and Brian Stafford became the Secret Service's twentieth director. Stafford was a "made man" of the Secret Service, and along with senior colleagues A. T. Smith, Julia Pierson, Joseph Clancy, and others, had been a ringleader of the agency's inner circle as it pushed back against the Kenneth Starr investigation. With Starr behind them, they looked to the future. They were ready to take advantage, eager to put what they called the "Master Plan"—or, as the Uniformed Division called it, the "Beltsville Plan"—into effect. Officially the idea was only to expand the agency's training center, the James J. Rowley Training Center, in Laurel, Maryland, but it turned into far more.

The Master Plan was designed to balloon the Secret Service to rival the size and mission scope of the FBI, even as that empire building sowed the Secret Service's eventual collapse. It was an expansive overreach that bogged down the entire service and distracted the agency from its real problems both inside and out.

The plan involved expansion in six areas: additions to the training center, new missions, new branding, a takeover of the Uniformed Division, a buildup of middle management, and greater international reach. We can piece together what we know about this plan from interviews with current and former personnel as well as government reports. Taken together, one thing becomes clear: as the Secret Service expanded in the 1990s, its decades-old problems remained: there were still too few agents and officers on duty, and they were overworked with too little sleep. As a result, President Clinton experienced some very close near misses, and the agency was put into a bad position in the tumultuous days after 9/11.

The first iteration of the Master Plan was building more than a dozen buildings at the training center. They included the Bowron Administration Building, the Magaw Tactical Training Facility, and the Merletti Classroom Building.*

More money—beyond the $500 million already supplied by Congress—was a critical ingredient of the expansion plan. The Secret Service got its hands on it by never letting a crisis go to waste. For instance, in 1997–98, several credible threats came in targeting the president's new chief of staff, Erskine Bowles. Bowles was greatly concerned and was flabbergasted to hear "Erskine, we can protect anyone in the world, but we can't do it for free." The agency claimed it couldn't afford more. Within the hour, he pushed for a meeting with the president, who gave the director access to the congressional terrorism fund of some $300 million.

Bowles was the victim of obvious Secret Service manipulation. While the threat was very real, it was preposterous to think

---

* Sound familiar? Instead of naming the new buildings after agents or officers killed in the line of duty, the new buildings were named after the three Secret Service directors who had served during the Clinton administration—and who had secured the funding for the buildings.

that the Secret Service could not find a way to give the president's chief of staff the protection he needed. Last-minute protective details had been set up before, including for the mother and wife of the alleged assassin of President Kennedy. Bowles and the president were willing to play ball. With the financial infusion secured, the Secret Service created far more than the simple protection detail for the chief of staff. The new buildings at the training center were planned, but other details of where the counterterrorism fund money went remain a mystery for one simple reason: the Secret Service did not have its own accountant.

Despite its rapid expansion, there was still nobody keeping track of the agency's funds. In fiscal year (FY) 1975, the Secret Service had a congressional budget of $82.8 million; in 1985, $192.6 million. Each decade, Congress just about doubled the service's budget. But in five years under President Clinton, as the Secret Service became his darling for fighting Starr's inquiries, the budget went even higher. In 1990, it was $366.1 million; in 1991, $412.7 million; and five years later, $555 million. This was done in part, starting in 1995 and ending in 2000, by the 1994 Violent Crime Control and Law Enforcement Act, which increased the Secret Service budget by an average of $18 million each year.

The next concerted effort in the Master Plan was changing the interpretation of "secret" in "Secret Service." In fighting Starr, the agency contended that "secret" referred to anything directly involving the president, but that didn't stop it afterward from sending out open invitations to cable news channels and programs to create TV spots and documentaries that highlighted the agency's prowess.

Dan Emmett, in his book *Within Arm's Length*, wrote:

"Subsequent to this [Joan Lunden Special], it became the norm for journalists . . . to regularly be on campus. There were times when so many of these visitors were on site that regular training had to be canceled and special agent class members used as extras in productions. It was not unusual on some days to be standing for an hour or more at the obstacle course with an agent class waiting for the signal to being the course while some cameraman filmed away. Even more irritating . . . was being forced to give up certain students for on-camera interviews . . . [the Secret Service's Office of Public Affairs] granted just enough [media requests] to interfere—significantly, at times—with our normal training schedule. . . . During this time many agents began to feel that the Service had lost touch with its mission by allowing this type of unnecessary exposure."

In the 1990s, the Secret Service lobbied the president and Congress to pass executive orders and legislation that would mandate the service to take on more missions, such as administering asset forfeiture, combating cybercrime, providing protection to individuals other than foreign dignitaries or those in the Executive Branch, crafting a national plan to protect schools against active shooters, locating missing or kidnapped children, assisting all law enforcement agencies with their investigations, and being the lead agency responsible for securing all major US events, such as the Olympics and NATO summit, for starters.

The Secret Service succeeded in getting power over forfeited criminal assets and created the Asset Forfeiture Program. It could thereby seize all property used to facilitate crimes, such as homes, cars, planes, boats, land, farm equipment, and so on. This opened up a Pandora's box of constitutional issues when it became clear that the Secret Service and other agencies were choosing investigations to pursue based on what they could financially gain from them and thus bolster their budgets. Litigations and countersuits flooded agencies using the practice as criminals and their victims tried to get their property back.

In May 1998, the Secret Service expanded again to take the lead role in protecting National Special Security Events (NSSE). This was a clear example of the agency's leadership taking on new missions at the expense of presidential protection, and it couldn't have come at a worse time. In his second term, President Clinton set out to travel the world nonstop, much as President Eisenhower had on his "Goodwill Tour," but Clinton went above and beyond any president before him. To keep up with his grueling schedule, the Secret Service was stretched to its limits.

In October 1998, Senator Larry Craig of Idaho summed up the serious uptick in presidential travel in a speech on the floor of the Senate: "President Clinton broke the Presidential record for foreign travel with his 27th trip abroad," he announced. "This year so far he has logged 41 days in 11 different foreign countries. Some say he is traveling in foreign countries to keep his mind off domestic problems . . . the president has now broken all-time Presidential travel records with 32 trips abroad, more than any other president ever . . . Bill Clinton also likes to travel around the country as well . . . the President has spent almost half of 1997, 149 days, as well as over half of 1998 so far, 155 days, outside of Washington, DC."

The men and women of the Secret Service were worn ragged protecting him. There simply wasn't enough manpower to protect the president correctly—yet the service higher-ups thought they could expand into new missions.

At the 1999 World Trade Organization Ministerial Conference, which, due to violent protests, became known as the "Battle of Seattle," the Secret Service struggled to secure the area before the president's arrival. Coordination with local authorities, specifically Mayor Paul Schell, was so difficult that as President Clinton was about to land, PPD threatened to turn around and head back if the mayor didn't get the situation under control. At the conference venue, rioters were getting out of hand and the Uniformed Division officers running metal detectors donned gas masks. The tear gas and pepper spray deployed by local police had seeped into the attendees' clothes and bags, causing officers to choke. Their eyes burned, their mucus membranes overloaded, yet they had to remain vigilant.

Just a block away, maddened rioters were flipping cars, smashing storefronts, and beating innocent people. The conference venue was a secure area, and many bystanders headed there for safety. Secret Service operatives kept working to make sure everyone was screened but were frustrated that they couldn't do anything to secure the situation beyond the venue.

Making matters worse, on their final sweep agents discovered an empty backpack big enough to fit a rifle and climbing equipment discarded and hidden in a closet. All Secret Service personnel were alerted, and they launched another sweep to find what appeared to be an unknown sniper or political stuntman in their midst. But soon afterward, with seemingly no substantiation, the agents declared the find a hoax, a way to intimidate the president and keep him from attending.

As the PPD threatened to turn Air Force One around, riot police stormed the protests with great force. The president arrived, and everyone in the Secret Service held their breath. The exit routes had been compromised. The streets were jammed. Tear gas still hung in the air. Whoever had left the backpack and climbing equipment behind was never found. Luckily, the president got through his appearance without a scratch, but it was another sign that the Secret Service was having a hard enough time guaranteeing presidential protection and wasn't in a position to guarantee the public's safety at large national events.

The same year, President Clinton insisted at the last minute on walking in the funeral procession of the deceased King Hassan II in Morocco. As CNN wrote, "President Clinton caused the Secret Service some anxious moments in Morocco Sunday, when he became caught up in the moment . . . and decided to continue walking with the funeral procession, as crowds pressed around him."

The story was filled with gross understatement. The "crowd" was an emotionally charged mob of at least two million. They were crying, screaming, running; the atmosphere was chaotic. It was as though the president were surrounded by a surging river of people. In the National Geographic documentary *Secret Service Files: Protecting the President* one of the PPD agents described how his improvised plan was to use the coffin and pallbearers as cover and concealment if any one of the 2 million unscreened Moroccans realized that he or she was next to the US president and attempted an attack. The PPD was also completely separated from the Counter Assault Team. The CAT and others had to disembark from the motorcade and try to stay parallel to the president. All of the equipment, time, money, and effort put into protecting Clinton could have been made worthless by anyone with a rusty razor blade or even a stampede that could have occurred at any moment. The procession was walking into the blinding sun in the driest month of the year in the desert country. Sand was being kicked up like a storm. The desert heat was unbearable for everyone in suits. If anything did go wrong, the closest adequate medical facility was back the other way—on board Air Force One.

The Morocco trip was a strategic failure brought on by a reckless prioritization of marketing over security. By putting himself into a dangerous situation, President Clinton put both the US government and the Moroccan funeral attendees at risk. Such a situation hadn't been dreamed of or planned for in even a theoretical sense. Some Secret Service personnel have speculated that the CAT and PPD would have attempted to shoot their way through the crowd of Moroccan civilians to get the president out—which prompts the question, why endanger the Moroccan people with such a selfish stunt? In footage of the event, the PPD agents and even the president are noticeably terrified, but they had no way out until the PPD pushed their way out, back to CAT and the motorcade. The advance team was blamed, but that was also ridiculous. The trip had been coordinated only in the few days since King Hassan had died. Within that window of time, no advance would have been adequate. Besides, it had been the president's last-minute decision to take part in the parade, and once he was committed, there was little chance of stopping him.

Since taking office in 1993, President Clinton had made the Secret Service so user-friendly—for himself—that it had been reduced to protecting him with little more than hopes and prayers. During the 1999 trip in Morocco, that's all that kept the American president alive.

Back stateside, President Clinton was on hand to dedicate the newly built Secret Service headquarters. He spoke of how the agency had a proud history and was "worthy of trust and confidence." His speech sounded so hollow, it was as if he were reading the agency's eulogy.

At the James J. Rowley Training Center in Laurel, Maryland, the "raw apples"—new recruits—were trained alongside agents and officers conducting their recertifications and continuing education. In 1999, Director Merletti invited about sixty National Football League employees and representatives to a Secret Service "dog-and-pony show," which had become so frequent they were like circuses that regularly came to town. The demonstrations had originally been put on for protectees to impress upon them the effectiveness and seriousness of Secret Service protection. Later, congressmen were invited so the agency could demonstrate to Congress how its ballooning budget was used.

The program consisted of a tour of the complex and large-scale demonstrations, with real pyrotechnics, of the Secret Service's defensive measures. It even included a mock "attack on the principal" with blank-firing guns and explosions. It was well known that the spectacle was put on at taxpayers' expense. Even if it was somehow justified in the accounting books to have the training center used to entertain NFL hotshots, real training had been sidelined and morale had suffered. The damage was done. The optics were that "worthy of trust and confidence" meant loyalty primarily to the Secret Service. Director Merletti joined the ongoing exodus of service personnel, leaving his successor in as tight a spot as the one he had inherited. Merletti took a job in security in the NFL and later became senior vice president of the Cleveland Browns.

During the Clinton administration, the Secret Service found itself in a desperate last-ditch effort to save itself. Director Merletti could have taken the agency to new heights instead of new lows if not for the power couple at the center of all the scandals, President Bill Clinton and First Lady Hillary Clinton.

Snipers, crowds, approachers, gate-crashers, and bombers have been common categories of violent threats facing presidents, but threats from the air have also hounded the president for more than a century and continue to this day.

The average reader reads about two hundred words per minute. That's a few paragraphs in this book. So just imagine seven seconds—that's how quickly an airborne threat can travel from outside the normal military or commercial air traffic lanes over DC and deviate to the White House. Small arms are useless against aircraft, so as soon as officers radio that an "unannounced" mystery aircraft is inbound for the White House and our president, seven seconds is all we have to realize what's being said over the radio, take the initiative, and "cover and evacuate"—fancy talk for getting the president from wherever he is to a secure area.

The airborne threat is far from new. During the Civil War, the Confederates launched blimps that posed threats to President Lincoln. Agent Mike Reilly had .50-caliber antiaircraft guns installed on the White House roof during World War II and wrote of them in his memoir. Then, as now, the Secret Service knew that the best protection was early detection so they could rush President Roosevelt into the bomb shelter, the only place safety was guaranteed if and when planes took aim at the White House. In Agent Reilly's memoir he noted very specifically how the capital's geography and monuments could easily lead any low-flying bomber directly to the White House, and the Secret Service consulted with experts and they even considered rerouting the nearby river to camouflage the White House from a bomber circling at high altitude. So the cat has been out of the bag on airborne threats for well over a century. Until the Secret Service and US government make it clear that airborne attacks are not possible on their watch, attackers will continue to see them as an opportunity, a chance to succeed.

One year, 1974, saw two significant near misses. That February, a disgruntled army pilot stole a Huey helicopter and headed for the White House. Thinking he could win his job back by impressing the president with aerial stunts, he engaged in two chases with police helicopters and twice performed low-flying acrobatics over the White House. On his second pass, Secret Service personnel opened fire with everything they had—handguns, shotguns, submachine guns—forcing the chopper to land and arresting the wounded pilot. That pilot was given just a few months in a military prison and was granted a "general discharge" from the Army, not even a "dishonorable discharge." Just five days later, a man attempted to hijack an airliner at a local airport with the intent of flying it into the White House. Wounded when police stormed the plane, the would-be assassin committed suicide like the coward he was.

By the 1990s, the Secret Service still had learned nothing but was in a worse position due to fatigue in its highest ranks and most important positions. There was, of course, the 1994 airplane crash at the White House. But another, relatively unknown incident placed President Clinton in danger, and it was made worse by the wrongly diagnosed problem of "freezing up." What most people call "freezing up" usually means that protectors lack rest, training, balanced psychological conditioning, mental readiness, or a mixture of all of those. But in a service where split seconds matter, "freezing up" kills.

The incident, which occurred shortly before Ken Starr's subpoenas started flying out of Secret Service fax machines, was kept secret even from President Clinton and amazingly never made it into the headlines.

A brand-new PPD agent stood just outside the closed door of the Oval Office. I stood next to her, standing the E-6 post outside the Oval Office. If and when the president moved, so did she and all of the PPD, who for the moment were downstairs in "W-16," the term for the PPD agents' break room and staging area. But as the officer at E-6, I would remain standing the post. President Clinton was inside and holding a meeting in his office. This agent was on her first shift on the job. She was new, but, like everyone else, she was overworked and desensitized. More important, she hadn't been there long enough for the shine to wear off, for the reverence of those hallowed halls and the VIPs in them to become mundane, part of just another workday. Yet, as she stood there, she and I were the last lines of defense for President Clinton.

The validity of that "last line of defense" was never more evident than when there was an airborne threat. Just as there had been nothing but air and the decisions of agents between

President Kennedy and a sniper's bullet, there was nothing but air, some building material, and our ability to react decisively that could save the president's life should we be alerted that an aircraft had left the unrestricted airspace, broken into the "P-56 area" of restricted airspace, and aimed at the White House.

The Uniformed Division officers at the Ellipse and on the executive mansion's rooftop radioed in fast. Per protocol, the president needed to be evacuated from the Oval Office to a more secure area in the White House immediately. The September 12, 1994, airplane crash at the White House was fresh for all the officers—several ERT officers had sprinted for their lives out of its path. This time we had a very large "unannounced" mystery helicopter coming in low and fast at the White House. It was flying up East Executive Avenue! No one knew why. Worse, unlike the small Huey helicopter shot down over the White House in 1974, this very large one was more than defensible against small-arms fire. Whatever it was up to, we were powerless—except to evacuate the president.

The radio warnings came in.

The PPD agent's response was astounding: "I'm not doing anything without the permission of my supervisor, and I'm certainly not going to open that door."

And just like that, seven seconds had passed. We might have missed our window to evacuate to a safe area. Still, we had to act. I opened the door and held up my finger to the president. President Clinton recognized the simple gesture that said "Be ready in a moment. We may have something that is more demanding of your attention." The president nodded and carried on with his meeting. I turned back and closed the door. The

PPD agent was furious and gave me the stink eye for having had the gall to open the door and warn the president, let alone look him in the eye.

As she dithered for a few seconds, the gray mystery helicopter with military markings went from a far off shape to take the form of a marine CH-53 heavy-lift helicopter, even bigger than the old white-and-green marine 1 SH-3 helicopters that flew the president.

But as that PPD agent had failed in a split second by choosing to ask her supervisors before acting, the Secret Service had an unwanted H-series helicopter approaching and flying overhead. If you haven't been near such a large helicopter landing and taking off, it's like a mini-earthquake. Everything shook. The reverberations were so loud that you had to raise your voice to be heard. But the shaking and noise diminished. The gate-crashing helicopter passed overhead and went on its way.

As soon as it did, the postgame show was on. The PPD agent and I saw the situation differently. She believed I had brazenly and disrespectfully interrupted the president, but I knew the Secret Service had completely failed to follow procedure and thereby failed to guarantee the president's protection. As soon as that Marine helicopter broke the airspace, we had roughly seven seconds to evacuate the president and get him to a hardened safe area. If that helicopter was intent on crashing into the White House, the president, the PPD agents, the West Wing officers, the West Wing staff, and all the visitors would be dead or wounded. There had been some light talk of the West Wing officers being formally trained to conduct the evacuation procedure in case the PPD couldn't for whatever seemingly inexplicable reason—but I had just experienced such a reason: a brand-new PPD agent who was more afraid to interrupt the president than protect him.

The PPD shift leader came up from W-16 and wanted to know what the hell had happened. Meanwhile, the officers in the Uniformed Division control center scrambled to hail nearby military and commercial airports to check flight rosters and find any explanation. Officers radioed in the tail number. I monitored the back and forth with the officers on the Ellipse, in the control center, and on the lawn to deduce details: how low, fast, etc.

"It said 'Duke' on his helmet," one officer said, half laughing. "That's how low he was."

Everyone wanted to know: Why the hell had a Marine CH-53 military helicopter flown past us?

Only one thing was certain: we had lost control of the situation. Our imaginations had raced to fill in the blanks. Some officers and agents were irate; others snickered, "That was weird. Another crazy day at the shit magnet, am I right?"

The agent's control center soon delivered an explanation: our mystery fly-by helicopter was discovered to be a legitimate Marine helicopter, though its route was anything but. Two marine aviators had taken a "check ride" of their CH-53 helicopter to test recent maintenance and figured that if they flew very low, no one would pick them up on radar—or at least no one would be monitoring. But their joyride and sightseeing tour around Washington, DC, had gone farther than they had planned. They had gotten lost but couldn't gain altitude lest their joyride be discovered by radar. Then they had traveled over the monuments and seen the White House up close, and only as they had traveled up East Executive Avenue, did they realize that they had really screwed up.

Back at the White House, the special agents in charge of the PPD, future director Lewis Merletti and Edward Merinzel, were working to figure out why the hell the PPD hadn't responded as it was supposed to. They eventually got someone from the marine unit or flight tower on the phone. I stood in W-16, offering what information I had gathered from the officers who had sounded the alarm on the helicopter. The person on the phone was explaining that the helicopter had been traveling much more slowly and higher than any of the officers were reporting, claiming that they were blowing things out of proportion and overexaggerating.

Merletti wasn't having it. "Who the hell is 'Duke'?" he demanded.

There was silence on the other end of the line. I knew I had done my job and passed on the right information. The PPD was about to give whatever marine unit and their aviators a licking. I didn't need to be there for that, so I left.

The hope after this incident was that the Secret Service would learn.

It had been another quiet day turned into a near miss. Air accidents happened far more than terrorist acts, and several dozen tons of fast-moving aluminum and steel loaded with aviation fuel was never something to take lightly. It was another failure to guarantee presidential protection that would be swept under the rug, another accidental success in keeping the country safe, another day counted as a "win" solely because the airborne gate-crasher happened to be friendly. But the damage to the Secret Service's morale and strategy was done: it proved that such an attack was possible and we were still no better off after decades.

The hope was that the Secret Service would harden up and be ready the next time. But it had been strategically distracted for so long, especially from 1998 to 2001, and eventually our time had run out and our bubble had burst. After decades of airborne incidents that had showed our weaknesses to enemies, the United States and especially the Secret Service had been distracted in all the wrong places. The airborne threat recognized in 1941, the two 1974 attacks, the CH-53 incident, and the 1994 Cessna crash into the White House had still left the Secret Service unprepared in January 2001 as President George W. Bush took the helm of the presidency.

Of course, the transition wouldn't have been complete without a final series of run-ins between the Uniformed Division and Clinton staff. A criminal investigation was looming, threatening to drag officers into court and Congress again to testify against the Clinton administration. On their way out, numerous Clinton staffers, bitter over Vice President Al Gore's loss, stole White House decorations and ornaments, drew graffiti in bathrooms and offices, and even removed the "W" keys on keyboards. Furniture was ruined, desks overturned, even glass tables were smashed. And then the big one: a key that only the Secret Service used was broken off in a door lock, making it inoperable. After the presidential transition was completed, the Government Affairs Office published a report entitled "The White House: Allegations of Damage During the 2001 Presidential Transition." Officers wondered if, yet again, they were going to be subpoenaed and have to answer the questions "Who did what?" and "How did this happen with the Secret Service present?" But the political currency needed to push the issue had evaporated.

Meanwhile, in New York City, the Secret Service was enjoying its modern office space in one of the world's most exclusive office complexes. Its old field office had been deemed so unsafe and unhealthy to employees—even the ceiling was collapsing—that the Government Services Administration (GSA) and Congress had prioritized the move to a new space over other federal agency projects. The process had taken eight years, but the agency magazine was finally able to say of the new office, "It's big, it's spacious, it's beautiful." It boasted that it had 8,000 additional square footage with backup generator, permanent emergency command center, voice mail, and bigger conference room and gym and was the first Secret Service office to be completely disability-friendly by the legal requirements. But what the service was perhaps most proud of was the new command center, which would be the hub of its latest expansion of authority: coordinating the protection of major national events, especially those in New York City, including the United Nations. The Secret Service had been very proud to move its area field office from World Trade Center Building 6 to Building 7.

The Secret Service internal publication continued with its announcement: "We all remember on Friday, February 26, 1993, at 12:18 p.m., a bomb exploded in the parking garage area near the New York City Field Office secure parking lot facility." Everyone in the field office had felt the explosion when the Al Qaeda bomb went off. The publication continued, "But one thing that came out of this tragic incident was that the GSA seemed to expedite our plans for relocation."

Like all federal law enforcement officials, everyone in the Secret Service was kept up to speed on the latest in enemy tradecraft. If a new kind of bomb or style of attack happened anywhere in the world—a suicide bus bombing or hostage taking in Israel or Myanmar, bombings that mimicked controlled detonations to collapse buildings on top of innocent victims—we were briefed on it. We were supposed to be thinkers and questioners of everything. Whether on a temporary assignment at a hotel or at the White House fence line, we would think to ourselves: Why is that wire in the ceiling there? When's the last time that lady with the stroller looked at her child? Are that man and woman in the corner of the room professional colleagues, friends, or intimate because they haven't looked at each other in minutes? We were professional people watchers, and we were on the alert. If some kind of attack had repeatedly proven successful around the globe, it was due to be tried in the United States eventually.

All agencies, including the Secret Service, were great at sharing general knowledge between directors and down to every post stander, beat cop, and ground-pounding agent or officer—because when the monster's new form appeared, aside from civilians, it would be those frontline agents or officers who would make the first contact.

And then, sometimes, the ground radically shifts under your feet. That's what happened on September 11, 2001.

As it always seems to go, this Tuesday started much like any other. The sky was cloudless and blue, the breeze pleasant, and most Americans had trivial complaints, such as dragging themselves through the workweek.

The War on Terror didn't start that Tuesday, just as World War II didn't start on December 7, 1941, with the attack on Pearl Harbor. Even that attack hadn't started on December 7; it had started long before the Japanese ships left their harbor. We were just ignorant about the war that had been declared on us. September 11, 2001, wasn't the beginning of the War on Terror, it was just the day when Americans realized we were in it. The War on Terror had finally reached us, and as every American witnessed the four hijacked planes used as ballistic missiles flying into key components of the US economy as well as its command and control structure, they now knew what sophisticated attacks by the worst kinds of monsters would look like—and what they would cost us.

The eighteen Al Qaeda terrorists (the nineteenth had been refused entry into the United States by a suspicious immigration agent) had studied piloting in the United States and then hijacked four commercial airliners. At 8:19 a.m., the FBI was alerted of the hijackings and readied its counterterrorist teams, but the Secret Service was not notified. American Airlines Flight 11 from Boston, with Mohammad Atta at the helm after he had brutally murdered the pilots, crashed into the North Tower of the World Trade Center (WTC) at 8:46 a.m. After the first crash, many people, including those in the Secret Service, believed it had been an accident. It wasn't until 9:03 a.m., when United Airlines Flight 175 crashed into the World Trade Center South Tower, that they realized the nation was under attack by terrorists.

Only three minutes before that had the Federal Aviation Administration (FAA) realized that simultaneous hijackings were occurring. It couldn't figure out what to do next. There had been a similar case in September 1970, when, in a three-day period, five planes, all scheduled to head for New York City, had been hijacked by terrorists. Despite that, the FAA had no protocols in place to alert aircraft to ground them. Furthermore, despite its own brushes with aerial threats to the White House, the Secret Service had no plans in place to respond to hijacked aircraft.

President Bush was in Sarasota, Florida, reading books to children in their school under PPD protection. He was notified of the first attack at 8:50 a.m. At 9:31 a.m., he spoke from Florida, announcing that the nation was under "an apparent terrorist attack." PPD agent Eddie Merinzel notified the president he had to get back to Air Force One and evacuate. As they boarded the plane, the plan was to head back to Washington, DC. Their specific destination was uncertain, but for some odd reason, Air Force One uncharacteristically had no fighter escort, even as it left Sarasota-Bradenton International Airport. They took off at maximum climb, gaining altitude almost like a rocket. Eddie Merinzel warned the pilots of his concern that this could be the beginning of a "decapitation attack," the likes of which the country had not faced since the 1865 plot that had killed Lincoln and nearly killed several other officials.

At 9:37 a.m., American Airlines Flight 77 crashed into the Pentagon. Had it been aiming for the White House, it would have hit its mark and killed scores of people, as the Secret Service had ordered an evacuation only at 9:45 a.m. United Airlines Flight 93, meanwhile, had left Newark International Airport twenty-five minutes behind schedule due to heavy traffic. As passengers learned of the attacks elsewhere, they bravely attempted to retake the cockpit, causing the plane to nose-dive into a open field in Shanksville, Somerset County, Pennsylvania. It crashed at 10:03 a.m. It is believed that the hijackers' destination for Flight 93 was the White House. Even leaving late, it would have arrived at Washington, DC, at 10:23 a.m., as the White House was still evacuating. Had it left on time, it would have reached DC and the White House at 9:58, when the evacuations had only just begun.

Meanwhile, Secret Service master special officer Craig Miller was fighting for his life in the smoke, rubble, and mayhem of WTC 7, inside the Secret Service Field Office. Craig resided in Virginia to be closer to where he was permanently posted in the Maryland-DC area, and when his family saw what was transpiring via television, they believed he was safe. But Craig had taken a last-minute special assignment in New York City. A veteran of Operations Desert Shield and Desert Storm and the recipient of two Bronze Stars, Miller had assisted in the evacuation efforts but had gone missing afterward. Though his family held out hope that he might somehow inexplicably be found alive or in a coma somewhere, his remains were identified three years after the attack. He was one of 72 officers from eight local, state, and federal agencies and one of 2,800 civilians who died that day at the site of the World Trade Center attacks.

At the James J. Rowley Training Center, all the New York recruits and agents receiving requalification training joined a handful of instructors, loaded up a few SUVs with food, water, ammunition, firearms, vests, and as much medical gear as they could fit in, and headed home to be of assistance any way they could. No one knew if this was the beginning and end of the attack or just the first wave.

In the Secret Service's possession today are several submachine guns recovered from the wreckage of the New York Field Office. The fire-rated safe had been burned through, and the barrels of the firearms had been turned into pretzel-shaped knots by the fire's overwhelming heat. It is kept as a reminder and a memorial to history, along with the memory of Craig Miller, the thirty-fourth Secret Service employee to die in the line of duty, the thirteenth to perish on duty by violence, and, as of this writing, the last to have died by violence.

At 1 p.m., President George W. Bush announced that the nation was on high alert from an Air Force base in Louisiana.

In the year that followed, the Secret Service had to contend with additional panic over the terror threat, on top of the flaws and gaps it had been contending with for decades. With so many new responsibilities taken on already as part of the Master Plan, the bloated middle management, and no idea how it spent its money, the agency had already been stretched beyond thin. After the attacks of September 11, 2001, the Secret Service's leadership tried to stretch the agency further. Defense of the White House again became a chief concern, and more officers were posted there. The security officers and trainers at the training center were even pulled from training duties. Officers were recalled from time off or ordered to take more overtime shifts to stand post at the White House. But what good was that? It just added more overtired officers to a location that was still just as unprotected from airborne threats as before Pearl Harbor.

That's when the agency's attrition problems went into over-drive and people started to recognize the situation for what it was: an exodus. No amount of money could justify the strat-egy of adding more officers to a target that was still defense-less from the air. For Secret Service personnel, what good was more money if you worked twelve-hour days seven days a week and had neither the time to spend with your family nor time to spend the money you earned?

So agents and officers flocked to the new Federal Air Marshal Service (FAMS) in droves. The attrition got so bad that the training center had the Internet technicians block the Transportation Security Administration (TSA) website to try to prevent officers and agents for applying to FAMS while at work—as if that were a solution.

SIX.

SHAKY WARTIME FOOTING

Immediately following the attacks of September 11, 2001, the nation reeled. Americans watched firefighters and first responders pull the living and the 2,976 lost innocents from the wreckage of four plane crashes. The question was: What now?

The Secret Service needed a strategic pause more than ever, a complete reevaluation of all it was doing and all it was still doing wrong. This could have been the time to fix the rift between the UD and the agents, fix the manpower shortages, give up the extraneous missions that detracted from presidential protection, tackle the airborne threats, make morale a priority, make sure personnel were well rested and trained, and even hire accountants to make sure the agency was using its budget correctly—or figure out how it was spending its money to begin with.

But like any national catastrophe, the attacks put an immediate and incredible strain on the Secret Service, especially in the first days after. The service had a number of immediate tasks: to rally the New York Field Office agents, protect all the foreign diplomats visiting the nation to pay their respects and coordinate the new war effort, and create new security details for everyone in line to succeed the presidency. Of course, it also had to bolster the defenses of the top terrorist targets: the White House and the president.

President Bush didn't hesitate to get moving. Just one day after the attacks, he did something very unexpected and against the wishes of many in the Secret Service. With Air Force One the only transport plane in the sky, he hopped from one military base to another to reach "ground zero," the site of the attacks on the Twin Towers. When he arrived on the scene, he gave a speech, visited firefighters, and roused the nation and the world to fight back and begin the War on Terror. The Secret Service and PPD would have preferred that he stay home at the White House or at Camp David or any one of the bases he had visited in the hours prior. But the goal of executive protection is not only to protect the president's life but to protect his or her ability to lead with confidence, and that's what Bush wanted to do.

Like the president and his administration, Secret Service director Brian Stafford and his managers had not expected to have their tenure defined by a major attack, despite so many past chiefs and directors being faced with major crises. All the men and women in the Secret Service found themselves standing in the shoes of their predecessors, facing yet another unexpected and terrible challenge, just as Chief Baughman in the Cold War, Agent Reilly in World War II, Agent Starling in World War I, and Agent Warne in the Civil War had. Now they were the ones "in it," and the president's life and leadership rested on their every strategic decision and split second reaction. The culture went from "all quiet" to a desperate "go-go-go" and "all hands on deck" mentality. Haste was the name of the game. Everyone felt that a second wave and another series of attacks were imminent. The Secret Service leadership found itself surprised by a war they had ignored, trying to figure out how to win it after it had already begun.

The New York Field Office agents and technicians were especially hard hit. Their beautiful brand-new office, one of the largest staffed in the agency, was completely demolished. Except for Agent Craig Miller, everyone on duty that day only narrowly escaped the ensuing inferno and collapse of World Trade Center Building 7 and the North and South Towers. Protocol dictates that if a Secret Servicer member is in so much as a serious on-duty car accident, he or she is pulled off duty and ordered to take time off for health services. But since the whole field office staff couldn't be taken off duty, that was swept aside. Secret Service leadership ordered the New York City agents to report and stand post to protect President Bush's trip to New York City on September 14 instead of pulling agents from nearby state offices. Some agents never reported, and others walked off the job then and there. It would be easy to blame this on the shock that came from facing such devastation as the New York agents witnessed on 9/11, but the sad truth is that the Secret Service has treated its employees like machines, often dispensable ones, so why change now?

Still, it was a new scenario for the Secret Service. It had protected presidents following each war after 1901, and it had lost six employees and its entire Oklahoma City Field Office in the 1995 Oklahoma City bombing. The New York City Field Office had been moved in part due to its acknowledged vulnerabilities after the 1993 World Trade Center attack. But none of those lessons had been enough to spur the agency to be ready for the total loss of a field office on 9/11.

A month after the towers and the Pentagon were hit, my boss's boss phoned me while I was an instructor at the training center. They were sending me a group of New York City Field Office agents, two men and a woman, to requalify on their handguns so they could go back on duty. Secretly, the service was so desperate for personnel that it was pressuring the shocked and wounded New York agents to get back on their feet. Management considered it "tough love" therapy; it was not a good mix.

As soon as I laid eyes on the agents when they arrived, it was clear that this was a horrible idea. I insisted our supervisors end the training; the agents needed mental health services, not a pressured "tough love" qualifier.

As we waited for the guns to return from the armorer, the agents wanted to tell their 9/11 stories. Every American had his or her own story from that day, and these men and women had some of the most harrowing. They needed to share them. The dissociated memories were clearly flashing in their heads and poured out of them, and I listened. Those agents had been buried, one person twice, and had had to dig themselves out. Each person had seen and experienced things he or she couldn't shake—certainly not as early as three weeks after.

The Secret Service agents in New York had a reputation spanning two centuries of harrowing investigative and protection missions. These three were some of the grittiest the service had had. Aside from some physical wounds, their eyes were red from stress; one agent said he couldn't "get the smell out of my head." It had been his first day back on the job. All instructors were trained first responders or had advanced medical training. I knew those three were still damaged. The armorer and I had to ask ourselves: Why does the agency want these agents back on the job? Does it really want someone back on the job protecting someone when he or she is visibly trembling? Passing the qualifier was going to prove on paper that the agents were fit to return to work, but no leadership is complete without seeing the state of things firsthand.

The armorer came emotionally unglued at the sorry sight of the agents' pistols. It was a red flag that spoke to their mental state. While the three agents were still in the hospital and couldn't report to protect President Bush on September 14 and thereafter, some of their colleagues could have been protecting the president with guns in an equally sorry state. The three agents' barrels were completely occluded by rubble. Dust had seeped in through the gun's orifices and been caked by gun oil and sweat, then packed against their holsters into a sort of concrete plug. Was that the kind of agent and firearm you want protecting the president? Though they had had their handguns on them after the attack, if they had ever had to fire them, the guns would've blown up in their hands. The armorer pulled himself together and returned the pistols, fully serviced.

During the firing range portion, the agents trembled and shook from feeling the reverberations of gunfire echoing around them. The once familiar sound of gunfire and the smell of gunpowder triggered the hell they had experienced only a month before.

All the agents were passed. They left the training center with prayers and hope that time would truly heal all wounds.

But the haste didn't stop there. The Secret Service set up a temporary New York City Field Office on some of the highest levels of a NYC high-rise. Many agents refused to enter the building or go up the elevator. When the agents' families heard of it, they broke out the phone book, called every Secret Service number they could find, and furiously berated anyone who answered.

After a series of misunderstandings, a small building in New Jersey served as the temporary New York City Field Office.

Agencywide, the future was just as uncertain as the wheels of the Secret Service began to completely fall off.

President Bush and Congress focused on the means, motive, opportunity, and intent of the 9/11 hijackers, and their solutions addressed each aspect of the attack. The attackers had been born of a festering and unhindered hateful ideology. They had infiltrated the country and slipped through the US intelligence dragnet due to lack of intelligence sharing. They were well funded and trained. Once in the country, at their flight schools, at the airports, and on the planes, nothing had stopped them—except for one planeload of passengers. Presuming they had been targeting the White House and the executive branch as well, it appeared that their plan had been to decapitate the nation's leadership structure and its economy. Following 9/11, the Department of Homeland Security (DHS) and Transportation Security Administration (TSA) were created, while the Federal Air Marshal Service (FAMS), and the National Security Administration (NSA) ballooned rapidly in a mad dash rush to create better security. FAMS went from around thirty air marshals on the payroll before 9/11 to the goal was to have enough to place one air marshal on every major flight within a year. Among those new organizations, future terrorists would have neither the resources nor the access to carry out further plots. The plan was that they would be hunted around the globe and, if they managed to get inside the United States, would be sniffed out and fought at every level.

DHS became the umbrella organization for most every federal law enforcement, intelligence-gathering, and counterterrorism organization. The FBI and US Marshals Service were excluded because they were under the Department of Justice. The CIA was also excluded, as it was the foreign espionage wing and forbidden to operate inside the homeland—without a homeland agency liaison, at least. The Secret Service argued that it, too, should be excluded from the umbrella because it was unique; its protective and investigative missions operated both in the homeland and abroad. As part of the Master Plan, the agency had established dozens of regional and national field offices in foreign countries that the president was likely to visit. The agency also conducted major counterfeiting and financial fraud investigations. The majority of counterfeit American dollars were printed in foreign countries and had been since World War II. Nigeria, Iran, and North Korea had become the biggest counterfeiters and perpetrators of defrauding Americans and stealing US citizens' identities; Iran and North Korea in particular were using those operations to sponsor nuclear programs and global terror and circumvent US sanctions. But for all its investigative efforts, the Secret Service was hamstrung to interdict those operations in any way. But the service was also viewed as an organization that was far too secretive and wasn't doing its part in notifying its fellow agency partners in the group efforts to fight terror. It was commanded to transition from the Treasury Department to the new Department of Homeland Security and to finally find a solution to the century-old problem of airborne threats.

After the temporary airport closings in the DC area subsided, the Secret Service's only answer to airborne threats was to create a committee or suborganization to find an answer. The "no-fly" area was extended, but it could be extended no farther than the two airports only miles away—Reagan National's runway was still pointed at the White House, and planes taking off still had to make a sharp turn to follow the Potomac River and not fly into the restricted airspace.

The Secret Service got the FAA to include it in the permitting process—not that 9/11 hijackers bothered with permits anyway—but it wanted as much notice as possible to evacuate the president. Extremely advanced blimps equipped with radar were set up in the area to increase the capability of detecting low-flying drones and small aircraft, and it was said that if someone dropped a tennis ball out of a high-rise window, the blimps' radar would record which way the ball was spinning. Representatives from the Secret Service, the FAA, and others joined the Office of National Capital Region Coordination (ONCRC) as part of the new Secret Service Airspace Security Branch (ASB). The Secret Service was finally giving itself the greatest possible notice of airspace breaches to evacuate the president, but what about other agencies?

In 2013, a man who had been investigated by the Secret Service and deemed not to be a threat landed his home-made gyrocopter on the Capitol lawn, completely unhindered by Secret Service or Capitol Police until he was pulled out from the copter and arrested. Unlike in the 1970s, none of the officers in DC was willing to shoot at airborne threats—because they were too afraid of their leadership not backing their decision to engage and protect.

The Secret Service was clearly having problems dealing with the realities of the post-9/11 world, as it had failed to prepare and, as the saying goes, it had prepared to fail. But there was one easy way for Secret Service agents and officers to deal with the problems that still faced their agency on the ground: get out—leave the Secret Service and transfer to another agency. When President Bush called on every able-bodied trained protector to join FAMS, no one was more willing than those who had been neglected by the Secret Service.

Leaving the Treasury Department to join the DHS meant that the Secret Service no longer had a patsy in the Treasury Department and Secret Service employees became employees under the DHS. The Secret Service's leadership and culture and the Master Plan to expand and consolidate power, paired with the transition to the DHS, was a recipe for collapse.

The Secret Service was gambling on the blind loyalty of its agents and officers. For the White House's defense, the Secret Service's reaction was to throw more bodies onto the White House's perimeter. The American people did not want the White House, "the people's house," a chief symbol of freedom, to be turned into an imposing armed camp, but within the agency, the likelihood of an attack on the White House seemed certain. The Uniformed Division was given greater permission to wear bullet-resistant and tactical vests and carry submachine guns or other long guns in full view of the public.

But the man-hours increased dramatically. The personnel shortages were already a problem, but they went from strained to desperate to dire.

Overtime went from sometimes voluntary to far more "volun-told," the sarcastic term for mandatory. Leaves were canceled. UD security details were pulled from the training center, Foreign Missions Branch (where the vice president lived), and all over the DC area to send more officers to the White House. Specialized training classes, courses, and seminars ranging from shooting in low light to new tourniquet practices, how to address civilians with possible disabilities, and even routine refresher trainings and qualifications for health, fitness, and shooting ability—all were slashed dramatically to get as many officers protecting the White House as possible.

Agents were mustered from all over the country to report for additional presidential protection duties and, for the first time, to stand posts around the White House. Those agents weren't hired out of thin air for that specific purpose, they were pulled off investigations into counterfeiting, white-collar crime, or the numerous new missions the Secret Service had acquired in the past few years. They were flown in from around the country to pull perimeter and basic area protection duties at the White House.

Agents and officers had a collective sense of dread and fatigue at padding the White House's defenses, a supposedly temporary measure that they knew would last indefinitely. Agents joined the Secret Service to serve on protection or investigations, not to stand post around the White House for twelve-hour shifts or longer. For the UD officers, many of whom loved their jobs as police officers around the White House, the work hours were crushing, as there were simply not enough people to do the job. However, there were plenty of people—some might say too many—in middle management who made those questionable decisions.

As far as the century-old lingering threat of airborne attacks was concerned, the Secret Service dithered and put its hope in the DHS, TSA, and FAMS to keep that angle covered. But so many of the UD officers and agents were facing crushing work hours that they felt were futile in protecting the president, so they decided to leave USSS and go where the nation needed them most: the TSA and FAMS.

The exodus was on.

In 2002, 130 UD officers left for the TSA alone. Not long after, about 300 UD officers left for TSA and FAMS in one year. The ranks of UD Training Center instructors, ERT, and Counter Sniper teams were especially hard hit, causing a massive shortage on those teams and a huge loss of expertise. FAMS hired anyone with advanced law enforcement or military experience, issued him or her a gun and badge, and put him or her onto aircraft to improvise on how best to protect the cockpit from hijackers. FAMS was willing to pay handsomely for such recruits, even $20,000 more than what they were making in the

Secret Service. For decades, the service's field office transfers had been notoriously corrupt, but FAMS would allow anyone to choose his or her field office—it needed air marshals in every large airport. The new air marshals knew they were entering a dicey environment—it could be just them alone in a plane with one or more hijackers, likely armed—but many Secret Service agents and officers figured that FAMS gave them a better chance to fulfill their mission to protect the public and the president from airborne threats. Unlike in the Secret Service, they could restore confidence in the nation's security.

The fact that both the Secret Service and FAMS were under the DHS umbrella made things easy. Transferring from one DHS agency to another was especially simple because all DHS employees were in the same computer system. Agents and officers were quitting the Secret Service and giving zero notice. Officers took advantage of their compensation time guaranteed by law for overtime served. Agents and officers started new jobs in FAMS seamlessly afterward. The migration from the Secret Service to FAMS became so bad that the service had its IT team block the DHS and FAMS recruitment website pages so that employees would stop applying during work hours. Still, the exodus continued. With the Secret Service working UD officers basically 24/7, the officers didn't have time to interview with TSA recruiters. So the TSA recruiters went to the White House at night to interview officers. It was like a fire sale on UD officers.

Not only had the Secret Service been unprepared to face the 9/11 threat and protect the president, the entire agency was set to collapse because of 9/11 and the corrupt choices in the Master Plan its managers had made leading up to it.

One thing helped stymie the exodus: as the DHS, TSA, and FAMS were created almost overnight, they needed to fill their entire leadership structure at breakneck speed. Guess who answered that call? Current and retired Secret Service agents.

Former Secret Service director John Magaw became the first director of TSA and built the agency we know today. Thomas Quinn, a former Secret Service agent, became the first director of FAMS. They brought some of the cronyism rampant in the service's upper ranks with them to their new agencies. Both Quinn and Magaw resigned suddenly after the air marshals basically mutinied, citing policies that put air marshals and the planes they were on at risk. It was rumored within the agency that the Transportation Secretary Norman Mineta began looking into allegations that Magaw was misappropriating government funds and engaged in cronyism. It was also rumored that Magaw wasn't misappropriating funds but that he was operating under the kind of nonexistent Secret Service budgeting protocols that TSA didn't allow.

Dana Brown became the second director of FAMS, but Brown's successor, Robert Bray, also entered into a settlement agreement that allowed him to retire without any disciplinary action amidst allegations of an illegal gun-selling operation within FAMS.

In 2006, Magaw of the TSA; Quinn, Dana, and Bray of FAMS; and FAMS's thirteen agency leaders as well as eleven of field office heads were all former Secret Service agents, and made men at that. Under them, Secret Service cronyism kept on chugging along.

Many officers and agents decided against joining FAMS, the DHS, or the TSA, not out of a sense of loyalty to the Secret

Service but because they knew that the worst of the service's made men were filling the ranks of those agencies. With the incestuous connections between the Secret Service and many of the other DHS agencies, recruits would be jumping from the frying pan into the fire.

The Secret Service's made men purposefully took advantage of post-9/11 "solutions" to establish cronyism in other agencies. Years later, those agencies, fraught with similar scandals and low morale, are following the same downward spiral. Even worse, former Secret Service agents—but not officers—took advantage of a loophole that allowed them to keep their Secret Service pensions even after they began working at the new DHS agencies.

Director Stafford was called into Congress to explain the problem. His goal was to convince Congress that the exodus was not as bad as anonymous whistle-blowers inside the agency were reporting. He acknowledged the shortages and attrition but in fact the Secret Service was "double-counting" its roster, which actually downplayed the severity of the exodus. Officers who quit were kept on the roster as if they had stayed on until the end of the quarter. The few officers who applied to become agents were counted on both the officer roster and the agent roster for the same period.

The exodus caused a domino effect that impacted the entire agency. The exodus put a greater strain on the UD officers who stayed, as they had to work more shifts of longer hours, with less flexibility of posts and rotations and less time for training and rest. Those who left did so immediately, but hiring replacements took on average well over a year and sometimes even longer.

Even if a candidate was recruited *and* took the job, "poaching" became a massive problem for the service even before its new employees ever stood a post. Secret Service recruits do their first leg of training at the Federal Law Enforcement Training Center (FLETC) in Glencoe, Georgia—where most other law enforcement agencies, such as the Border Patrol, ICE, and the ATF, also do their training. Since the ATF, ICE, Border Patrol, FAMS, and others were all at FLETC, recruiters from each agency would pay visits to the gyms and locker rooms to persuade Secret Service recruits to transfer to them while still at FLETC. They didn't have to worry about doing background checks on the poached recruits because they had already been cleared by the Secret Service. It was cheaper and more efficient for those agencies to steal from the Secret Service than recruit brand-new agents for themselves! ATF poachers would even brag to Secret Service supervisors, "I got three of your guys. Keep treating them the way you are. Don't change a thing." Then, as class sizes shrank by the time they arrived at the Secret Service Training Center, everyone would know that the missing recruits had been poached.

The rift between agents and officers widened as more agents were pulled from field offices around the nation to do UD jobs. The agents had not been trained for police jobs such as traffic stops, leading to tension with the UD officers, who did know what they were doing. To make matters worse, many agents viewed those kinds of duties as grunt work, beneath their lofty feelings of self-worth. Many agents and their families were seriously perturbed to discover that after graduation from agent training their stints on perimeter detail at the White House were becoming more frequent, increasingly long, and mandatory.

They were flown out for weeks at a time and put up in hotels to fill in for UD jobs they had been promised they'd never have to do. Naturally, all this was extremely expensive. The solution of the service's leadership was to create barracks-style housing at the training center for agents to be bused to and from each day. That solution was not received well.

Recruitment had its own problems, which had gone back years. Delegating UD recruitment to agent field offices had been a disaster. Recruitment was a part-time responsibility that was in addition to field office agents' investigations or protective duties. The Secret Service had very stringent prerequisites, and the administrative approval process sometimes made hiring take years. Many of the recruitment steps were also out of order. Why conduct a week's worth of background investigations on someone who can't pass the physical?

But the response from the highest ranks of the Secret Service to 9/11 was "more": more officers posted at the White House, more agents surrounding the president, more collective hours on the job. It hadn't been sustainable before 9/11, and it was even less so afterward, and the broken recruitment process didn't help.

Agents and officers had to ask themselves, "Will the additional hours served do anything to stop the kind of attack that spurred this response in the first place?" And the answer was absolutely not.

President George W. Bush thought extremely highly of the Secret Service based on the image that PPD presented and had earned. What the presidents saw of PPD was not indicative of the rest of the Secret Service or even behind the scenes of PPD, CAT, and the rest of those who protected him closely. The president assumed that there was careful oversight of the PPD and other divisions. But in truth, the Secret Service had always inspected itself. Still, his trust remained.

In 2005, President Bush traveled on a five-day, four-nation European tour commemorating the end of World War II. On May 10, he gave a speech in Liberty Square in Tbilisi, the capital of the nation of Georgia. The crowd estimate for the event was 10,000. In reality, there were more than 150,000 people in the crowd. It was the same scenario that had faced the Secret Service protecting President Eisenhower in India in the 1950s. Georgians came from all over the country to cheer and see the US president who had become a hero to many of them. President Bush had become so popular for fighting the war on terror that the highway leading to the country's main airport was renamed George W. Bush Street.

In the days after the speech, news reports ran headlines of President Bush drawing one of the largest crowds in the former Soviet republic's history, the largest since its independence. The event was praised for going off without a hitch. It was seen as another job well done, another success by default, as no one had made an attempt on the president—except that someone had. In the hours and days following, it was discovered that behind the stirring scene, the event had been a systematic failure and the president had only narrowly survived by luck.

One man in that crowd carried an old Russian-made hand grenade wrapped in a handkerchief. It was the smallest item in the cache of weapons he kept in his apartment. He was willing to trade his life for the smallest chance to kill the president, and he figured the grenade would be an ideal weapon of choice due to its balance of small size and serious firepower. Once the pin was pulled and the grenade thrown, so long as it landed within ten feet it stood the best possible chance to kill. To the assassin's surprise, the metal detectors, run by the Secret Service Uniformed Division, were turned off and the crowd of thousands was being waved through into the square. The security checkpoints had been inundated, and the Secret Service and Georgian authorities faced a crushing mob of people rioting their way through the metal detectors. Once the security checkpoints had been so grossly overwhelmed, they faced a choice: shut down the metal detectors and let people through unscreened, or cancel the president's appearance. They let everyone through and informed the president of the situation. The president's protection thus relied almost solely on a buffer zone, the president's armored podium, behavioral analysis of people in the crowd, and luck.

As the agents and local Georgian military and police scanned the crowd of 150,000 cheering frenzied Georgians, the assassin worked his way through the crowd to get as close as possible. He then pulled out his handkerchief with the grenade wrapped inside, took the grenade in his hand, pulled the pin, and hurled it at the president. But nothing happened. No one noticed. Police never closed in. The grenade never went off—as if some Secret Service magic had made it disappear. Panicked, the assassin simply walked out.

But the grenade had not disappeared. It had hit a little girl in the back of the head and landed at the feet of a Georgian police officer, fifty feet shy of the president. The grenade had a kill radius of ten feet and could inflict severe wounds on people up to fifty feet away. Though the president had his Secret Service Technical Services Division–issued podium, which was highly resistant to high-caliber bullets, it wouldn't have stopped anything from being thrown over or around it. The officer picked up the item, immediately realized it was a grenade with the pin pulled, and, fearing it could explode any moment, he, too, simply walked off through the crowd without even informing his fellow officers. He went to a park underpass and hid the grenade in a brick wall. In case it went off, it would mitigate the damage to others nearby.

It was later found that the grenade's safety lever, known as the "spoon," had been tightly wrapped by the handkerchief. Even as the lever had released and the grenade had been activated, the grenade's primer had been lightly struck, and the detonator had not gone off. The president had been saved by the Secret Service's buffer zone, a quick-thinking Georgian officer, absolute luck—yet again.

As the agents believed that the grenade had been a hoax when they learned about the attempt hours later aboard Air Force One, it is unknown when the Secret Service informed the president.

In the aftermath of the event and the investigations that ensued, numerous Secret Service officials swore that "to the best of their knowledge" this was the first time metal detectors had been shut off. It was an utter lie.

In the ensuing manhunt, led by Georgian authorities with the help of a US task force including FBI and Secret Service representatives, one journalist's photo from that event held the key to the would-be assassin's identity. In the raid on the man's apartment, one Georgian officer was gunned down, but the man was finally brought to justice.

As President George W. Bush survived two terms, most of which played out in the tense post-9/11 environment, it seemed as though the Secret Service was improving and evolving to meet the challenges of the modern era. But the consequences of strategic follies often become clear only decades later. Though all seemed quiet, the catastrophic cocktail of the Clinton years fighting the Starr investigation, the exodus, the transition to the DHS, and the Master Plan were taking effect. All these together had done more than add strain to the Secret Service—they had exacerbated the worst of the agency's culture, which valued complacency, arrogance, and keeping secrets for the sake of the Secret Service "brand," even at the expense of presidential protection.

Agents and officers who rocked the boat were squashed and pushed to the agency's fringes or pushed out entirely, while agents and officers who knew how to play ball thrived. The culture was even willing to overlook criminal misconduct, as long as the perpetrators were willing to tow the "secret" line. Those agents were rewarded and rose in the ranks to become middle managers or even the made men of the upper ranks, who only made the culture worse.

SEVEN.

LOSING CONTROL

*The Art of War teaches us to rely not on the likelihood of
the enemy's not coming but on our readiness to receive him;
not on the chance of his not attacking but rather on the fact
that we have made our position unassailable. . . . Victorious
warriors win first and then go to war, while defeated
warriors go to war first and then seek to win.*
—SUN TZU, SIXTH CENTURY BC

When President Barack Obama took office on January 20, 2009, the nation witnessed a historical milestone, but there was concern in the air as well. Since his election, headlines had declared that as the first African American to hold the office, after a racially charged election, Obama would be the most targeted president in history. That could not have come at a worse time for those charged with protecting him.

Yet again, just as the nation needed the Secret Service more than ever, it was falling apart and setting up a new president for failure. President Obama just happened to take the office when the Secret Service was at its worst. The truth about the agency's inner workings was finally getting out.

Though many pundits focused on exploring the possible motives behind the surge in threats against President Obama, it was often overlooked that behind each new crop of threats against a president is some increase in the means to make the threats. There had been threats against President Kennedy, for instance, for being the first Roman Catholic president. But as technology advanced, the number of avenues for making threats to the president increased. In the past, they had been made mostly by mail, telegram, or phone, and it had been far more difficult for threateners to travel to see the president or visit the White House. But the Internet and social media have increased the platform for hate spewing, and advances in travel have made it easier for words to become real-world dangers, be they spontaneous acts of rage or premeditated attacks.

The media often purports upticks in threats, attempts, and demands on the Secret Service as surprising, but in reality these are routine. There are always new threats to look out for. While the Secret Service does experience upticks in threats, attempts, and demands on time during election cycles, it is a complete myth that there is ever a lull for the Secret Service. The president never stops traveling, and too often at the last minute. There is never a shortage of the stupid, dangerous, crazy, violent, or methodical would-be assassins.

The Secret Service had still never had the time to take a strategic pause to look seriously at its internal operations. Even in 2009, it still didn't have an accountant to analyze how it spent the taxpayers' money. But around the time Obama took office, the curtain began to be pulled back, bit by bit, revealing the inner workings of this "secret" agency.

It took plenty of guts to start to bring the truth to light. Some Secret Service insiders spoke out anonymously to their home-state representatives in Congress, and they knew the risks: if the agency discovered any employees "speaking out of school," the repercussions would be brutal. On the outside, the journalist Ronald Kessler conducted a series of mostly anonymous interviews with former agents, which he turned into a series of books on the Secret Service. The most damning was *In the President's Secret Service*, published in August 2009, which contained what *USA Today* called "often disturbing anecdotes about the VIPs the Secret Service has protected and still protects." *Newsweek* pointed out that Kessler also addressed "why the under-appreciated Secret Service deserves better leadership."

Kessler revealed how President Obama was in danger as the Secret Service's management was supposedly "lax." However, the book didn't reveal why, and so, of course, nothing changed. Each revelation was swept under the rug as anecdotal.

But 2009 marked a turning point. It was the year when the consequences of terrible leadership began to seep out.

Ten months after President Obama's inauguration, on November 24, two wannabe reality TV stars and one audacious local businessman penetrated every Secret Service protective layer at a White House state dinner. The guests of honor were Indian prime minister Manmohan Singh and his wife. The reality TV couple had not colluded with the other man, but all three of them made it into one of the (supposedly) most secure sites in the world, simply by dressing nicely and insisting that they should have been included on the list.

In 1901, the same thing had happened when a tuxedo-wearing deranged gate-crasher pressured his way into a meeting with President Theodore Roosevelt. One hundred and eight years later, with $1.6 billion a year being spent on the Secret Service, what had changed? This time not one but three uninvited guests entered a White House state dinner simply by pretending to have been invited.

The lone gate-crasher, Carlos Allen, had been turned away twice, but, undeterred, he had gone to the Willard Hotel nearby and meandered onto a bus of invited guests from India. Once at the White House, he had simply walked in behind them.

The wannabe TV star couple, Tareq and Michaele Salahi, simply walked in and insisted that the Secret Service was wrong, that they had been invited, and it worked.

After the event, the Secret Service brazenly blamed its failure on the State Department, saying that it had been its lack of a checkpoint at the Willard Hotel that had allowed the one breach to occur. As for the gate-crashing couple, they were subpoenaed to testify before Congress but pled the Fifth Amendment. The Secret Service habitually downplays incidents or neglects to press charges so that its methodologies—and screw-ups—are not made public through court trials.

That marked the moment when the American public, the DHS, and Congress wanted to know how a $1.6 billion agency with 6,732 employees could not carry out such a simple task as making sure only invited guests got into an event. Worse still, the Secret Service had promised Prime Minister Singh, his wife, his security detail, and the nation of India that the prime minister's security was guaranteed under its watch. The only thing that protected any of the actual guests and the president from the three gate-crashers was that their motivation for crashing happened to be self-promotion rather than violence. The couple wanted to be featured on *The Real Housewives of D.C.*, and the other gate-crasher just wanted to "party." Those motivations were the only thing that kept the president, the prime minister, and the other guests safe from an attempt on their lives.

That was the first scandal in an increasing series of scandals that brought major scrutiny by the DHS, Congress, the public, and the media—most notably the *Washington Post*'s investigative journalists.

In 2006, Secret Service director Mark Sullivan took the helm of the agency. Sullivan believed he was untouchable, and that sense of arrogance led him to preside over one of the most bizarre episodes involving the agency during President Obama's tenure.

"Prowler" was the code name of a team of Secret Service agents specifically tasked with perimeter security around the White House. Prowler agents are supposed to be especially watchful when the president enters and exits helicopters on the White House lawn, a situation when the president is exposed and thus demands the utmost care on the part of all Secret Service personnel on duty. But suddenly, in 2011, the Prowler agents found themselves reassigned to an unlikely post: a long dirt road in the heavily wooded suburb of La Plata, Maryland, an hour away from the White House. What could be so important as to abandon the president as he was most vulnerable entering the White House?

In the first place, Prowler had been another Master Plan addition and redundancy. For a century, the White House's perimeter defense had been the responsibility of the Uniformed Division and the White House Police officers who had come before. The UD had already had a vehicle patrol for decades, and it had been part of the 1960s expansion of the UD to assist the Metro Police in fighting DC crime. UD officers saw Prowler for what it was: a Master Plan takeover designed to steal the UD vehicle patrol and part of the reckless plan to dismantle the entire UD.

Prowler agents were not only trying to horn in on UD duties, they couldn't even provide much help to the UD once they got there. Prowler agents were not even empowered to make arrests in areas where officers were, such as the enforcement of traffic laws. Prowler agents and the UD patrol were even on separate frequencies and communicated with two separate radio rooms. Whenever the Prowler team did catch someone, they had to call UD, the Park Police, or the Metro Police to make the arrest anyway. In the 1990s, one director had thought it would be efficient to merge Prowler and the UD vehicle patrol. But the UD officers had retaliated against the encroachment by embarrassing the agents for not being able to make arrests. Numerous suspects were caught in the argument as agents tried to find a nearby officer who could actually write so much as a ticket. When the Metro Police got involved as well, things became even more complicated.

The tensions between the UD and Prowler patrols got so heated that the two patrols were split again—just another example of the long-standing rift between them and how the agency's culture jeopardized the mission.

But Prowler remained in place—until Director Sullivan assigned them to some unique duties down a dirt road in Maryland, a mission called "Operation Moonlight." He ordered them to survey and intimidate his old secretary's neighbor for months, day and night, with at least two agents in two separate vehicles. Not only was that a wanton abuse of power, it came during the worst manpower shortage in Secret Service history, which threatened to collapse the agency. After a neighborly dispute resulting in a restraining order, somehow the Secret Service felt it had to get involved. Prowler's victim happened to be a retired FBI secretary of twenty-two years. Her neighbor, the one the Prowler agents were supposed to be "protecting," was the secretary to the Secret Service director. For the duration of Prowler's secret policelike intimidation tactics targeting a private citizen, the president and White House were without Prowler—which prompted the question: Why did Prowler exist anyway?

The Prowler agents knew their activities were wrong and illegal. Instead of refusing the orders, they contacted DHS acting inspector general Charles K. Edwards, the head of the "watchdog office" that was supposed to rout out corruption. Instead, he did nothing. Three days before Edwards was to testify before a Senate Subcommittee about his alleged derelictions of duty, he resigned from the service.

While Operation Moonlight was going on, it was known to many in the Secret Service. It was yet another blow to the agency's morale to learn that agents had stooped so low and jeopardized their mission, and that the director had eventually gotten away with it in exchange for leaving his post. It also cemented what everyone in UD had known from the beginning—that Prowler agents were a needless redundancy. That explained why the director had chosen them to leave and harass a civilian in what would at most have amounted to a local police issue.

It stands to reason that if the director of the Secret Service was involved in something so petty, the agency still had some serious problems. But the worst of the scandals were about to cascade like an avalanche.

Aside from the usual confrontational crazies that UD Officers dealt with on a daily basis, Friday, November 11, 2012, at the White House perimeter was quiet. The day was cold, with zero wind. By 8:50 p.m., it seemed as though another day might pass with the only ones at war being the groundskeepers fighting the leaves that fell and were swept up each day. President Obama and the first lady were not at home, but inside the executive residence, the younger first daughter and the first lady's mother were cozy, believing the Secret Service leadership and protectors on site had them as their first priority.

Inside were agents on the first daughter detail and officers standing their fixed posts. Outside were many Uniformed Division officers on the fence line, at entry control points, at security booths, at the perimeter of the White House, and on patrol in a vehicle around the area. The officers outside kept their bodies moving to keep their blood pumping in the chill. Uniformed Division officer Carrie Johnson was on post under the Truman Balcony, which overlooks the South Lawn. This was UD domain.

A taxicab passed the Ellipse, the long circular roundabout in front of the South Lawn of the White House. It stopped at a stoplight. A car at the intersection in front of it stopped abruptly, oddly. The cab driver and passenger looked suspiciously at the mysterious stopped vehicle. Inside the car was a madman with a rifle, full of conviction. He'd driven more than 2,400 miles from Idaho for the slimmest chance of success. His motivations were bizarre. His intent was to kill or scare the president. In his hands was a Romanian state-manufactured Cugir Arms Factory AK-47, chambered in 7.62 × 39, the same cartridge and family of rifle that was used in the 1994 attack on the White House. That's when the cab driver and passenger witnessed the unexpected. The man in front of them began shooting at the White House, firing five times.

Officer Carrie Johnson was on the receiving end of the bullets. As the Truman Balcony took fire and debris hit the ground around her, she drew her handgun and took cover. The attack was on. Officers hearing the shots went into action. Officers at booths, entry control points, and fixed posts drew out their keys, popped their gun boxes, and brought out the long guns. The officers closest to the shooter drew their handguns and flashlights and pushed toward the gunfire as other officers closed ranks to prevent additional gaps. The UD vehicle patrol raced to the site of the reported gunfire as Park Police and Metro police converged on radio calls of "possible shots fired."

The madman threw the rifle into the passenger seat, sped off, and abandoned his car nearby. Meanwhile, as the cab drove away from the shooter, the passenger in the back seat began tweeting frantically at the Huffington Post and *New York Times* as he wondered why the police were taking so long to respond. In a nearby office was the special agent in charge of the Secret Service's governmental and public affairs, Ed Donovan, who was immediately alerted by his team to the witness's tweets. He immediately forwarded the tweets to the Protective Operations Intelligence Center and began tweeting back to the witness for more information as to the shooter's location. The witness responded that the shooter was at Constitution Avenue at the Ellipse, some seven hundred yards in front of the White House and not directly in front of the fence.

Five minutes after the shots were fired, officers converged on the Ellipse lawn. As soon as two UD patrol officers disembarked their patrol car to follow the sound of the gunfire on foot, they recognized the familiar smell of gunpowder. They noticed that the attacker's muzzle had blasted the leaves to each side. They moved on the nearby abandoned car and discovered the rifle in the passenger seat and several shell casings in the car, several loaded magazines, and hundreds of rounds of ammunition. The shooter had been ready for a serious attack but had run like the coward he was. Another UD patrol officer caught a glimpse of a man in dark clothing heading in the direction of the Theodore Roosevelt Bridge, less than a mile away, and notified Arlington PD.

But the cover-up had already begun.

Soon after the shots struck the White House, someone from the comfort and ignorance of the Joint Operations Control Center inside the Old Executive Office Building notified all agents and officers that "No shots have been fired . . . stand down" and said that it had all been the result of a car backfiring. That order and claim had zero substantiation, but because of it, the officers' response was seriously hampered. The shooter got away, fleeing into Arlington, Virginia, because Secret Service middle managers refused to put out a lookout—why put out a lookout for a man's description if it was just a backfire?

The Secret Service then got its wires crossed. The Park Police officers who had assisted the UD officers' response to the shooting issued a warrant for the owner of the vehicle—not because of the shooting but because the rifle was illegal in Washington, DC. Based on that search warrant, other Secret Service agents interviewed the man's family and friends and learned that he had intended to kill the president. Only then, five days later, did the service finally issue a BOLO (be on the lookout) to hotels and other businesses, and one hotel clerk in Pittsburgh made the connection. Pennsylvania state troopers made the arrest, and the man was tried and prosecuted for attempting to assassinate the president.

The day after, officers were told to ignore what they had seen, smelled, and experienced as they were under fire. Because of the Secret Service culture, none of them spoke up to correct management's side of the story.

The subsequent investigations were all set up for failure as the service did everything it could to cover up or make excuses for its lack of response, including omitting what the officers had seen, smelled, and knew to be true. Within the service, the incident was disputed and set to be swept under the rug, despite two witnesses having seen the shooting and reporting it to authorities and newspapers. Four days after the shooting, a White House cleaner reported to the usher the discovery of three bullet impacts in the glass and one hole in the concrete around the window on the Truman Balcony. Only then did the Secret Service open an "spot report," acknowledging an incident, but the event was not formally investigated until after the *Washington Post* reported on the fumbled response and cover-up three years later. The formal investigation by the Inspection Division did not open a case file until October 2014.

Then came two major scandals that gave some hope that finally, after decades of failing in secret, the Secret Service might finally be forced to turn the corner.

President Obama was eager to attend the 2012 Summit of the Americas in Cartagena, Colombia, to meet with more than thirty heads of state from various countries from South, Central, and North America. As was standard protocol, the Secret Service sent an advance detail of agents to the meeting site. It would be their job to follow the president's schedule and plan for every contingency, such as ground or air attacks, NBCR (nuclear/biological/chemical/radiological) attacks, explosives, fires, and even natural disasters. Then the findings of the Secret Service, the five branches of the military, and the State Department would be coordinated to make sure that security and diplomacy worked in tandem. The president's security rested on that advance work, but, as the Secret Service demonstrated, far more was at stake.

"FFNs" is an espionage term meaning "female foreign nationals," and agents are supposed to avoid them when traveling abroad. Spy, terrorist, drug cartel, and petty criminal networks use FFNs to take advantage of male federal agents away from home and destroy their common sense—and they've been very effective at doing so. Their goal is to compromise federal agents. They can use blackmail, drugs, pickpocketing, bribes, burglary, vehicle theft, bugging with tracking or listening devices, kidnapping, or even murder—and it usually involves a potent mix of more than one of these. But being compromised can occur far more easily. Even a federal agent honestly answering the friendly question "So what brings you here?" can lead to disaster. Though agents' travel is not clandestine, they are on the clock 24/7, expected to be quiet professionals doing their job and otherwise rest up.

Even if they behave just as they're supposed to, the risk of identity theft of federal employees abroad is very real. The public has no idea how bad this is—and it affects every federal agency. Government-issued credit cards—which are considered government-issued property and equipment—are routinely targeted. Terrorists and criminals bug, infiltrate, and even run hotels, bars, cafés, and restaurants in a several-mile radius of tourist traps, beach fronts, and chain hotels used by governments, anywhere with Wi-Fi hotspots or credit card machines. They infiltrate those venues via bartenders, servers, and other staff to steal equipment, financial information, and even identities. Networks inside hotels learn and report on the coming and going of agents, making the practice very effective. Once identities, credit cards, equipment, phones, radios, badges, and other materials are stolen, unlike locals, who can go to the police, agents have to return to their home country. That makes it more difficult to investigate the criminals. Who is tasked with tackling this plague of identity and credit card theft in foreign countries? The Secret Service. This makes its culture of partying hard and pursuing FFNs above and beyond gross negligence—it's a serious security risk.

Yet meeting women had always been standard protocol

during travel. If senior agents couldn't be reprimanded for having affairs with Clinton staffers, how could junior agents be held accountable for cavorting with FFNs, even sex workers—especially as their supervisors doing it, too? The culture of "Hear no evil, see no evil" was rampant. Even the most professional Secret Service operatives would have trouble reconciling the behavior set by Presidents Kennedy, Lyndon Johnson, and Clinton—and even as early as Andrew Johnson. It was the "Secret" Service after all, right?

For the 2012 Cartagena advance detail, the State Department made the arrangements at the Hotel Caribe, a luxury beachfront resort, which also provides rooms by the hour and is prostitution-friendly. Two weeks before the president was set to arrive, the hotel managers took notice of how the advance agents were especially hard partiers and drinkers. It was hard to miss. Then more agents and PPD arrived two days ahead of the president's arrival.

One agent on that particular detail was quite the player, having already "scored" on presidential trips to Italy, Ireland, Russia, New York City, and Colombia—and those were just the FFNs. He had even hooked up with an American in the Republic of Korea on another taxpayer-funded vacation, a Secret Service advance presidential detail. Another agent preferred the convenience of sex workers, having twice solicited them in El Salvador and Panama. Most people in law enforcement call that "sex tourism."

The "misconduct" was very well known and accepted within the agency. One senior agent forwarded an email to fifty-four of his fellow agents that "Our motto for this trip is *una mas cerveza por favor*," meaning "One more beer, please." Another agent responded, saying "Swagg cologne-check. Pimp

gear-check. Swagg sunglasses-check. Cash fo dem hoes-check."
Agents carried on in Spanish, saying "I'm dying for the report
from last night," and "Tonight we ride."

Between thirteen and seventeen agents—many of whom
were married—drank, partied, and became the center of attention for hours into the night at a nearby strip club in Carten-
ega—at some point soliciting at least twenty sex workers—and
kept repeatedly showing off their abs. The party then continued back at the Hotel Caribe, where many of the agents checked
their sex workers in at the front desk. Partying with the agents
were at least five military Special Forces members. They partied together and then went to their hotel rooms with the sex
workers. Afterward, a few agents tried persuading the sex workers to stay the night after the services were rendered. But that
wasn't the problem in the eyes of the "secret" Secret Service.

Their problems began the following morning, when one
agent, who had persuaded his sex worker to stay the night with
him, refused to pay her and kicked her out of the room. Some
believe the agent had done so in an attempt to save money, as
he might have thought that sex work was illegal and the woman
would not turn to the hotel or police. But she returned, and the
Caribe hotel manager demanded to speak with the agent in his
room. He refused, so the manager pulled the list of all seventeen
Secret Service agents and even the five Special Forces operatives members and called the police. When the hotel and police
got involved against the agents, the agents had to fall back on
their diplomatic immunity to keep from being arrested. Agents
and police then took the matter up with the State Department
and US Embassy, which had issued their diplomatic identifica-
tion granted by the Colombian government.

That day the Secret Service recalled eleven of the agents to DC. and sent out replacements. The military recalled the five Special Forces members and confined them, pending its own investigation. The local Colombian police, the US Embassy, the State Department, the president's administration, and the Secret Service were now in diplomatic contention, all because of one agent's exceptional arrogance.

It became a diplomatic nightmare when an anonymous someone alerted Ronald Kessler. He then alerted the *Washington Post*, which broke the story the very same day with the headline "U.S. Secret Service Agents Recalled from Colombia." The media went wild, covering the story for weeks. The Secret Service contended that the recall had not impacted President Obama's security while on the trip. Not only was that claim far too premature to be certain, it also posed the question: If those agents (and Special Forces operators) didn't matter, why had they been there in the first place? As the media ate the story up, revelations poured out.

Some White House aides knew of Secret Service agents who used the trips for sex tourism. One of the sex workers even landed an interview on NBC's *Today* show. On Comedy Central, Jon Stewart ran the headline "The Bangover." Six Secret Service agents resigned and were allowed to retire without punishment. The media found that one of the supervisors involved in the scandal, Agent David Cheney, had posted a picture of himself on Sarah Palin's detail with the comment "I was really checking her out, if you know what I mean?" He, too, was allowed to retire with full benefits. The media learned many of the details as four of the agents contested their dismissals. One of their rebuttals cited cavorting and partying as a long-standing USSS habit. Another told investigators that he knew the Secret Service condoned hiring sex workers and picking up "nonworking" FFNs because in other countries he had translated the negotiations between PPD agents and high-ranking supervisors. "Wheels up, rings off" had been a motto for at least decades.

Neither the DHS inspector general nor the Secret Service interviewed the women involved, because the Department of Justice believed that the DHS should have pursued the investigations as part of a criminal investigation. Instead, the inspector general only pursued the interviews with the FFNs as they related to congressional queries. As the DOJ and the DHS inspector general played chicken, neither budged, and the FFNs were never interviewed by anyone other than the media.

Then Director Sullivan, appearing before Congress, got himself into a jam four different ways. When asked about the flagrant abuses, he said that he "[did] not believe [the agents] did it because they believed that this type of behavior would not be tolerated." But with the emails being known to investigators before his testimony, the brazenness of the agents' actions, and the incredible history of prostitution and extramarital affairs within service going back decades and climbing to its highest ranks, it seemed that either the director was either completely out of touch with his own organization's present and past or he was covering for the sake of the agency's future—his future.

Next, Director Sullivan told Congress that none of the twelve agents had had any sensitive documents or equipment in his hotel room—a dubious assertion considering that agents are supposed to keep their radios, cell phones, pagers, identifications, wallet contents, commission books, guns, and other standard-issue items with them at all times. The congressional investigators later decided that Director Sullivan was either lying or out of touch with his agency, having learned that, naturally, the agents had had their standard items on them. Something as rudimentary as an agent's cell phone could be a treasure trove of information for a terrorist planning an attack or a foreign spy organization wanting to gain intelligence that would give its country an edge against the United States.

The third "inaccuracy" from Director Sullivan was his assertion that none of the sex workers or other FFNs involved had known associations with drug cartels, human-trafficking organizations, terrorist Columbian revolutionary forces, or the like. In fact, one of the women did have a partial association with such a group.

The fourth jam was the Secret Service's defense as a whole. The service had recalled eleven agents back to DC, yet in its internal investigation of thirteen agents, despite not interviewing the FFNs, only three agents had been proven to have taken FFNs to their rooms and engaged in "sexual activity." But those agents claimed not to have known that the women they took back were prostitutes. Perhaps that explained the argument that started the mess for the Secret Service? But those three received only slaps on the wrist and were fully reinstated afterward, without so much as a permanent blemish on their personnel record. They also fell back on the preposterous excuse that the incident had been the result of not having clear guidelines, for which they claimed the solution had been found when a chart had been created explaining that prostitution and FFNs were, in a word, bad.

If those "elite" agents couldn't understand this on their

own and the Secret Service's "elite" leadership couldn't make it clear, are they really so "elite," and is the president really safe in the hands of people so systematically moronic?

Because of the director's less-than-forthcoming answers, Congress referred him to the Department of Justice's Public Integrity Section, which believed it wasn't enough to prosecute the director.

Two years later, the DHS investigator working on the Cartagena scandal moseyed into a brothel under surveillance by the sheriff's department in Broward County, Florida, and a prostitute positively identified the investigator as a customer.

One unanswered question: Did the agents use their personal funds, voucher money, per diem expenses, or even government cards at the hotel or when they visited other businesses—legal or otherwise? It's standard procedure to ask a business where a fed is using a card "What will this charge show up as on my credit card statement?" because every purchase has to be justified to a supervisor. The agents had to pay in some way, and each method, even paying large sums in cash, violates protocol and training.

Such a clear desire on the part of the Secret Service to sweep the scandal under the rug, such little punishment, and Director Sullivan's cavalierly inaccurate responses to Congress under oath make it clear that the service holds criminals to a much higher standard than it does its own agents. It shows how little importance it places on pursuing the truth and being "worthy of trust and confidence."

Not only was the incident a potential major security breach, but the Secret Service completely failed the president because his trip to Colombia was overshadowed by the scandal, which kept him from making the most of the trip on behalf of the United States.

Many congressmen's and pundits' proposed solution was to pressure the agency to hire more women, as if simply hiring more women would solve the service's long-standing ills.

There was no doubt for many inside the Secret Service, that this was a factor in Julia Pierson replacing Director Sullivan on March 27, 2013. During my time in the service I knew Pierson and I have mixed feelings about her, but there can be no doubt that she was set up for failure. She was forced into the quagmire in which the Secret Service still exists. To toe the Secret Service line is to watch it tiptoe toward collapse and catastrophe, but turning her back on the agency's made men and reforming the agency might not end well. The jungle of problems doesn't need a butter knife, it needs a chain saw. Pierson tried the butter knife and lasted until October 1, 2014, after a year and six months amid even worse scandals that she couldn't adequately explain to Congress.

Had the culture changed, as Secret Service leaders promised?

In March 2015, there was the Amsterdam mission, when one Counter Assault agent passed out drunk in a hallway. The next day, that agent and two others, despite Director Pierson's presence, got so drunk again that they made public fools of themselves like a bunch of juvenile frat boys and had to be sent home, put on administrative leave, then given twenty-eight- and thirty-day suspensions. One agent even admitted that he had done the same exact thing, getting so drunk as to pass out, during a presidential visit to Chicago.

But most of all Director Pierson was set up for failure by the Master Plan put into place by made men years before. The plan degraded the Uniformed Division and therefore the White House's defense. On September 19, 2014, a fence jumper hopped the White House's North Fence and sprinted several hundred feet across the lawn unhindered. He ran up the stairs leading to the White House's front door, opened it, plowed into an officer, who was surprised to see him and with whom he wrestled as far as the Green Room, where he was finally tackled and stopped by an off-duty agent. The DHS and Secret Service blamed failures of equipment including their radios alarms and even the White House's infrastructure.

The truth was that the officer in the interior of the White House had neglected to hear the alarm because the Secret Service had rolled over for the ushers' request to turn the pesky intercom volume all the way down. Protocol had been to lock the door at the first sound of an alarm, but the service made no adjustments to its plan even after it turned off the intercom. Its operators had never bothered to ask themselves: Does the plan still work with the intercom turned down? The radios would in theory have worked, except as with any radio, when several people hit the transmit button at once, it interrupts the signal. The radios were also vulnerable to cutting one another off as the encryption caused a one-second delay in transmissions. But that, of course, could still be mitigated if the officers were well rested and focused enough to be alert and yell out to others when a fence jumper made an attempt.

Director Pierson's responses to Congress were so unbelievable that many congressmen felt she was insulting their intelligence. They became frustrated because her responses and answers lacked any clear substance. She especially got into trouble when she seemingly contradicted herself and the Secret Service's arrest report with two conflicting stories of whether the intruder had been stopped at the White House entrance or as far into the building as the Green Room—which latter had been true.

Things didn't get much better for Pierson in the wake of the September 16, 2014, incident at the Centers for Disease Control and Prevention in Atlanta, Georgia. That day, while under Secret Service protection, President Obama was as close to death as any president has ever been. All that stood between life and death was the whim of several armed men whom the Secret Service *assumed* were unarmed and one armed man who placed himself next to the president—not once but three times. Anyone who asserts that this was an isolated incident doesn't know the details that the service tried desperately, pathetically to keep secret.

Since the CDC houses many of the world's worst diseases and helps cure them around the world, it maintains its own 24/7 security, including armed guards. When the president visits a facility such as CDC, the Secret Service doesn't replace the existing security; it augments it and adds its own layers, such as plugging into the organization's security cameras and assigning employees to augment the organization's security as needed. The CDC employed numerous armed security contractors for its daily defense. The Secret Service had to make sure it didn't interfere with the CDC's operations while still guaranteeing presidential security.

For President Obama's visit in Atlanta, the Secret Service

asked the CDC Security Services for a spreadsheet with the names of its guards and their basic information (birth date, sex, Social Security number, and so on) and then did nothing more. It didn't even run a background check on the names on the list—despite those employees being armed with handguns. It even sent a questionnaire to the CDC asking if its guards were armed. The CDC answered "Yes." Still the Secret Service failed to follow up.

Here's how bad things got: in the after-action report, while agents were scrambling to figure out how they had screwed up and how they could downplay the issue, one senior agent wrote to another, "No other armed CDC security officers were in our secure areas. They were in non-secure areas. We did have unarmed CDC officers in our secure area. They were not name checked and should have been." But there were in fact no unarmed CDC officers—all of them had guns. The Secret Service leadership had no idea that the men were armed, and the agents on site assumed they had all been vetted and were trustworthy. Therefore they didn't bat an eye at the guns all around them. It was a volatile cocktail, a complete and catastrophic systematic failure.

Things got worse. Against Secret Service policy, despite the officers' not being on the service's checklists, the service handed out "shift pins"—lapel buttons that serve to identify screened personnel—to all the unscreened armed guards. That meant agents would even be less likely to question them. Some guards did not get pins, but nobody seemed to notice either way, despite the pins' being central to the president's security.

The utility elevator operator, an armed, unscreened guard, did not have a shift pin, but Secret Service agents took no notice. Unbeknown to the service, he had a criminal history of three arrests (but not convictions)—one of which was for, according to the congressional report, "reckless conduct with a weapon, when [the guard] intervened in a shooting incident at a neighbor's apartment by shooting at and hitting a fleeing suspect's vehicle while a three year old was in the back seat, though this charge was Nolle Processed due to the death of the defendant (the fleeing suspect) and a primary witness." The other two arrests were for domestic disputes with family members.

The Secret Service's survey plans included no mention of an elevator operator, yet on the day of the event, some agents knew that the elevator operator was armed; others did not. But against all policy, PPD allowed the president to board the elevator with the mystery armed guard who did not have an identifying shift pin. They rode the elevator together, and by the grace of the guard's goodwill the president and his Secret Service agents left unharmed. The special agent closest to the president didn't even realize that the guard was armed.

But after the doors opened and the president and his protection detail exited, the guard left his post and followed them. PPD's special security formation was thereby compromised. The guard managed to follow the president closely, creating gaps in the president's protection, then began rudely taking pictures of the president with his cell phone as they left the building and went into a nearby security tent. Only then was he noticed and escorted out of the tent by an agent. The lead agent would only later discover that the guard had been armed the entire time.

How the Secret Service and CDC handled the fallout from this incident says a great deal about the two agencies. Once the CDC learned of its guard's behavior, that he had lied in an follow-up interview and had left his post in the elevator, it immediately fired him. The Secret Service, on the other hand, went into tried-and-true cover-up mode. No one was fired or disciplined. Instead, it blamed the CDC, as if it had been its job to guarantee that everyone surrounding the president was up to the Secret Service's security standards and protocols.

In the aftermath, the disconnect continued. The Secret Service chose not to inform the president of the series of lapses at the CDC, except for the cell phone photos. Director Pierson did not inform the president or his staff, who found out about it two weeks later, when the story broke on the news. The day after the president was made aware of the danger he'd been in, he accepted Pierson's resignation. Joseph Clancy, appointed acting director after Pierson left, swore that the guards in the secure areas had not been armed except for the elevator operator—but he was wrong.

But what was the central reason for the lapsed advance preparations? The agent in charge of the advance had been "overwhelmed." The same reason applied to everyone else involved.

The shameful excuses only got worse when Pierson's replacement, Joe Clancy, who had been brought out of retirement to head the agency, blamed the Secret Service's inability to keep intruders out of the White House on its lacking a mock White House to train in. His proposed solution was to build a $8 million mock White House to scale, including realistic shrubbery and landscaping. The proposal was a mockery and an insult to everyone's intelligence. They already had a building that resembled the executive mansion on one side and an embassy/hotel on the other. The truth was that officers and agents (flown in on temporary assignment) were too distracted, complacent, and exhausted to do more than watch, yell, and radio when faced with a real-life intruder.

The Obama White House was threatened yet again on the night of March 4, 2015. At least, that's what it looked like at first— an attack pitting the Secret Service against a crazed individual seeking to attack the White House. But the resulting conflict actually ended up pitting the Secret Service against itself.

That night, Officer Samuel Mason of the Uniformed Division was approached by woman who pulled her car up to his post, got out, and, after a brief exchange, dropped a package at his feet, declaring that it was a bomb, and ran back into her car to flee. Mason didn't hesitate; he ran up to the car, yelled for her to get out, and even reached in and put the car into park. She fought him and reversed, taking Officer Mason with her, as he was halfway into the car. He pulled out at the last second, and she sped off. He radioed the situation in and gave a description of the car but couldn't make out the plates. Meanwhile, the bomb was still at his feet.

The alert went out. All Secret Service mobile phones were updated that the White House was at "condition yellow," meaning there was an active investigation of a serious crime. Mason's post was cordoned off. Washington Metropolitan Police's Bomb Squad was suiting up and on their way.

Meanwhile, two Secret Service supervising agents, Marc Connolly and George Ogilvie, had been the last to leave a fellow supervisor's retirement party and had racked up quite a serious bar tab. In Ogilvie's government car, they drove to the White House. These were not two "low-ranking" agents. Connolly was the deputy special agent in charge of President Obama's PPD, making him one of the most powerful men in all of the Secret Service. Ogilvie was a senior supervisor for the DC Field Office protection squad. According to interviews of Secret Service personnel on-site that day and the DHS Office of Inspector General, the two supervisors, made men of the Secret Service, were driving drunk. And they ended up in the middle of a suspected bomb site.

Belligerent and arrogant, they drove past a UD officer who had tried to wave them away. They never bothered to check their phones and never saw the "condition yellow" update. They drove past police tape and numerous barriers.

The two agents had come within inches of the bomb when officers, at first in total disbelief, ran bravely toward the car, trying to save their fellow Secret Service members' lives. At least they hoped it was a Secret Service car—they had no idea who else would be either so stupid or so crazy as to try to breach the White House's barricades. That's when the confrontation began. According to interviews with anonymous Secret Service members, the agents were furious at the officers and accused them of abandoning their posts. Equally furious and afraid that the bomb might explode at any moment, the officers coaxed the arrogant agents to a vehicle blocking gate a hundred yards further into the White House complex. There they could contest the issue among themselves and away from the bomb. The officers, seeing the sorry state of the agents, knew them to be drunk and sought to breathalyze them as soon as they exited their car.

The agents, on the other hand, doubled down, threatening the livelihoods and careers of the new officers. The officers sought backup from their chain of command.

But guess where the Uniformed Division chain of command led to now, thanks to the Master Plan rules? To the same agent they were trying breathalyze, Marc Connolly.

As the bomb was found to be a hoax, Agents Connolly and Ogilvie pressured their way into not being arrested or even so much as written up. As they were the highest ranking on-site (once they arrived), the Secret Service supposedly expected them to "self-report." Having been thoroughly intimidated despite Ogilvie and Connolly having admitted that they were indeed driving drunk in their government car, none of the high-ranking UD officials passed the report on to the DHS OIG, and neither did Ogilvie or Connolly. For days it seemed the incident was going to be kept a secret. Meanwhile, the woman, arrested several days later after Secret Service agents missed her several times, was likely going to get a lesser sentence to keep the Secret Service's catastrophic failure from coming to light.

In the days that followed, word of the incident spread like wildfire throughout the Secret Service. Many agents and officers were ashamed. The entire incident underscored the fact that the service's made men held themselves in much higher regard than the White House's and president's safety and that the agency that purported to be "worthy of trust and confidence" was anything but.

The entire incident was going to be swept under the rug. The director only happened to catch word of the incident through an offhand mention on an internal message board.

The story broke publicly when an anonymous Secret Service source leaked it, and the director and every person involved were called before DHS OIG investigators and a congressional investigation.

During the investigation, the Secret Service relied on a collective sense of stupidity to thwart investigators when asked to explain why no one had passed on the incident to the DHS OIG, the Office of Integrity, or the Office of Professional Responsibility. None of it had been passed along, neither the gross dereliction of duty and crime of drunk driving nor the endangerment of other Secret Service members, the public, the White House, and the investigation. When Congress asked UD deputy chief Alfonso Dyson, the third-highest-ranking officer in the UD and the highest ranking at the White House, why he hadn't passed on the incident to the agency's Office of Integrity, he replied, "There is a wide range of things. If an officer violated some policy, but that's not necessarily always going to go to Integrity. It really varies. It's kind of difficult. There's no set rule on every single misconduct issue."

Of course, the rules for everyone else are much clearer. Whereas any normal employee or citizen would be in severe trouble and face serious jail time for driving under the influence (DUI) the Secret Service holds its men to the lowest of standards. Then, even when their dirty laundry is shown to the world and numerous agents and officers are pulled in to testify before Congress, they play stupid and claim that there is not a specific policy to deal with driving drunk over an active bomb investigation, intimidating officers, withholding information related to an investigation, and so on.

And despite specific training just two months prior detailing exactly the limitations and protocols of using a government car that stipulated that all government-issued cars were supposed to have a mileage log to make sure they were not being used for personal purposes, Ogilvie admitted that he never updated the log for any personal trips. As congressional investigators reported the "misunderstanding," "USSS personnel may have employed creative means to circumvent this ethics rule; Ogilvie told DHS OIG that he understood that government-owned vehicle driving logs were not to record any mileage other than the drive from home to office or office to home. As a result Ogilvie's driving log for March 4, 2015, listed no usage of the government-owned vehicle to drive to the retirement party and back to the White House Complex." These are the people worthy of the agency motto?

And what happened to the two Secret Service agents? Not much: Connolly retired as planned; Ogilvie was transferred, demoted from GS-14 to GS-13, and received a small suspension. A few other supervisors were given letters that stayed in their personnel files for three years. DHS OIG, even when it uncovered the fact that many who attended the retirement party had also driven drunk and even returned to work, did not pursue the investigation.

This is the Secret Service's "plantation mentality." The agents consider the Uniformed Division as subservient and "less than." No matter what an officer's rank and no matter what an agent's rank, USSS has cemented a culture in which agents are always above officers. Not all agents wear that mentality on their sleeve, but "UD bashers," such as A. T. Smith and Brian Stafford, did. New officers with naive notions of justice and accountability would try to push their limits, but as older officers tried to educate the new guys, some agents would make it their prerogative to hammer the plantation mentality home, making it clear that like the fence, the White House presidential helicopter, and most every Secret Service pillar, the service was stuck in its ways and loathed accountability more than anything else.

Instead of changing the plantation mentality, the service's made men sought to expand it. In the weeks afterward, several dozen agents conspired and lashed out against the leading congressmen on the House Oversight Committee. Those agents were so arrogant and cavalier that they even used their government emails to hatch their plot: The Federal Law Enforcement Officers Association (FLEOA), a nonprofit law enforcement advocacy group, attempted to coerce Congressman Jason Chaffetz by releasing a sealed job application file from when Chaffetz had applied to the Secret Service in 2003 but been rejected. The leak of the application was designed to create a story to embarrass Chaffetz, as if to send the message that he had no right to critique and provide oversight to the Secret Service when he had not been accepted as an agent himself. Members of the service and FLEOA contended that Congress—which had the mandate to conduct oversight—had no right to conduct its oversight while the DHS was supposedly investigating the March 4 incident. The assertion that the Secret Service was above Congress was beyond absurd. Forty-one Secret Service agents were lightly disciplined, but the culture remained. As no one was severely punished or let go, the service's made men essentially got away scot free.

The media almost missed the story entirely, but the *Washington Post* carried the scoop, as it has with many other Secret Service mishaps. But it was around this time that the media's role in the relationship among the Secret Service, the president, and the public was in the midst of change. A new, potent weapon against the president was emerging. The Secret Service had become a tool to manipulate the presidency by cavalierly writing off endemic failures as if they were unrelated scandals and by blaming the service's failures on new presidents that are at the agency's mercy; then, of course, there's the demagoguery, the "soft endorsements" of assassination by celebrities and the media, that drives the mentally ill and easily manipulated onto a collision course with the Secret Service.

But it might be that the media know exactly what they're doing. The trend of treating Secret Service mishaps as presidential scandals is only getting worse.

EIGHT.

THE SECRET
SERVICE SWAMP

In April 2009, New Yorkers once again evacuated buildings and ran for their lives, fearing that another plane was about to crash into New York as they looked up and saw two F-16 jets and a Boeing 747 inexplicably flying low, circling over the waters off lower Manhattan. The planes flew off and the public, furious, demanded answers.

It turned out that ninety-seven days after President Obama's inauguration, unbeknown to the president, someone in the administration thought it would be a nifty idea to have the backup plane for Air Force One fly low over the Statue of Liberty to pose for a photo. The plane was not transporting the president or anyone else; the flight had been solely for a photo that was to be printed on souvenir cards sold at the White House gift shop. The head of the White House Military Office, who had approved of the flyby, resigned.

A souvenir photo? Such a preposterous reason left the public demanding more explanation. How could "elite" government agencies—the FAA, the air force, the FBI, and especially the Secret Service—have allowed this or been so careless as to keep the flyover a secret from the people they were supposed to protect?

The answer: the FAA had made the trip secret and threatened to jail anyone who leaked advance notice of Air Force One's movement. In the aftermath, the Secret Service and other agencies apologized and pledged never to let "secret" get in the way of doing the right thing by the people they are supposed to serve.

President Obama made it clear that he had had no knowledge of the flyby, but the media hounded him for weeks, expecting answers and solutions. It was his office's plane, after all; the photo was for the White House gift shop; and the president was the man at the top.

With time the public outcry subsided. The media later found new distractions, but the damage had been done: weeks of President Obama's political agenda had been hampered as the media and the nation focused on the flyby scandal.

This mishap spurred a change in the attitude of the media that came about during the Obama presidency and now seems poised to define the tenure of Donald Trump. During the Obama years, journalists and political operatives in the DC media world had an epiphany. A new form of "killing" a presidency came into its own. Even if a scandal was the fault of the Secret Service, in the future it could be used to hamper, impugn, malign, distract, and obstruct a president. As the Cartagena scandal demonstrated, a Secret Service scandal could be pinned to the sitting administration and become a presidential scandal. As the Secret Service spiraled downward, the agency responsible for protecting the president would soon become the vehicle by which political opponents attempted to blame the next president.

Political opponents were going to use the Secret Service to politically assassinate the president, and Donald Trump is now in the crosshairs.

One of the candidates in the 2016 election, Hillary Clinton, had been protected by the Secret Service nonstop since 1992. As a first lady and former first lady she had had a Secret Service detail for twenty-four years—every former first lady, like every former president, will have Secret Service protection until she passes away or decides she no longer wants it. When she became secretary of state under President Obama in 2009, after losing to him in the Democratic primary, she had a mix of State Department and Secret Service protective details.

As Ronald Kessler correctly reported, Secret Service agents regarded her detail as a form of punishment. During the 2016 election, candidate Clinton had an incident in which she appeared to collapse, faint, or, stumble after she unexpectedly left a September 11 remembrance event in New York. For most pundits the word used to describe her fall depended on their political affiliation or their Secret Service expertise. Her detail agents caught her, braced up her limp body, and lifted her into her van as discreetly as possible without causing extra attention. Had one passerby not filmed the incident, the Secret Service would never have made the episode public. Aside from that incident, which called her health into question, she then coordinated a staged photo op outside her daughter's New York apartment, where she greeted a little girl in an attempt to head off the scandal of her fainting spell.

She had instructed agents to be far outside the viewing angle of the cordoned-off camera people across the street. After all the talk of the Secret Service leaders citing the "executive protective function privilege" during her husband's tenure to be a matter of life and death, candidate Hillary Clinton put her protectors far beyond arms' length for a mere photo op.

But the Secret Service agents on her detail despised working it for so many reasons more than her indignant behavior toward them. For decades, agents had suffered the tirades and disrespectful attitudes of Presidents Johnson, Nixon, and others. They were exasperated with candidate and former first lady Clinton for not wearing the standard-issue belt designed as an aid for agents to use in extricating a protectee in a hurry—not that the Secret Service had ever planned ahead for a different style that would be favorable to a female candidate. Body armor for all female protectees had always been a nonstarter over the protectees' concerns of "looking fat," and the service's leadership had given up on the issue. But most of all it was things such as the unarmored van she insisted on using. The belt, body armor, and especially the van were part of a litany of examples where candidate Clinton jeopardized her protection for a mix of optics and comfort without the Secret Service being able to provide adequate alternatives.

The van was a security nightmare. It was unarmored; its double doors, known as "suicide doors," opened in different directions, one before the other, making extrication more dif-

ficult. The unarmored small engine could hardly take on gunfire or accelerate away from danger fast enough or ram other
cars—that being the most important. Because of the reduced
ground clearance due to the small tires and low running boards
and bumpers, the van wouldn't be able to run over an attacker,
hop a curb, or power over loose terrain. Even if it had been
armored, armor is extremely heavy, and the armor would have
had to be minimal—that's apparent to anyone with even a bit of
expertise. So how much weight could that rear-wheel-drive van
handle? How fast could the van extricate a protectee from an
ambush? The bottom line was that the agents on her detail felt
one of two ways: futile and angry or futile and in denial.

During the Reagan assassination attempt, the presidential
limousine had stopped one bullet from hitting President Reagan directly and saved his life; a sliver of the other bullet had
ricocheted into his lung, but his armored limousine, which had
powered him to the hospital in the nick of time, was prepared
to ram anything that got in its way. It could even take a direct
rocket hit. While not the presidential limo, candidates had specially made armored Secret Service SUVs that were tanks in
their own right, only with greater ground clearance and better
maneuverability. Clinton's van, with its tiny wheels and high
roof, was top heavy. Any armor or added weight would have
made that worse, which meant it would have become more
unstable at higher speeds and more likely to flip on a sharp
turn.

That made Clinton's "soft-skinned" unarmored van a death
trap ready to be sprung by an approacher with so little as a
small-caliber handgun, and it was a clear indication that the
candidate, for whatever reason, had insisted on it. Agents had

to ask themselves: Would the Secret Service's protective plan still work without its core piece of equipment? They hoped and prayed, because that's all that would make the difference should someone target that ridiculous van. In actuality, Clinton's insistence on the van was no different from President Kennedy's insistence on riding in a convertible and in some ways even more dangerous. That is exactly the kind of thing that drives protectors' morale down and should not be tolerated by the public or Congress.

In true Clinton fashion, even as a candidate—in an election she was expected to win handily—she involved the Secret Service in yet another series of scandals. The 2016 Clinton email scandal created a firestorm. Just like the allegations of her and her husband's bribes and perjuries and allegations of his sexual misconduct going so far as to involve the Secret Service in criminal investigations by the DOJ and FBI, everyone wanted to know whether her "private" yet government-hosted email servers were physically and digitally under Secret Service protection. In addition, there was an intrusion into Clinton Foundation servers and theft of information on them. The subsequent investigation by the FBI revealed that a Secret Service agent on the former president's detail had aided the Foundation's private investigation.

The twists and turns of the Secret Service's involvement are many, but after Clinton lost the election, it seemed as though the political capital to investigate the service's involvement in various campaign intrigues fizzled out. But there can be no doubt that the agency barely dodged being dragged into another series of Clinton scandals and investigations.

Then there was candidate Trump. Much of how he treats his detail is unknown. Officers and agents interviewed for this book have reported good things, but it is still early in the administration and the protector-protectee relationship has yet to fully form. But Trump has been known to make nice gestures. For example, he assigned a private concierge exclusively to assist Secret Service personnel stationed at Trump Tower in New York City, but that service was turned down after it was deemed improper for the agency to accept it.

There have been some difficulties, too. The Secret Service signed a lease with Trump Tower in 2015, but that ended during negotiations for a new lease when both sides wouldn't budge over some unknown clause.

The main problem, however, is not how the Secret Service interacts on a day-to-day basis with President Trump. The more systemic issue is that the collapsing Secret Service is setting President Trump—and future presidents—up for failure.

President Trump was inaugurated on January 20, 2017. Immediately, he found himself facing a trifecta of threats unlike any president before him: the collapse of the Secret Service, which is supposed to protect him; a national trend of "soft endorsement" of violence against the president; and political operatives using Secret Service mishaps in their efforts to assassinate the president's political reputation.

The chief concern among this trifecta is that President Trump remains under the care of a protection agency that has spiraled out of control. The 2015 House Oversight Committee Report spoke of an impending "collapse" in the agency's future.

The service's leadership has succeeded in exhausting its officers with overtime and crushing their morale with poor working conditions, undignified treatment by management, and attempts to replace officers with agents as much as possible. Only the agents don't want to go along.

President Trump is surrounded by agents who are likewise overworked and exhausted, engulfed by a culture that values showboating, arrogance, and complacency over proper rest, training, readiness, morality, and family. All of those factors put him at risk of harm due to negligence or madness on the part of his protectors. Suicide, divorce, and psychological disorders are rampant, at rates unique to the service. It should be the exact opposite: the Secret Service should have the strictest standards of any agency. Our president needs to be protected by the best, brightest, and most ready—not the most tired, downtrodden, pissed off, disgruntled, and on the edge. More, the culture of corruption has allowed agents to blackmail the agency into further corruption while its made men drive whistle-blowers so far as to suicide, as we will soon see.

In 2016, Agent Kerry O'Grady, the head of the Denver Field Office, left a long-winded post on Facebook, saying "I would take jail time over a bullet." There can be no debate over whether she violated USSS and DHS agency policy and even the law, specifically the Hatch Act, which regulates public political endorsements by protectors, when she ended her comment with "Hatch Act be damned, I am with Her," meaning Hillary Clinton.

Agents informed the Secret Service leadership of the comments. Nothing happened. Then, on election day, she changed her profile picture to a *Star Wars* photograph with the words "A woman's place is in the resistance." Still nothing happened.

Eventually her posts became public, and only then did the Secret Service respond—by making the situation worse.

Civilians can tout "resistance" all they want. But a Secret Service agent, especially one who pledged her allegiance to the losing candidate and retracted her oath to defend the office, should be judged by the Secret Service's standards of evaluating a potential threat. Using "means, motive, opportunity, and intent," Agent O'Grady checks all boxes. She would be the ideal assassin, if only she weren't brazen and unprofessional enough to make her thoughts public—but so many past presidential assassins (and would-be assassins) have done so in writing, posting, and calling in threats. Many agents and officers have resigned because they no longer value the mission, and that's a good thing—they shouldn't be there if they feel that way. But Kerry O'Grady's continued paid vacation with no punishment demonstrates that the Secret Service culture remains a threat to President Trump. Her story is not unimportant; at her rank, she helped set Secret Service culture.

Yet the service never fired her or even really punished her. It said she had been "removed," but in fact she was placed on "administrative leave" pending an investigation that will last indefinitely, until she retires with a full pension. She's been in the service for more than twenty-three years. The service is running out the clock for her for another year and a half, until she transfers to DHS or simply retires with maximum benefits. That's the truth. It's a well-known practice that the service runs out the clock on criminal investigations and then allows suspected wrongdoers simply to resign. That was done for Director A. T. Smith following pressure from Congress to fire him due to the security failings.

Though many in the media have mistakenly confused the action taken against O'Grady for her actually being fired, she was really put on a Secret Service–approved taxpayer-funded paid vacation. She's on "administrative leave," but that doesn't stop her pay, because, according to Secret Service, the internal investigation is not finished. That investigation is narrowly focused on trying to figure out if she made the posts while she was at work. Her Facebook posts are time-stamped "Sunday, 11:06 PM." Either the Secret Service is incompetent at doing investigations and shouldn't be entrusted with them, or its protective efforts are corrupt and it shouldn't be trusted with them.

So the agency in charge of investigating the most serious financial crimes has gone months without concluding whether Agent O'Grady made her time-stamped posts at work or not?

Morale has taken another hammer blow and the agencywide culture of corruption has been further cemented. The spouses and family members of the agents in her office and under her command circulated a petition to Director Clancy to oust her immediately, saying that she was "no longer worthy of trust and confidence." After all, her "soft endorsement" of violence directed at Trump put her Secret Service brothers and sisters, possibly even those in the Denver office, in the line of fire.

Compare that to the service's treatment of the officer who brought in a cake that said in icing, "Congratulations on making 305 out of 305," making light of the Secret Service being declared the worst place to work in the federal government for morale and confidence in mission performance, as rated by each agency's employees. He was given several days of administrative leave *without* pay.

In 2017, another internal scandal broke out at the Secret

Service. It turned out that the agency was fast-tracking disability retirements for its own nefarious purposes. Despite begging Congress for $200 million to $300 million more annually, the service tried to defraud taxpayers by falsifying disability-related retirement for agents in exchange for dropping their complaints against it. It was hush money, yet no one was fired or disciplined. Agent Robert MacQueen, a twenty-four-year veteran of the agency, saw his life and the life of a colleague become hell after they reported complaints of investigative misconduct to a Secret Service internal investigator. The service retaliated, accusing the two agents of collecting more overtime pay than they had earned and misusing a government car. MacQueen's security clearance was revoked, and he was put on indefinite unpaid leave. The other agent, who was subjected to psychological torture from higher-ups, including "wife baiting"—calling the agent's wife's cell phone and asking her about the allegations of fraud—eventually committed suicide. DHS officials have noted that these tactics are seemingly reserved exclusively for whistle-blowers.

In 2017, after my book *Crisis of Character* came out, the Secret Service called in White House officers, many of whom were my former colleagues, and repeatedly asked them to sign nondisclosure agreements that extended until after retirement. They were the same type of NDAs that Congress had ruled in 2015 violated whistle-blower laws—not to mention creating serious First Amendment rights issues. That was another form of the service's soft intimidation.

So there can be no doubt that the Secret Service is more concerned with crushing whistle-blowers than with reining in a culture that promotes self-preservation over missions, especially that of protecting President Trump and his family.

All of the ills that led to all those scandals are still there and getting worse. Adding insult to injury, the service's leaders give the public and Congress ridiculous excuses and promise solutions such as reminding agents that prostitution is bad and against policy and that from now on drinking before a president's arrival in a foreign country will be allowed only in "moderate" amounts. *Seriously?* This is the same culture that preceded President Kennedy's assassination.

The Secret Service is needed now more than ever as "soft endorsements" of violence against the president become more mainstream. Though every election and advance in technology brings an uptick in threats made against each president, President Trump faces the soft endorsement of assassination by numerous celebrities, supposed role models, and even government officials.

Celebrities have sought fame with gross "artistic" representations of violence against the president and have made statements in speeches before hundreds of thousands of people and posts to their even larger online audiences that endorse and normalize the idea of punching, killing, or beheading President Trump or even blowing up the White House. Though inappropriate depictions of violence occurred in the past, they were acts by individuals with zero or small followings. When one fringe political commentator threatened President Obama with "I'll be dead or in jail," that was an individual making his own threat against the president public. That celebrity was investigated by the Secret Service and warned, and many inside the service argue over whether it should have pressed charges. But soft endorsements are far worse.

Hollywood celebrities have put large budgets and professional camera crews into depictions of shooting, beheading, and stabbing President Trump to death. For the beheading photo shown by comedian and former CNN host Kathy Griffin, though she was fired over the stunt, the photographer is still allegedly entertaining six-figure bids for original prints of the former CNN host holding up the effigy of the president's decapitated head. Though such "artistic" statements are constitutionally not illegal, certain celebrities have made it clear to their large fan bases that they favor the idea of the president being attacked. This kind of soft endorsement is the means by which cowards give themselves legal deniability but simultaneously achieve their intended result: directing their fans to target the president.

There are also many in the media who also make soft endorsements of violence, such as *Rolling Stone*'s depiction of one of the Boston Marathon murderers as a "rock star" on its cover. Whenever a tragic attack like that occurs, too many in the media shamefully pursue ratings by obsessively focusing on possible revelations and endless commentary to frightened Americans desperate to make sense of it. In doing so, they have made it clear that they are all too willing to make celebrities out of mass murderers and presidential assassins and thereby are complicit in exacerbating attacks and attempts.

Current and former government officials should know better than to engage in soft endorsements, but obviously they don't, hence Kerry O'Grady's Facebook rant, which made a soft endorsement of agents failing in their protective duties for political motivations. Similarly, CNN's counterterrorism analyst Phil Mudd, formerly of the CIA and FBI, cavalierly told CNN host Jake Tapper on air that "As a former government official, the government is going to kill this guy," meaning the president.

He continued, "Government is going to kill this guy because [the president] doesn't support them," meaning the politics of people inside the government. Though Mudd later said he had meant "killing" figuratively, he then doubled down, referring to the "deep state" of government officials entrenched in agencies for twenty or thirty years, and said that this deep state is going to politically assassinate the president and his policies.

Such statements result in society's most vulnerable, the mentally ill, who are susceptible to these ideas, throwing themselves more willingly at officers on the White House fence line or at agents surrounding the president. Many celebrities put out public service announcements for antibullying, suicide prevention, and politically correct terminology, all grounded in the idea that words matter and, if abused, can cause great harm. So it's incredibly ironic that many of the same celebrities are making statements that result in those who are mentally ill or emotionally disturbed throwing themselves at the Secret Service in attempts on the president's life. There are millions of Americans and foreigners whose mental and emotional faculties hang on a thread. Any soft-endorsement of violence against the president can trigger an incident that pits them against the Secret Service. It happens all the time at the White House fence line, where officers typically take the offenders to St. Elizabeth's Hospital for treatment or, sadly, have to resort to using their firearms. Soft endorsements are incredibly reckless and get people killed. In October 2017, while the president visited the Capitol building, one man infiltrated the press pool and, from concealment, threw Russian flags at the president, shouting "Traitor!" The screaming man was not mentally ill, only pushed too far by the media. Though he had been screened by Capitol police, the incident created an extremely tense moment for the Secret Service, which had to identify: stunt or attack, flag, cell phone, camera, or nonmetal knife or gun that had been snuck through. In 2016 especially, several maddened approachers made attempts on the White House gates, giving officers little choice but to shoot them. Hyperbole and demagoguery seem to have been what pushed one man to make an attempt to assassinate several Republicans as they practiced for a bipartisan baseball game in Alexandria, Virginia, in June 2017.

The newest tactic is using the Secret Service to politically assassinate the president, as if President Trump, having been in office only since January 2017, is responsible for all that is wrong with an almost two-hundred-year-old agency. Though preposterous, that could be the most dangerous threat of all.

President Trump's liberal opponents are already on the warpath. American Bridge 21st Century is a political action committee (PAC) that describes itself on its web page as "a progressive research and communications organization committed to holding Republicans accountable for their words and actions." It was founded by former Clinton operative David Brock in 2010 under the umbrella of Media Matters for America. In the Roll Call article "American Bridge 21st Century Super PAC Is Hub of Left," Janie Lorber reported the PAC's communications director as describing its role very simply: "Our existence means that [Democratic politicians and their committees] don't have to put trackers out there and they don't have to do research." Lorber noted that "Much of the organization's most effective work goes on behind the scenes, as it quietly feeds material to reporters all over the country" and that its millions of dollars in funding were provided by fewer than fifty donors, the biggest being George Soros. One former employee was quoted in the article as saying that between Brock's Media Matters for America and American Bridge 21st Century, "They try to create their own echo chamber. It's a fabulous strategy."

Now that echo chamber is directing its efforts at the Secret Service, submitting Freedom of Information Act requests, digging up dirt, and reporting on many of the Secret Service's ills. But instead of directing them back at the Secret Service, they're spinning them in an effort to blame President Trump. They're spinning the service's long-standing waste as if it were the fault of President Trump. They fault the president for having a large family that needs protection, for traveling to his residences, which demand protection, for leasing space to the Secret Service in New York City, and for no longer leasing space to the Secret Service in New York City. They blame the president for New York agents working out of a contractor trailer, for the Secret Service renting porta-potties, golf carts, and cars, and for the expense of Air Force One's jet fuel. The practice of blaming the president for the service's big expenses certainly grew under President Obama but is now rampant with claims that President Trump is "ruining" and bankrupting the Secret Service.

When Director Randolph Alles went to the media for an exclusive interview to drum up political capital for a "legislative solution" for Congress to remove the pay cap on overworked agents, the media ran with headlines such as "Secret Service Depletes Funds to Pay Agents Because of Trump's Frequent Travel, Large Family."

Add to that the Russia "scandal," an overly complex allegation of collusion between Russia and the Trump campaign, not to swing the election but to discuss possibly obtaining information from Russian sources about Hillary Clinton's criminal wrongdoing. There are mountains of echo chamber commentary but only three sources. The oldest son of then-candidate Trump, Donald Trump, Jr., had a "bombshell" exchange of emails with a person he believed was a Russian attorney who offered physical proof of Clinton's criminal wrongdoing—but he released those emails himself and admitted to trying to set up a meeting, which never actually happened. There was also a meeting between Trump Jr. and two scam artists that ended after thirty minutes when the son realized it was a hoax. Also contributing "evidence" are Fusion GPS and a British journalist, Louise Mensch. Both cite anonymous sources without any real evidence and basically ask the American people to trust them. Fusion GPS is pleading the Fifth Amendment before Congress's investigation into questions of its political donors and ties. Mensch, who works for News Corporation, is also citing anonymous sources and nothing more. Even with FISA warrants executed and one campaign staffer being raided by the FBI, there is still zero physical evidence to be had other than what Donald Trump, Jr., served up.

Many of the same organizations and media power players that have woven the Russiagate web together based on zero clear evidence are the same ones that would weave a similar web asking the public to sweep scandals regarding Trump's political opponents under the rug. The media organizations that are all too happy to dig into the Trump-Russia connections are altogether uninterested in exposing the collapse of the Secret Service even as their work pushes more mentally ill and unstable people to target the president.

Hyperbole runs rampant. The media echo chamber and some cable news networks cycle a constant fixation on the topic. Some reckless government officials and news sources have accused the president of being a traitor or colluder, rigging the election, sabotage, dooming the planet to Armageddon, even genocide. Every president since Truman has probably been accused by some of "being" Adolf Hitler, but the trend is growing, serving as the most widely used soft endorsement. The Hitler comparison is a soft endorsement, yet still a call to murder. The situation has gotten so bad that a North Carolina councilwoman compared the first year living under President Trump to living under Hitler and one Puerto Rican mayor accused the president of perpetrating something she considers "close to genocide."

Such hyperbole being aimed at the individual—Donald Trump or any other—and not the office or larger political ideology creates a paradigm in which many feel that the problem is that individual and that the solution is the elimination of that specific person. Similar hyperbole directed at policies, though inappropriate, doesn't directly levy the blame on human beings, let alone a very specific human being.

In the age of social media, Twitter, Facebook, YouTube, and leagues of other websites abound where anyone can make threats against the president. The Secret Service used to investigate all threats against the president, but it has changed its focus to going only after "serious" threats. "Serious" is characterized by a person having the means, motive, opportunity, and intent to make an attempt. If an elderly disabled person confined to a wheelchair, who does not own any firearms, has no zero military or relevant experience, has few funds, and has zero access to bombs or vehicles were to make threats, that person would not be considered a serious threat. But if a threat is made by a wealthy, able-bodied, military-aged male with some military experience, access to guns and explosives, access to a car, and a criminal history, that man would be considered a very serious threat. The Secret Service is inundated with threats and it has to pick and choose which threats to investigate.

President Trump is the most targeted and most at-risk president because of an increased trend that has put presidents at ever-greater risk because of the Secret Service's screwed-up priorities—a list topped by protecting its own "brand."

So what is being done?

In October 2014, the DHS secretary, Jeh Johnson, ordered the creation of a United States Secret Service Protective Mission Panel, or USSSPMP, to investigate the Secret Service's White House defense, recommend candidates for the next director and "subjects for further review," and would "provide a roadmap for reform that a new director and newly invigorated Secret Service will need to implement." Though the media had long been distracted by other, juicier stories, the results of the USSSPMP were released two months later, and they were dire.

The report seemed to contradict itself. Sandwiched between high praise and flattery were acknowledgments that the Secret Service had refused to implement needed changes, but it offered no explanation and said that the service was in great disrepair.

It told of how the White House fence was extremely scalable, yet the service had never tackled the issue going back to World War II. It said that the service was "starved for leadership," not resources. It made abundantly clear that the service's only hope would be to bring in a director from the outside. It revealed that the "average special agent received only forty-two hours of training" and that "the Uniformed Division *as a whole* received 576 hours of training, or about 25 minutes for each of over 1,300 Uniformed Division officers." The situation was so desperate that the report recommended that the future director should "shed" nonessential missions.

Then came the blockbuster revelation: "the Panel has been hamstrung to some extent by the lack of complete data. Put simply, the Service does not have systems in place to make the most prudent budgeting choices." It continued diplomatically, "the Service has, for years, looked at its base budget and tried to ballpark how much more it might be able to get through the OMB [Office of Budget and Management] and congressional processes. The result, however, is that no one has really calculated how much the mission, done right, actually costs. That is why one of our most important recommendations is that a new director start with a zero-based budget. Forget about what the Service has asked for in the past." And the Secret Service still didn't even have an accountant!

It recommended, as an interim first step for the sake of the president and the White House, that the service hire 85 more PPD agents and 200 Uniformed Division officers to protect the White House. But the report didn't end optimistically. It said, "Many of the recommendations set forth below are not new. Indeed, some of them precisely echo recommendations that the

White House Security Review made in 1995 . . . but that remain concerns today. Others even harken back to recommendations by the Warren Commission Report following the assassination of President Kennedy." It acknowledged without explanation the fact that Secret Service leaders had recognized glaring problems but had never implemented solutions. The USSSPMP staff kept referencing their inability to understand how the service had fallen so far and why its directors were asleep at the wheel. The answer that eluded them was the Master Plan; the downfall had occurred in large part due to the service's made men.

In December 2015, the House of Representatives Committee on Oversight and Government Reform released its report *United States Secret Service: An Agency in Crisis.* The document was 437 pages long with numerous footnotes, which was probably why no one in the media decided to bother with its findings or recommendations. The congressional hearings and interviews with representatives had yielded an occasional juicy article, interview, or video snippet, especially as representatives grilled directors and Secret Service supervisors and dressed them down on C-SPAN. Once the report was issued to the media, the Secret Service and Congress seemed to consider the service's problems settled, put to bed. The members of the oversight committee felt they had done their job.

Some of the highlights of the report were:

- After one of the two female assassins who had targeted President Ford, Sara Jane Moore, was released from prison in 2007, the agent assigned to her to make sure she was no longer a threat became close friends with her. She was invited to his son's wrestling matches, to a Labor Day event at his home, and even to his wedding to another agent, where many Secret Service agents were in attendance. Several agents involved were punished, excluding the supervisor who had permitted it.

- The service had fewer total personnel in 2015 than when the Protective Mission Panel had recommended a hiring increase in December 2014.
- In 2012, the same year in which numerous scandals occurred, the service officially listed protection as "Goal 2" and financial investigations as "Goal 1."
- The service has a big problem with incidents of physical abuse and sexual misconduct by agents, such as supervisors assaulting subordinates and agents having sex with informants and suspects in exchange for reduced sentences—and not punishing the agents for it.
- Even though a Special Services Division agent pointed a gun at his wife during a domestic dispute, had a long list of abuses toward his wife, failed a polygraph, had extramarital affairs with eight women and was a "swinger," the service failed to levy any charges against him and allowed him to retire.
- Though driving under the influence is a serious crime for civilians, the Secret Service holds itself to a far lesser standard and even routinely saves employees arrested for it from being charged by local police.
- The service publicly announced that Deputy Director A. T. Smith had accepted a position with another

agency but kept him on the payroll so he could continue to be paid.

Though the oversight and investigation were theatrical and the report's findings glaring and incredible, the recommendations put forward by Congress were a joke, even lazy:

- The committee found rampant abuses of misconduct at the middle management level were followed up by the excuse that "USSS supervisors lacked clarity about when to report possible misconduct to the Office of Professional Responsibility." Its recommendation was that "Supervisors should receive formal training on the new guidelines for promptly referring allegations of possible misconduct to the Office of Professional Responsibility."
- When the committee found that low morale and the exodus to other agencies had harmed the service, it recommended that "USSS should report to Congress on additional proposals to decrease attrition and improve morale."
- The committee found that the DHS's Office of Inspector General panel was staffed almost exclusively by former Secret Service agents, despite prior recommendations to diversify the panel. It recommended that "USSS should be more proactive in pushing DHS to appoint non-USSS employees to the Board."
- The committee found that the Secret Service had a corrupt habit of keeping made men on the payroll

while investigations into their misconduct went on indefinitely, until the agent could retire with full benefits. It recommended that after an investigation, "USSS should review its disciplinary processes to find ways to streamline and make them more efficient and effective."

- The committee found that the service had a continued hiring crisis. It recommended that "Congress should ensure that USSS has sufficient funds to restore staffing to required levels, and USSS should ensure that it has systems in place to achieve these goals."

- The committee found that the service's Security Clearance Division was understaffed and recklessly cutting corners to hire unqualified or unfit recruits. It recommended that "USSS should take care to minimize risks to national security throughout the hiring process."

Really? Talk about catching the fox in the hen house and then putting him in charge! The findings go on, becoming increasingly more bizarre, exposing unprofessional and irre-sponsible conduct. The recommendations amount to nothing more than "USSS should stop doing the wrong thing and try to do the right thing." It was an shame that a report so well founded was so feckless. The committee essentially found an agency that was willfully "collapsing" due to incompetency, misconduct, arrogance, and self-interest and kept the abusers in charge to turn the agency around. Legislatively, the only thing Congress forced the Secret Service to do about all its wrongdoing at the expense of the president's security was take more money.

This is the agency that is in charge of protecting President Trump. We're in trouble.

After his inauguration, President Trump made an incredibly bold move that had been unprecedented for nearly seventy years. Taking the recommendations from the 2014 Protective Mission Panel and 2015 House Oversight Committee report, he appointed a new director who had never served with the service. He went against the grain of the made men, and things seemed hopeful when he appointed Randolph Alles as Secret Service director. Alles took charge on April 25, 2017.

Alles wasn't quite the outsider many had hoped for. He had been acting deputy commissioner and chief operating officer of US Customs and Border Protection, but he had improved that agency's morale. Before that he had served thirty-five years in the Marine Corps and retired as a major general in 2011 after he and his units had earned numerous commendations and medals.

Early in his directorship, Alles made the rounds at the White House, speaking to Secret Service employees everywhere—a very welcome sign. But officers and agents revealed that they had been hopeful before. All the made men now under the new director are the same who carried the torch that burned the agency down. Only time will tell whether Alles will join the ranks of the service's made men and adopt the deeply flawed and dangerous Master Plan as his own or whether he'll take a chain saw to the organization's bloated bureaucracy and cut the anchors that hold presidential protection back.

He showed signs of falling into the pattern of the made men, his current inner circle, when he told the media that he blamed the president and Congress—anyone but the Secret Service itself—for the agency's problems. He told *USA Today* that "the president has a large family" and that the solution is for Congress to get rid of the pay caps on agents' salaries. But the problem was never the pay caps; the problem was having too few agents and the decades of the service's leaders prioritizing taking on new missions over preparing for future presidencies.

Understaffed agents have to work twice as hard. The solution is more difficult than obtaining more funds. It requires fixing all the long-standing ills pointed out by Congress, the DHS, and even former outspoken agents and officers. Seeing how Director Alles might turn toward the dark side by endorsing the pursuit of quick-fix solutions, many in the service believed he would be just another typical director.

Perhaps the best hope, just maybe, lies in the new, highly unorthodox president, the unafraid establishment bucker. If the mainstream media, a candidate as formidable as Hillary Clinton, and even insiders within his own party weren't a match for him, perhaps the Secret Service's made men won't be either.

One incident seemed to have especially pissed off President Trump. In March 2016, two Secret Service agents assigned to the youngest first grandson, who is only eight years old, abandoned their posts to take a selfie with the protectee while he was sleeping. The first grandson awoke and was startled to see the agents hovering over him. The Secret Service responded by investigating the agents, not for criminal wrongdoing but for possibly abandoning their posts.

President Trump made an announcement in October 2017 that he plans to allow the unsealing of the remaining files pertaining to President Kennedy's assassination, including the files of the CIA, which has continuously fought their release and had succeeded in persuading each previous president to keep them sealed.

It seems now that the "secret" will be let out of the bag. Maybe there's nothing in the old documents, but doing away with the secrets that have lent credence to conspiracies, doubts, and questions is an incredible gesture. As Secret Service reports have demonstrated, the service had even neglected to implement solutions recommended by the Warren Commission, and as a result, presidential protection has been jeopardized ever since. Perhaps it is foolish to be hopeful, but one thing is certain: the more transparent the story of the Kennedy assassination becomes, along with the details of the Secret Service's involvement, the better.

Whether they are mistakes of the past, such as losing President Kennedy, or mistakes of the present, such as not preparing properly to cover the Trump family, the Secret Service's problems need to be shared with the public. Like every other taxpayer-funded agency, it must be transparent to the American public. While some in Secret Service management might fear this, in truth it will only make the agency stronger. We can hope that President Trump and the Secret Service finally make the changes necessary to ensure a presidential protection that is "worthy of trust and confidence"—one that has strong morals and faith in its mission and whose agents and officers are well rested, well trained, and alert. We need the service to be as strong as it can possibly be—not just for the sake of current and future presidents but for our nation.

NINE.

MAKING THE SECRET SERVICE GREAT AGAIN

"Snowflakes."

The word evokes either snickers or defensive rebukes. It's an insult usually used to call out juvenile complainers who perceive slights and prejudices in the smallest of social interactions, often where there is none. Snowflakes believe their self-worth is contingent on how entitled they feel, rather than the services and value they create that they can exchange with other producers. Snowflakes are people who can't reconcile themselves to the real world, where risk and hard work equal reward.

Though millennials are often the objects of this insult, I find that it far more fitting for the old stalwarts within our government.

Ask yourself: When you listen to music, do you judge how "good" or "moving" a song is by how many hours the artist tells you he or she put into it? No, because that would be absurd.

When you shop for a car or refrigerator, do you consider how hard the company said it worked on the product? That would also be absurd. A consumer wants to know two things: What will the product achieve for me? and Is it within my budget?

If we don't accept this "snowflake mentality" anywhere else in our society, why should we accept it from a congressman, an agency director, a post-standing White House officer, or a Presidential Protection Division agent?

Snowflakes within the government, no matter what their political affiliation, cite how hard or how many hours they've worked. How many times have you heard "My office and I will work tirelessly"? It's the easily spotted trademark of political snowflakes. When someone questions their results and fulfilling the campaign promises they made, snowflakes take offense and talk about how hard they've worked.

But only one thing matters: results.

Before we get into exactly how the United States can achieve good results in the Secret Service's two core missions, we must first promise ourself that we will not accept the petty arguments of snowflakes; instead we will accept only what will achieve results and coldly cast out what is failing.

President Reagan said, "No government ever voluntarily reduces itself in size. Government programs, once launched, never disappear. Actually, a government bureau is the nearest thing to eternal life we'll ever see on this Earth!"

President Kennedy said, "There are risks and costs to action. But they are far less than the long-range risks of comfortable inaction." That same president also said, "Victory has a thousand fathers, but defeat is an orphan."

Coincidentally, both of those presidents were shot while under Secret Service protection. One survived.

If we take their wisdom to heart and apply it to what we know about the Secret Service's history, its present, and its near future, the guidelines for changing that future are apparent. The solutions will be uncomfortable; we must be willing to destroy what we have built and start fresh; and we must change our culture to embrace our defeats as much as our victories.

If we do the opposite and seek to achieve results by acting within the confines of what is convenient and comfortable for everyone at the table and are not willing to cast out what is broken, we will have to ask ourselves: Would we rather repeat the worst of our history or the best? All Americans who have achieved greatly had two things in common: they embraced the discomfort involved in taking risks, and they took decisive action.

Our political representatives should take government agencies down a peg—or down entirely—with the same fervor as they create and expand them.

Numerous presidents, from Presidents Reagan and Clinton to, most notably and recently, President Trump, have proudly proclaimed, "Let's make America great again!" President Trump also promised to "drain the swamp." He knows that when you drain the swamp, you're left with alligators. He promised that "America will start winning again, winning like never before." Where better to start than with the most failing, bloated, downtrodden, and critically important federal law enforcement agency?

The Secret Service will never fix itself. We cannot rely on the same people who are responsible for making the Secret Service fail to make it succeed. But right now and for the past few decades, that's exactly what we've been doing—and it needs to stop. After two decades of Congress asking politely that the Secret Service stop failing, it is clear that it needs to stop being polite and start demanding.

The Secret Service argues that it is unique and that its responsibility of executive protection is so important that Congress is playing chicken with catastrophe if it tries to make changes. Its leaders argue that only made men should be able to make changes to the service—*yet aren't they the people responsible for its downfall?*

This is especially ironic considering that Congress created the service and continually expands and funds it. Moreover, the Secret Service exists to protect the constitutional system, which includes a legislative branch, meaning that the legislature should and does have some say in managing the agency. Setting aside the political cynicism that Congress and the President have been bought by Secret Service lobbyists or that consensus can be garnered only via sudden tragedy, only Congress can save the two core missions of the Secret Service.

Before we can address solutions, we must first define the problems. These are the major ones:

- The Secret Service cannot be relied on to protect the president. Assassinations, near misses, and continued gross misconduct refute the claim that all of these are a series of isolated incidents.
- The Secret Service is antitransparency and anti–First

Amendment. This is unacceptable. We must recognize
that the only reasons we know the Secret Service is
failing is because of whistle-blowers, memoirs of former
employees, and dedicated journalists such as Carol
Leonnig and Susan Crabtree at newspapers such as the
Washington Post who refuse to be intimidated.

- The Secret Service is repeating the same mistakes that
  allowed for assassinations of the past, going back to
  President Lincoln and before.
- When internal or third parties review the Secret Service
  and make recommendations, those recommendations
  are ignored.
- The Secret Service has a long-standing culture issue
  that values pridefulness, arrogance, complacency,
  groupthink, and blind loyalty to the agency.
- The Secret Service culture has issues with numerous
  prejudices. Its most common is the rivalry between
  agents and officers, and between ranks, but the racism
  faced by Agent Abraham Bolden or the sexism faced
  by Sue Ann Baker is not isolated (as they revealed in
  their memoirs). Though the service has become much
  better in this area than it was several decades ago, we
  must also recognize that the politically correct solutions
  of forcing the agency to meet quotas and prioritize
  diversity of appearance have only made the "plantation
  mentality" worse. All of these prejudices serve a greater
  goal: to boil the frog so slowly that it doesn't realize it's
  being cooked. Today the prejudices are symptomatic
  of a much greater cultural issue. As long as agents
  and officers are forced to accept inhumane working

conditions and hours, agents and officers will treat each other with equal spite. The agency has prioritized chasing self-imposed diversity goals by prematurely hiring agents and officers without security clearances pending background investigations. Those agents and officers are routinely placed in areas such as the West Wing, where they routinely come in contact with top secret information.

From this day forward, there are only two ways this situation is going to go.

First, I offer you the risky and uncomfortable Plan A. Plan B, which seems far more convenient, can be implemented as early as tomorrow. If you are a political or Secret Service snowflake, brace yourself for Plan A.

Strategic Restructuring

These changes are for Congress and the president to institute by law, not recommendation.

The Secret Service should be split into two separate groups by mission. The Secret Service by name will no longer be "secret," since that has been part of the excuse for horrible abuses. Eliminating the "secret" culture is the only way to make clear that it is at an end and that the president's security, not the agency or its made men, is priority number one.

The two missions, protection and investigative, should be split entirely and made into two separate agencies. The protective side of the new agency would be given a new name. We'll call it the Executive Branch Protection Service (EBPS) for now, but

Congress and the president can rename it whatever they want. The goal should not be a "cool" name, just a simple name that is descriptive of what the agency is and does. "Secret Service" as a name no longer adequately describes what the agency does. It hasn't applied to the organization since Abraham Lincoln's and Andrew Johnson's presidencies, when the group was created to fight counterfeiting only. The EBPS would remain under the Department of Homeland Security to conduct presidential protection and protection of foreign dignitaries. Securing and protecting the public at major national events is a part of the DHS's mission, so it should be taken away from the Secret Service and delegated to the DHS entirely.

EBPS would establish new field offices in every major city for the sake of tracking down threateners and threats and aiding in advance protection work. But agents, whether they keep that name or not, will go back to the pre-1937 Secret Service mentality of "operatives," operating alone, in pairs, or in small groups, tracking down threateners and then, when necessary, calling upon local authorities for their assistance and muscle. But those offices should be small and contain no more than a handful of agents who work with local and nearby federal police forces.

The new EBPS force, being focused on protection only, should truncate its management extremely and completely ax superfluous branches, divisions, and offices that do nothing but take responsibility away from supervisors who should be holding their subordinates accountable. The agency does not need both an Office of Professional Responsibility and an Office of Integrity. The practice of dispatching bad agents to indefinite and fraudulent investigations that go on forever as a way to insulate them from punishment must be abolished. EBPS should have only three divisions: an Agent Division, a Uniformed Division, and a Technical Services Division—that's it.

Congress must mandate that all federal agencies post their agencywide hierarchy in a graphic representation based on manpower, rank, and mission and make it available to the public online. This visual representation must include every office, division, bureau, branch, committee, and team. Ideally, each hierarchy should appear in a pyramid shape that is widest at the bottom. Many agencies are bloated and top-heavy, and the graphic representation will reveal what agencies are the fattest, the most cantankerous, and the most structurally ineffective.

Ideally, agencies should be widest at the bottom, so there are enough officers and agents to do the job with rest and adequate training, and narrowest at the top, where there is one director and his deputies.

As for the investigative side of the Secret Service, that should be renamed the Treasury Investigative Service and be moved back where it belongs, within the Treasury Department. Financial crime in whatever form, whether it be electronic intrusions into banks or retirement frauds, identity theft, or counterfeiting of money, is the responsibility of the Treasury, not the DHS, the department designed to thwart terrorism. Financial crimes can be the result of terrorism, but they are always a Treasury matter. The old Secret Service field offices could be retained by the new Treasury agency.

Evolving Protection and the Agency That Fulfills It

The new era in presidential protection needs to foster a culture of selflessness, a military mentality in which everyone is trained to be replaceable so that if, for whatever reason, one person is out of action, another can seamlessly fill his or her place. It needs to be made clear that no one is above oversight, sickness, days off, etc. All agents and officers must have both primary and secondary capabilities, such as advanced medical or marksmanship capabilities. All agents and officers could serve twenty to twenty-five years and would then be required to retire. There would be no waivers, except in the most extreme of times. There would be no more "double dipping," whereby agents or officers retire from one agency and transition to another to restart the clock. Federal law enforcement must always be a young person's game whose leadership isn't afraid to mix it up and keep their teeth sharp on the front lines, so their agency can fulfill its mission. Part of a service member's later years of service need to be spent transitioning his or her knowledge, expertise, roles, and responsibilities to new recruits. Mandated turnover will help keep the agency's performance sharp and resolute.

That's why standards must become performance based— based purely on test scores in physical, tactical, aptitude, and other areas. Not only must every agent and officer meet the basic standards to maintain employment, but everyone's scores should be posted for the rest of the agency to see. PPD agents need to be chosen based on tryouts. Competition increases pride and camaraderie and grounds protectors in realism as opposed to arrogance. That practice would foster hard competition to be the best.

A performance-based scoring system for agents and officers would also force management to treat employees fairly based solely on how well they do their jobs. At present the Secret Service's leadership works its employees like machines, treats them as if they are inferior and with contempt, while simultaneously expecting them to be glad to be there and perform as it pushes them to fly closer to the sun.

The service still has trouble treating all its workers fairly. In 2017, it settled a racial discrimination lawsuit with a hundred agents for $24 million. The first female agents weren't given proper holsters, and decades later female agents have been eyed by opportunistic presidential staffers as the means of increasing a president's likability with female voters. Yet agencywide, the worst is how the service subjects its lowest-ranking employees to sensitivity training while flagrantly letting higher-up agents get away scot free with sexual abuse of their female subordinates. Performance-based scoring would also help with the service's greatest prejudice: the rift between UD and agents.

If and when an employee does not meet the minimum score requirements, there would be a probationary period, then penalties would be imposed, and if the employee does not improve, he or she would be fired. As long as firings get rid of nondedicated, unfit, or bad characters, they are good.

There would be no more supervisory positions for agents who have not served in the role they are supervising. This would be an easy way to push out the undesirables who have been moved to supervisory positions, a process in which corrupt agencies promote bad apples instead of firing them or referring them to the Department of Justice for criminal proceedings. Too much of the protection side's manpower is tied up in paper pushing and redundancy. That has to stop.

Fraternization rules need to be enforced. If two Secret Service members start dating, they must formally notify their supervisors. Dating of protectees, including presidential and facilities staffs, agents, and officers must also require notification of supervisors—so that the personnel can be removed from the detail. Adultery cannot be tolerated by the agency because it creates drama and poor morale, deteriorates integrity and trust, and creates an imbalance between the workforce and its performance.

Uniformed Division Solutions

To understand the heart of the issue that has led to the worst morale in the federal government today, you must understand the typical workday of a Secret Service Uniformed Division officer.

The typical day of a UD officer usually begins with a 1.5-hour commute to work, 30 minutes spent finding parking, an 8-hour shift *before* overtime, typically 4 hours of overtime, and then a 1.5-hour commute home, repeated six to seven days a week. That's 14- to 17-hour days, six to seven days a week, during which officers are expected to perform like athletes and think like lawyers and are treated with contempt by many on the street and many more within their own agency. On top of that are the real dangers of the job.

This is simply not a sustainable practice for most any human being.

Secret Service officers' salaries are between forty and eighty thousand dollars per year before overtime, for which there is no annual cap. The annual income before overtime is not enough to live within DC, so officers live in Maryland, Virginia, or even as far away as Gettysburg, Pennsylvania. For emergency response purposes they're supposed to live within less than a 25-mile radius away, but that ideal has long been swept aside. Officers are supposed to have eight hours from the time they turn the key on their home door to the time they leave their home to ensure that they're well rested, but that too has been thrown out the window. Numerous government agencies receive public transportation subsidies to incentivize the use of public transportation, but with officers living so far away and with their odd schedules, public transportation hasn't filled the gap. In all, officers at the White House are spending more time on the job than with their families.

Though some might argue that UD officers should "suck it up" because there are more demanding jobs that pay less, that is to completely miss the point. It is true that there are jobs in the military that pay less, where soldiers face far greater dangers and see their family far less—but military men and women have what Secret Service officers and agents don't: a sense of fulfillment. Secret Service officers and agents don't do the job for the money. Some exceptional officers work so much overtime that they make more than $230,000 a year—one officer interviewed made more than the head of DHS at $250,000—and they are still quitting. In 2017, pundits are predicting that if only Congress would stop being stingy, the Secret Service would no longer have a morale, mission, or hiring problem; they couldn't be more wrong, especially since UD officers, who have no pay caps, are leading the charge to leave. Secret Service officers and agents do the job because they believe in the service's mission, but as soon as they find out that their leadership doesn't believe in the mission themselves, they decide to make their money and quit. They transfer to an agency that gives them a sense of fulfillment: serving their country, maintaining their dignity, and giving them time to be part of their families' lives. When the sense of fulfillment is lost, officers and agents quit.

The question is: Who do you want protecting the president, someone who is well rested and balanced or someone who's exhausted and on the edge? Divorce, suicide, stress-related deaths such as falling asleep at the wheel, and heart attacks are rampant within USSS, as is being emotionally distraught.

In the late 1980s, an investigation began on the White House grounds when groundskeepers began to discover dead squirrels that had been mutilated. All manner of animals from hawks to foxes live in the White House grounds, but the mystery continued until the culprit was discovered to be a UD officer. To keep himself awake, he would use his security booth, his workplace home for eight to twelve hours a day, six to seven days a week, as a trap. He would set bait and one by one coax squirrels inside. Once they entered the booth, he would shut the door and crush them with the bottom of a fire extinguisher, then chuck the carcasses onto the lawn. Once his activities were discovered, he was fired.

After one officer had a "negligent discharge"—a term for firing one's weapon by mistake due to not paying the firearm the respect it deserves—a routine investigation ensued that was expected to result in a formal slap on the wrist. Upon inspection of the handgun the investigators discovered the primers on the back of the bullets to be slightly dimpled, the results of light strikes from the revolver's hammer. It turned out that the officer, exhausted and bored, had been practicing western-style tricks, cocking the hammer of his service pistol. As the habit became more outlandish he got quicker, and each time he would let the hammer down easy and repeat—until the hammer finally got away from his thumb fast enough to hit the primer hard enough and the gun went off. He, too, was let go.

But agents were no different. One agent, through a mix of stupidity, fatigue, and lack of training, duct taped the backstrap safety on his Uzi submachine gun. His excuse was that he felt it might slow him down if the president were attacked. With the backstrap safety, which served as a drop safety, permanently depressed, it dropped while the agent was inside a military transport plane and the Uzi emptied its entire magazine in the aircraft.

The driver on First Lady Clinton's detail, distracted by an argument with his wife, neglected to put his Uzi back in the limo after checking it. It fell into the street as the limo turned to enter the White House complex and was discovered by a very alarmed officer. Another agent had a negligent discharge with his 870 shotgun as he believed that keeping it in the Secret Service's "gunbox" condition (no round in the chamber, safety off) would slow him down, so he kept the safety off and a round in the chamber. One day, as he grabbed the shotgun, it discharged, putting a large hole in the ground around other people.

Training matters. Time off matters. Morale matters. Yet the Secret Service's leadership has a proven track record of neglecting those essentials and then keeping secret all incidents that occur as a result of neglect.

One officer revealed that each day there are typically thirty posts at the White House that are unfilled due to the manpower shortage. Those thirty shifts have to be covered by officers on overtime or by agents who are not trained to fill those jobs. In the 1990s, if there weren't at least two extra standbys, it was cause for serious concern and review. But the Secret Service, instead of making its desperation known and tackling the issue by calling for help, keeps its problems secret and, as a result, creates even more problems.

Even the most basic environment is often in disarray. The Secret Service locker room has continuously been held to be in substandard conditions. The service continually moves the locker room, as it has not found a suitable location in either the Old or the New Executive Office Building. In one area underneath the Old Executive Office Building, the hallway leading to the locker room had so much wiring and conduit added on haphazardly that the ceiling height was lower than six feet and jagged. Officers often cut their heads on the conduit wiring. A fire exit sign that hung at a level of only about five feet, six inches was a notorious culprit. Officers had to hunch over and walk close to one wall, where the ceiling height was manageable. It's almost unbelievable that basic OSHA and labor safety standards are not being met in the most important buildings in the nation. Another secret of the Secret Service.

Once in uniform and on duty, after a briefing, officers "push" the officers of the previous shift off so that they can go home or begin working another shift for overtime. That means that if an officer is late for whatever reason, the previous officer has to keep working. Overtime can be issued anytime by the assignments office, and stories abound of officers leaving the locker room and being called right back in for overtime, even on holiday weekends.

It is clear that the Secret Service does not value a balanced home life for its protectors, despite it being a key element in having focused, well-balanced agents and officers.

All this explains why the Secret Service, and most especially the Uniformed Division, is using the word "collapse" when talking about its workforce, its attrition, and its employees' readiness to do their job. This is dangerous and must be turned around, which makes bolstering the Uniformed Division a major focus of Secret Service reform.

- The UD's first priority is the White House's defense.
  As a temporary measure to ensure the White House's defense, the leaders of the protective mission need to put their egos aside and consider calling in military police forces until the long-standing White House defense problem is resolved by bringing Uniformed Division staffing numbers up to the level that they need to be to get the job done properly.
- All UD working areas must meet OSHA standards and labor law requirements.
- UD management must be split from special agents.
  Just as UD officers aren't allowed to work at Secret Service field offices, agents should not be supervising Uniformed Division units. UD should report to UD and agents to agents. The only exception should be during "integrated" temporary details and assignments such as dignitary protection and presidential travel and PPD.

- The management structure should be trimmed down.
  The presence of too many middle managers only
  complicates and bogs down the chain of command.
  For instance, the UD chief should report directly to the
  Secret Service director.

Morality and Cultural Issues in the Secret Service

Creating a culture in which workers are valued is essential in
any workplace, especially when those workers are tasked with a
serious national security mission. To combat the Secret Service's
cultural rot, a number of new policies should be implemented.

- Numerous law enforcement officers and agents have
  been killed or injured taking part in Secret Service/SSD
  operations from investigations to protections. Many of
  them died participating in security efforts that protected
  the president's life. At least six motorcycle officers
  have died while taking part in presidential motorcades.
  The Secret Service memorial needs to be expanded to
  include any officer who has died taking part in Secret
  Service operations, especially thanking and honoring
  officers who died while protecting the president. They
  deserve to be honored in equal part or on a separate
  list for their service and sacrifice to the mission of the
  Secret Service.
- For the sake of transparency and the future safety,
  morale, and security of the service's protectors and
  protectees, *all* suicides, including off duty, must be
  tracked and made public.

- For the same reason, *all* off-duty deaths related to fatigue and stress and other factors related to fulfilling the extremely demanding job need to be tracked and be made public.
- *All* officers, operatives, and agents who are seriously wounded "by an instrument of violence" in the line of duty or in the direct act of protection must be tracked and reported. Despite many of these operatives, officers, agents, and employees receiving commendations and medals for valor and sacrifice, the Secret Service has not made this proud part of its legacy known. My friend "Reverend" was injured in a motorcade while protecting the Clintons' reputations but was never honored because disclosing the details might have damaged the Secret Service "brand."
- The Secret Service must reinstate and restore the UD Benefit Fund in keeping with President Truman's wishes to honor and pay tribute to the officer who died to protect him, Leslie Coffelt. His story needs to be told and its value cherished.
- The Secret Service leadership expects its employees to treat the service as if it were their first family and their actual spouses and children as if they were a lesser second family. Law enforcement agencies should embrace the modern culture of respecting their workers' mental and emotional well-being, and the first step in that is to respect the "nuclear family" ideal. It's not about whether someone is gay or straight, married or single, etc.; it's about valuing an officer's, agent's, or other employee's right to have a family and a support

network. Every Secret Service family serves the mission in its own right, and that needs to be appreciated, not ignored. The mental, emotional, and physical well-being of employees would rise as a result.

- It should become standard practice for all agencies to create an intranet system whereby oversight can be conducted by frontline agents and officers, who can recommend cost-saving and efficiency solutions. This has become standard operating procedure in many private businesses, and it is only because of ego and incompetence that the Secret Service hasn't done so. It usually isn't a good idea to ask a government agency to "create" something new, but a system like this would cut through lots of waste and mismanagement almost immediately.

- Agents and officers should have to learn their agency's history. This is a seemingly simple idea, but as the old adage says, "Those who don't know history are doomed to repeat it." Officers need to learn about Officer Coffelt, just as agents need to read the memoirs of Urbanus Baughman and Mike Reilly.

Congressional Oversight

Congress needs to stop finding the fox in the henhouse and then putting the fox in charge of it.

Congress needs to establish a "carrot-and-stick" plan for agencies across the board to succeed and operate within their budgets and fulfill their goals. Agencies should feel as if they are competing with one another to meet the goals set for them by Congress. If they go over budget or don't meet the goals outlined by Congress, they should lose power and funding while successful agencies roll over their savings, increase their budget, and can take on new missions. If an agency is losing, it loses. If it's winning, it wins. It's that simple, yet the Secret Service has routinely been rewarded for losing catastrophically.

Each year, directors need to submit performance evaluations and budget reports, including expenditures, to Congress, just as civilians are expected to report and submit their taxes. Incentives and bonuses should be awarded by Congress for agencies that are overachieving, while for agencies that don't meet basic standards, Congress should freeze their budget, pay, and benefits, bar them from taking on new responsibilities and expanding, and force them to fix whatever problem exists. If an agency's director does not produce its financials in a suitable and legitimate manner, the director and others responsible within that organization should not be paid their salaries. This incentive/disincentive program should especially be applied to directors and anyone else in the Senior Executive Service (SES) pay scale. If they don't perform and achieve the goals and milestones they agreed to as part of their position, their retirement and pension would be at risk. If they achieve, they should be rewarded.

Congress shouldn't be afraid to legislate specific changes to agencies such as key leadership firings. This hammerlike tactic should be used especially against managers who seek to punish whistle-blowers who report to Congress and those who try to keep criminal personnel on indefinitely so they can retire with full benefits.

There should be no more "dog-and-pony shows." Members of Congress should exercise their ability to inspect government facilities and agencies without giving much advance notice. But taxpayer-funded sideshows serve no purpose. Each congressperson should make a habit of interviewing employees at random. That not hard. If anyone wants to find out more about the Secret Service, he or she need only walk over to the White House fence line and chat up an officer. They're so disgruntled that some will have no problems letting their feelings flow freely. Just as food health inspectors don't announce their arrival to restaurants in advance, Congress would learn more if its members made surprise checks. If members of Congress want to schedule their arrival, they should give several windows in the calendar during which they may or may not show up unannounced at Secret Service facilities and the training center to observe normal activities. They have every right to bear witness to everything the Secret Service does because that's what oversight is.

If need be, whistle-blower protection laws should be strengthened. Right now agencies, especially the Secret Service, are using illegal nondisclosure agreements regardless of legal limitations because they believe that Congress is helpless to stop them. The Secret Service is abusing whistle-blowers, applying a grossly disproportionate level of scrutiny and intimidation to whistle-blowers while simultaneously aiding and clearing agents who commit horrible crimes. Any agency that abuses whistle-blowers should be punished by Congress. If necessary, Congress should mandate the firing of any staffer found to be abusing his or her oversight position by mercilessly intimidating whistle-blowers or allowing criminals on the payroll to hang on in investigative limbo until they retire. Congress needs to allocate an emergency fund for whistle-blowers whom it believes have been wrongfully punished by their agency after speaking to Congress. Congress needs to have a backbone about this issue and stop leaving whistle-blowers high and dry when agencies retaliate against employees who report their concerns and abuses to Congress.

Here's how you stop the "old boys' club," deep state entrenchment, or agency made-men culture: make a law that caps all federal law enforcement tenure at twenty to twenty-five years with no exceptions. A military service member leaving the service and beginning a new life in federal law enforcement would not count, just as it would not count for someone to transfer the opposite way. No longer can we tolerate Secret Service employees infecting other agencies.

As mentioned earlier, "double dipping" between agencies should be prohibited. Staff of the Inspector General Office especially should not be "double dippers"; they should be more like the "Untouchables" of cinematic fame. If you want a fresh apple, pick it straight from the tree—straight from training— don't rehire old timers from the Secret Service, the most "secret" agency with the worst morale, mission performance, and accountability.

One of the biggest responsibilities for agents and officers, as for any leader, is ensuring that their knowledge and skills are adequately passed on to the next generation. There should be no more petty coveting of positions and setting one's successor up for failure. Federal law enforcement is a career, not a lifelong lifestyle or welfare system.

Just as the "Annual Best Places to Work Report" is an incredible indicator of the government's best and worst agencies, Congress needs to create a governmentwide public report that categorizes the goal fulfillment and success of federal agencies in terms of high, medium, low, and critical. That way Congress and the public would be able to recognize problem agencies as well as agencies that perhaps hold the key to the future. As the Secret Service is annually over budget, doesn't currently have the ability to evaluate its current spending, has the lowest morale, and is in the midst of an employee exodus, it would be listed as a "critical" poor performer.

In critical agencies, a director's pension and benefits, as well as those of assistant and deputy directors, should be performance based. Whenever a poorly performingr director testifies, he or she should no longer do so in a vacuum but should be accompanied by a devil's advocate, either a whistle-blower or part of an oversight group that can call out the malarkey that has risen to insulting, ludicrous levels.

A new law should require the agency in charge of presidential protection to report near misses to the president and Congress, just as hospitals have to report near misses to government watchdog groups. Congress needs to establish a law that anytime the Secret Service shuts down a metal detector at an event anytime other than at the end of the event, Congress needs to be notified.

Likewise, Congress must demand that it and the public be notified when the Department of Labor or the Office of Management and Budget makes exceptions for critical poor performers such as the Secret Service. The practice of skirting congressional mandates must end. Any waiver for a critically failing agency must be made public and reported to Congress.

Congress should make a law mandating that all federal agencies create and upload a hierarchy chart that includes every committee, council, board, branch, division, and other groups by similar name, organizing them by the rank of each supervisor's rank and government pay scale (GS 1 to 15 and SES 5 to -1). By their doing so, watchdog groups, Congress, and the public will be able to see their structures. While normal businesses have a pyramid-shaped hierarchy, with the CEO or director being the point at the top and the frontline employees being the widest portion at the bottom, much of our government agencies have turned into upside-down pyramids in which the management structure far exceeds the number and scope of the frontline agents and officers who actually implement the mission. Graphic representations will help clearly show the fat and bloat.

The Executive Branch and Presidents of the Future

While the presidential protectors are learning to live under new rules, there are a few similar rules that should be shared with anyone who might fall under their protection in the future. Think of it as a "never-do list" for protectees. Based on tried-and-failed attempts, it is a commonsense approach to staying alive.

- Never ride in an open convertible.
- There are to be no more unplanned "walk-offs," "rolling the dice" in unscreened crowds on a whim. This means never deviating from your planned walking route, even if it is to shake hands, see a nearby friend, or for any

other reason. Don't do it. It is impossible to guarantee your protection while you are in front of a crowd.

- Even with unannounced surprise visits to local businesses, the Secret Service will need a certain window of time to plan and place a security detail in advance. Crime happens everywhere. Just because a visit to a local establishment is unannounced doesn't mean you won't have the bad luck of crossing paths with a robber or violently mentally ill person. Oftentimes only half an hour is necessary, but the discipline to plan accordingly can be the difference between life and death—not just of the protectee but also of the protectors and the public.

- There is to be no more shutting down of metal detectors. If they are important enough to install, they are important enough to keep on. Eliminating the ability to turn them off when they are needed most will help eliminate the poor planning that creates the cocktail of failures that gets them turned off.

Protectees should also seek better communication and understanding with their protectors. This includes:

- The protectee should communicate a set routine or habits that are necessary for mental and emotional balance, such as jogging or visiting a friend, to the Secret Service so it can adequately adapt existing protective plans or create new ones. There are to be no more last-minute changes where a critical link is removed from the plan, throwings it in jeopardy.

- All staff members who work for the president must
  sign a contract with the Secret Service making them
  aware of what rules they are expected to follow and
  the consequences of not following them. This contract
  should be made public if need be.

Protection of Former Presidents

For the first year or two after leaving office, past presidents
should be given Secret Service protection; after that they should
be weaned off with a stipend for private security. It is true and
reasonable that when a president becomes a former president, he
or she may still be the focus of violently mentally ill, disgruntled
people or even something as extreme as state-sponsored plots.

Historically, such threats have existed, albeit they are
extremely rare. But former presidents are no longer within the
executive branch's chain of command. It is unwise to have a
highly inflexible government agency protect a former president
who is now free to do as he pleases. Real protection is comprehensive and depends on adhering to an agreement between protector and protectee. But the Secret Service–former president
relationship is not consensual, and as a result former presidents
and first ladies as well as their families are draining resources
while jeopardizing their own protection.

Having a private-sector company chosen by the protectee
ensures that the two will have an informed consensual relationship that will give the protectee the protection he or she wants
instead of the government wasting very limited resources on
a disproportionate and noncomprehensive protection plan.

There are countless former agents who would be willing to protect a former president and even far more private security firms that can provide the latest and greatest in security. The obvious benefit to protectees that they would be able to hire their ideal protection (or lack thereof) and sign private security companies to nondisclosure agreements that are not required to adhere to whistle-blower protections.

President Nixon rescinded his detail after a few years as he had been humbled by his resignation, yet Lady Bird Johnson maintained her detail for decades at taxpayers' expense despite no threats to her. It's simply outside the crumbling budget of finances and manpower for the current failing Secret Service—as well as a government that is over $20 trillion in debt and climbing—to maintain permanent protection for all former presidents and their family members.

Wasteful Pet Projects

There are plenty of "perks" that can be trimmed in order to conserve limited money and resources and foster greater discipline among presidential protectors, including:

- **Take-home cars in lieu of increased pay:** Letting anyone but agents doing active investigations take home government cars needs to stop. The purpose of a take-home car is so agents doing investigations are available 24/7. But for everyone else, it's a complete waste of taxpayer money. It's also a form of fraud since the Secret Service is gifting take-home cars to skirt pay caps and as incentives for a number of things it shouldn't.

Special agents in charge of field offices don't need take-home cars because they drive to and from the office. The practice is rampant within the Secret Service and Congress, and the public is none the wiser because on the surface it seems legitimate.

Evolving the Protection Strategy

Uniformed Division officers need to be integrated into PPD and PPD's inner circle. A uniformed presence serves as an increased arresting authority, intimidation, and distraction tool to thwart potential attackers. Uniformed Division officers have the ability to wear tactical gear and body armor over the uniform as part of the uniform to better protect the president. Without modern rifle–rate bullet-resistant vests, many modern bullets can't be expected to be stopped before hitting the protectee. Including Uniformed Division Officers in the diamond formation that closely surrounds the president as he moves would increase the effectiveness of the diamond formation's "bullet sponge" protection of the president by putting agents and officers in the direct line of fire of would-be attackers as a last-resort protective measure. It's just like the concentric circles they do at the White House.

If all of this sounds too painful and complicated, too different from the "way we've always done it," there is always Plan B. Plan B is far more simple and convenient:

First, do nothing. Second, act as though changes are being made when the results amount to the same tired repeat of history. Put on a "big show," another shake-up, another round of talk about convenient solutions. All the while, the renowned and beloved Secret Service slowly collapses and rots from the inside out, in front of the world.

And another president will die. The tragedy of assassination *will* come to our modern era. After that, solutions may finally come, but it would be beyond insane and foolish to think that *this* time a solution will present itself and our presidents will be safe, feel safe, and trust that their protectors will do their job so that they can confidently do the bidding of the people who put them into office.

The truth is that short of swift, dramatic, seemingly scorched-earth changes, another president will fall. It is up to the American people to see whether we can create solutions to problems before they happen or we have lost our way so much that we have to wait until tragedy strikes and lives are lost to do the right thing.

We'll have to see, but now is not a time for waiting.

ENDNOTES.

Introduction

1. Chaffetz, Jason E., and Elijah E. Cummings. "House Committee on Oversight and Government Reform Report U.S. Secret Service: An Agency in Crisis." Committee on Oversight and Government Reform, December 9, 2015.

2. Partnership For Public Service. "Overall Rankings." Best Places to Work in the Federal Government, 2016.

1. Clinton Characters

1. Aldrich, Gary. *Unlimited Access: An FBI Agent Inside the Clinton White House.* Regnery Publishing, 1998.

2. Lardner, George, Jr., and Susan Schmidt. "Livingstone Resigns, Denying Ill Intent." *The Washington Post*, June 27, 1996.

3. Fatzick, Josh. "Q&A with Dan Emmett, Former Secret Service Agent, Author of 'Within Arm's Length'." *The Hill*, March 26, 2012.

4. Byrne, Gary J., and Grant M. Schmidt. *Crisis of Character: A White House Secret Service Officer Discloses His Firsthand Experience with Hillary, Bill, and How They Operate.* New York: Center Street, 2017.

5. Friedman, Thomas L. "Haircut Grounded Clinton While the Price Took Off." *The New York Times*, May 21, 1993.

2. Kenneth Starr Targets The Secret Service

1. Office of Independent Counsel. "The Starr Report on the Death of Vincent Foster." Failure of the Public Trust, FBIcover-up.com, October 10, 1997.

2. *Memorandum from J.C. Frier to Mr. Potts*, 3 (1993) (testimony of Unsub: Vincent W. Foster, Jr., Deputy White House to the President - Victim: 7/20/1993; PPSAKA - Staff Member, Obstruction of Justice (OOJ); Preliminary Inquiry; OO: WMFO).

3. Novak, Robert D. "Government Lawyers, Private Matters." *The Washington Post*, December 21, 1995.

4. Fritz, Sara. "Search of Foster's Office Is Revealed : Whitewater: White House Aide Tells Senate Panel She Sought Suicide Note After Deputy Counsel's Death. She Denies Interfering with Probe." *Los Angeles Times*, July 26, 1995.

5. Post, Washington. "1996 Fund-Raising Scandals Bring Stiff Penalty." *LA Times*, September 21, 2002.

6. Journalists, Staff Investigative. "Chinese Got Long Beach Deal." *The Daily Republican*. March 7, 1997.

7. Drudge, Matt, and Michael Isikoff. "NEWS KILLS STORY ON WHITE HOUSE INTERN, BLOCKBUSTER REPORT: 23-YEAR OLD, FORMER WHITE HOUSE INTERN, SEX RELATIONSHIP WITH PRESIDENT." *The Drudge Report*, January 17, 1998.

8. Gormley, Ken. *The death of American virtue: Clinton vs. Starr*. Broadway Books, 2011.

9. Broder, John M., and Stephen Labaton. "Shaped by a Painful Past, Secret Service Director Fights Required Testimony." *The New York Times*, May 30, 1998.

10. Byrne, Gary J., and Grant M. Schmidt. *Crisis of Character: A White House Secret Service Officer Discloses His Firsthand Experience with Hillary, Bill, and How They Operate*. New York: Center Street, 2017.

11. Court, U.S. District. "Secret Service Grand Jury Testimony, Jun 25 1998 | Video." C-SPAN.org. June 25, 1998. https://www.c-span.org/video/?117044-1%2Fsecret-service-grand-jury-testimony.

12. Broder, John M. "Secret Service Officer Worried About Lewinsky." *The New York Times*, April 24, 1998.

13. King CNN, John. "Sources: Complaints By Secret Service Agent Resulted In Lewinsky Transfer." CNN. April 24, 1998.

14. "Secret Service Secrets: Are They Worth Telling? Judges Rule: Testimony from Agents is Required, No Matter the Merit of the Case in Question." *The Baltimore Sun,* July 9, 1998.

15. Staff CBSNews.com. "Rehnquist: Agents Must Testify." CBS News, July 16, 1998.

3. First Successes, First Failures

1. Shattuck, Gary. "Plotting the 'Sacricide' of George Washington." *Journal of the American Revolution*, July 25, 2014.

2. "1778 Ipswich Journal Newspaper Archive." 1778-1779 Ipswich Journal FDLHS newspaper archive.

3. BAKER, WILLIAM S. ITINERARY OF GENERAL WASHINGTON: from June 15, to December 23, 1783 (classic reprint). Philadelphia, PA: J.B. Lippincott Company, 1892

4. "Guarding the White House." White House Historical Association.

5. "Saving History, Dolley Madison, The White House & The War of 1812." White House Historical Association.

6. Fleming, Thomas. "When Dolley Madison Took Command of the White House." Smithsonian.com, March 1, 2010.

7. Jennings, Paul. A Colored Man's Reminiscences of James Madison. Brooklyn, NY, 1865.

8. Dept. of the Treasury United States Secret Service. Service Star, 1995.

9. Dept. of the Treasury United States Secret Service. Service Star, 1996.

10. Dept. of the Treasury United States Secret Service. Service Star, 2000

11. McBride, Robert W. Lincoln's Bodyguard, The Union Light Guard of Ohio. 1st

12. Norton, Roger J. "The Shot Through Abraham Lincoln's Hat." The Shot Through Abraham Lincoln's Hat. http://rogerjnorton.com/Lincoln86.html.

13. Klein, Christopher. "Lincoln's Battlefield Brush With Death, 150 Years Ago." History.com.

14. Boyes, Christina. "5 Failed Assassination Attempts on President Lincoln You Didn't Know About." *Travel Thru History*, February 27, 2015

15. Fishel, Edwin C. *The Secret War for the Union: The Untold Story of Military Intelligence in the Civil War.* Boston: Houghton Mifflin Co., 1996.

16. "History." Pinkerton, June 29, 2016.

17. Quarles, Benjamin, and William S. McFeely. *The Negro in the Civil War.* New York: Da Capo Press, 1989.

18. History.com Staff. "February 23, 1861: Lincoln Avoids Assassination Attempt." History.com, February 23, 2009.

19. Taylor, John. *William Henry Seward: Lincoln's Right Hand.* Harper Collins, 1991.

20. Mogelever, Jacob. *Death to Traitors: The Story of General Lafayette C. Baker, Lincoln's Forgotten Secret Service Chief.* Doubleday, 1960. Davis, Curtis Carroll.

21. "The Craftiest of Men: William P. Wood and the Establishment of the United States Secret Service." *Maryland Historical Magazine*, 1988, 111-26.

22. Tarnoff, Ben. "A Counterfeiting Conspiracy?" *The New York Times*, March 27, 2012.

23. "Brockway's Career of Crime." *The Brooklyn Daily Eagle* (Brooklyn, New York), February 16, 1896. Newspapers.com.

24. Loy, Lawrence. *The White House Beat: The United States Secret Service, Uniformed Division Commemorates 75 Years of Presidential Protection.* Washington, DC: U.S. Secret Service, Uniformed Division Benefit Fund, 1998.

25. Starling, Edmund W. *Starling of the White House: The Story of the Man Whose Secret Service Detail Guarded Five Presidents from Woodrow Wilson to Franklin D. Roosevelt, as Told to Thomas Sugrue.* Chicago: Peoples Book Club, 1946.

26. Reilly, Michael. *Reilly of the White House.* New York, New York: Simon & Schuster, 1947.

27. Coop, Austin. "Did FDR and Al Capone share the same armored Cadillac?" *Roadtrippers.* November 04, 2014. https://roadtrippers.com/stories/al-capone-car.

28. Baughman, Urbanus Edmund. *Secret Service chief.* 1st ed. Harper, 1962.

29. Smith, Merriman. *President's Odyssey.* 1st ed. Greenwood Pub Group, 1975.

4. Bullets from Dallas to Washington

1. Tzu, Sun. *The Art of War.* Translated by Thomas Cleary. Boston, MA: Shambhala Publications, Inc, 2003.

2. Ayton, Mel. *Hunting the President: Threats, Plots and Assassination Attempts From FDR to Obama.* Regnery History, 2014.

3. Channel, Smithsonian. "Kennedy's Suicide Bomber." Smithsonian Channel. 2013.

4. Baughman, Urbanus Edmund. *Secret Service chief.* 1st ed. Harper, 1962.

5. Wilson, Chief Frank J., and Beth Day Wilson. Special Agent: 25 Years with the American Secret Service. 1st ed. London, England: Frederick Muller Ltd, 1966.

6. Delich, Helen. "The Shadow Man." *The Baltimore Sun* (Baltimore), March 30, 1947.

7. Hersh, Seymour M. The dark side of Camelot. Boston, MA: Back Bay Books, 1997.

8. Parr, Jerry. In the Secret Service: the true story of the man who saved President Reagan's life. Carol Stream, IL: Tyndale House Publishers, Inc., 2013.

9. Salinger, Pierre. *P. S.: a memoir.* 1st ed. New York City, NY: St Martins Press, 1995.

10. Kessler, Ronald. *In the President's Secret Service: Behind the Scenes with Agents in the Line of Fire and the Presidents They Protect.* New York City, NY: Crown Forum, 2009.

11. Bolden, Abraham. *The Echo from Dealey Plaza: The True Story of the First African American on the White House Secret Service Detail and His Quest for Justice After the Assassination of JFK.* New York: Three Rivers Press, 2008.

12. Reilly, Michael. *Reilly of the White House.* New York, New York: Simon & Schuster, 1947.

13. Venker, Marty, and George Rush. *Confessions of an Ex-Secret Service Agent.* New York: D.I. Fine, 1988.

14. Palamara, Vince. *The Not-So-Secret Service: Agency Tales from FDR to the Kennedy Assassination to the Reagan Era.* Walterville, OR: Trine Day LLC, 2017.

15. "A Chronicle of Carriages." Secretservice.gov. https://www.secretservice.gov/about/history/motorcade-basic/.

16. Youngblood, Rufus W. *20 Years in the Secret Service; My Life with Five Presidents.* New York: Simon & Schuster, 1974.

17. Warren Commission. *Report of the Warren Commission on the Assassination of President Kennedy.* McGraw-Hill, 1964.

18. Haggin, Joseph, Thomas Perrelli, Danielle Gray, and Mark Filip. "United States Secret Service Protective Mission Panel (USSSPMP)." Department of Homeland Security, December 15, 14.

19. Loy, Lawrence. *The White House Beat: The United States Secret Service, Uniformed Division Commemorates 75 Years of Presidential Protection.* Washington, DC: U.S. Secret Service, Uniformed Division Benefit Fund, 1998.

20. Meyer, Lawrence. "President Taped Talks, Phone Calls; Lawyer Ties Ehrlichman to Payments Principal Offices Secretly Bugged Since Spring 1971." *The Washington Post.* July 17, 1973.

5. Transition and Tragedy

1. Gormley, Ken. *The death of American virtue: Clinton vs. Starr.* Broadway Books, 2011.

2. U.S. Secret Service. *James J. Rowley Training Center Master Plan Environmental Assessment Laurel, Maryland.* By AECOM, August 2012.

3. Service, Secret. "United States Secret Service Budget 1975-2002." DOJ: JMD: BS: Budget Trend Data, United States Secret Service. https://www.justice.gov/archive/jmd/1975_2002/2002/html/page133-135.htm.

4. Emmett, Dan. *Within Arm's Length: A Secret Service Agent's Definitive Inside Account of Protecting the President.* New York, NY: St. Martin's Press, 2014.

5. U.S. Secret Service. *Making Schools Safer,* May 2013.

6. U.S. Secret Service. Dept. of Education. The final report and findings of the safe school initiative: Implications for the prevention of school attacks in the United States. Washington D.C., July 2004.

7. Dept. of the Treasury United States Secret Service. *Service Star,* 1995.

8. Dept. of the Treasury United States Secret Service. *Service Star,* 1996.

9. Dept. of the Treasury United States Secret Service. *Service Star,* 2000.

10. Congressional Research Service. *National Special Security Events: Fact Sheet.* by Shawn Reese, January 25, 2017.

11. USA. U.S. Congress. Government Publishing Office. Presidential Travel. by Larry Craig. No. 137 ed. Vol. 144. 105th Congress, 2nd Session. DC, DC: Congressional Record, 1998.

12. Bohn, Kevin. "Clinton Walks in Moroccan Funeral Procession, Meets Other World Leaders." Cable News Network, July 26, 1999.

13. Freeze, Christopher. "The Time a Stolen Helicopter Landed on the White House Lawn." *Air & Space Magazine,* April 2017.

14. United States General Accounting Office. *The White House: Allegations of Damage During the 2001 Presidential Transition,* 2002.

15. History.com Staff. "9/11 Timeline." History.com, 2011.

16. "The Dangerously Delayed Reactions of the Secret Service on 9/11." Shoestring 9/11, October 2, 2013.

17. Keefe, Mark. "A Tribute to a Quiet Hero." *American Rifleman*, September 11, 2014.

18. Miller, Brian. "ECHOES OF 9/11: Secret Service Agent Craig Miller." *The Enterprise*, September 4, 2011.

19. "September 11th Terror Attacks Fast Facts." CNN, August 24, 2017.

20. Kessler, Ronald. *The Terrorist Watch: Inside the Desperate Race to Stop the Next Attack*. Crown Forum, 2007.

6. Shaky Wartime Footing

1. Graff, Garrett., Jack Shafer, Jeff Greenfield, and Anna O. Law. " 'We're the Only Plane in the Sky'." *POLITICO Magazine*, September 9, 2016.

2. Cenciotti, David. "Air Force One Journey on September 11: No Escort During the Attacks, 11 Fighters When the Airspace was Completely Free of Airliners." *The Aviationist,* September 9, 2011.

3. Ungerleider, Neal. "There Are Secret Blimps Protecting Washington, D.C." *Fast Company*, December 23, 2014.

4. Meeks, Brock N. "Head of Federal Air Marshal Service Resigns." NBCNews.com, January 6, 2006.

5. "Thread: Air Marshals Complain of Secret Service Cronyism." LEO Affairs Forums RSS. August 25, 2006.

6. Anonymous Federal Air Marshal (For Fear of Reprisal). "Air Marshals and The Secret Service Factor By An Anonymous Federal Air Marshal." Scribd. 2006. https://www.scribd.com/document/122150590/Air-Marshals-and-The-Secret-Service-Factor-By-An-Anonymous-Federal-Air-Marshal

7. Becker, Andrew. "Air Marshals Say a Party-Hearty Attitude Prevails at the Agency." *Reveal.* August 3, 2017.

8. Associated Press. "Retired Secret Service Agents Use Loop Hole to 'Double Dip'." *North Hills News Record*, June 20, 1998.

7. Losing Control

1. Johnson, Kevin. "Secret Service: Trump Faces Same Number of Threats as Obama." *USA Today*, June 2, 2017.

2. Haggin, Joseph, Thomas Perrelli, Danielle Gray, and Mark Filip. "United States Secret Service Protective Mission Panel (USSSPMP)." Department of Homeland Security, December 15, 14.

3. Chaffetz, Jason E., and Elijah E. Cummings. "House Committee on Oversight and Government Reform Report U.S. Secret Service: An Agency in Crisis." Committee on Oversight and Government Reform, December 9, 2015.

4. Kessler, Ronald. *In the President's Secret Service: Behind the Scenes with Agents in the Line of Fire and the Presidents They Protect.* New York City, NY: Crown Forum, 2009.

5. Shamma, Tasnim. "'In the President's Secret Service: Behind the Scenes With Agents in the Line of Fire and the Presidents They Protect'." *Newsweek.* August 04, 2010.

6. Amy Argetsinger, and Roxanne Roberts. "Reliable Source: Tareq and Michaele Salahi crash Obamas' state dinner for India." *The Washington Post.* November 26, 2009.

7. Thomas, Pierre, and Sarah Netter. "Alleged White House Crasher Carlos Allen: 'I Got an Actual Invite in the Mail'." *ABC News.* January 11, 2010.

8. Leonnig, Carol D. "Secret Service agents pulled off White House patrol to help protect a top official's aide." *The Washington Post.* May 10, 2014.

9. Ragavan, Chitra, and Christopher H. Schmitt. "The Secrets of the Secret Service." *U.S. News & World Report,* June 11, 2002.

10. Martin, Adam. "How to Party Like a Secret Service Agent in Cartagena." *Yahoo! News.* May 23, 2012.

11. Wyler, Grace. "Here are the wild details from the secret services prostitution scandal" *Business Insider.* April 14, 2012.

12. Leonning, Carol, and David Nakamura. "Secret Service scandal: Colombian woman describes night of carousing with agents" *The Washington Post.* May 4, 2012.

13. Nakamura, David, and Joe Davidson. "U.S. Secret Service Agents Recalled from Colombia." *The Washington Post,* April 13, 2012.

14. Leonnig, Carol D., and David Nakamura. "Aides Knew of Possible White House Link to Cartagena, Colombia, Prostitution Scandal." *The Washington Post,* October 8, 2014.

15. Reporter, Daily Mail. "'Check this out . . . you're fired!': Sarah Palin hits back at the disgraced Secret Service agent who joked about her on Facebook." *Daily Mail Online.* April 20, 2012.

16. Martin, Adam. "Fired Secret Service Agents Will Not Go Quietly." *The Atlantic,* May 23, 2012.

17. Leonnig, Carol D., and David Nakamura. "Secret Service Sex Scandal: Several Say They Didn't Break the Rules." *The Washington Post,* May 22, 2012.

18. Nakamura, David, and Ed O'Keefe. "Secret Service Imposes New Rules on Agents for Foreign Trips." *The Washington Post,* April 27, 2012.

19. Kessler, Ronald. "Secret Service Agents Are Not Polygraphed." Newsmax, May 7, 2012.

20. Schmidt, Michael S. "Investigator in Secret Service Prostitution Scandal Resigns." *The New York Times*, October 28, 2014.

21. Tucker, Eric. "Prostitution Scandal Highlights Lack of Women in Secret Service." *The Newark Advocate*, April 29, 2012.

22. McVeigh, Karen. "Julia Pierson: Pioneer Out to Restore Secret Service's Tarnished Reputation." *The Guardian*, March 28, 2013.

23. "Statement of Julia A. Pierson Director, United States Secret Service Department of Homeland Security. Before the Committee on Oversight and Government Reform United States House of Representatives." Committee on Oversight and Government Reform. September 30, 2014.

24. Dept. of Homeland Security. Office of Inspector General. *2014 White House Fence Jumping Incident*, 2014.

25. Kessler, Ronald. "Something Is Rotten in the Secret Service." *POLITICO Magazine*, September 30, 2014.

26. Lowery, Wesley, and Carol D. Leonnig. "Secret Service Director Pledges Full Security Review After White House Breach." *The Washington Post*, September 30, 2014.

27. Kessler, Ronald. "White House Security Breach: The Secret Service Thinks We Are Fools." *Time*, September 23, 2014.

28. "Oversight Hearing White House Security, Sep 30 2014 | Video." C-SPAN.org. September 30, 2014. Accessed November 04, 2017.

29. "Secret Service Seeks $8 Million to Build Fake White House for Training." *Fox News*, March 18, 2015.

30. Crabtree, Susan. "Trade Group Slams Chaffetz as Secret Service Subpoena Showdown Intensifies." *Washington Examiner*, April 1, 2015.

31. Rein, Lisa. "41 Secret Service Agents Disciplined After Leaking GOP Congressman's Personnel File." *The Washington Post*, May 27, 2016.

32. "DHS Inspector Confirms Secret Service Director's Changing Story." *CBS News*, October 23, 2015.

8. The Secret Service Swamp

1. Bazinet, Kenneth, Alison Gendar, and Christina Boyle. "Feds knew flyover might spark panic - but didn't care." NY Daily News. April 29, 2009.

2. Leonnig, Carol D., and David Nakamura. "Aides knew of possible White House link to Cartagena, Colombia, prostitution scandal." *The Washington Post*. October 08, 2014.

3. Cheney, Dick. "Dick Cheney reflects on the difficult decisions of 9/11." NBCNews.com. March 27, 2013.

4. Parr, Jerry. *In the Secret Service: the true story of the man who saved President Reagan's life.* Carol Stream, IL: Tyndale House Publishers, Inc., 2013.

5. Takala, Rudy. "Hacked: Clinton's newest email address revealed." *Washington Examiner.* October 06, 2016.

6. Bier, Jeryl. "Clinton aide asked secret service agent to assist with securing Hillary email server." *Weekly Standard.* November 01, 2016.

7. Fandos, Nicholas. "Secret Service Post Moves From Trump Tower to a Trailer." *The New York Times.* August 03, 2017.

8. Chaffetz, Jason E., and Elijah E. Cummings. "House Committee on Oversight and Government Reform Report U.S. Secret Service: An Agency in Crisis." Committee on Oversight and Government Reform. December 9, 2015.

9. McVeigh, Karen. "Julia Pierson: pioneer out to restore secret services tarnished reputation." *The Guardian.* March 28, 2013.

10. Crabtree, Susan. "Secret Service Offered to 'Fast-Track' Disability Retirement for Able-Bodied Workers, Several DHS Sources Say." Washington Free Beacon. September 08, 2017.

11. Hodge, Mark. "Female Secret Service agent reveals she wouldn't risk her life to protect Donald Trump." *The Sun.* January 25, 2017.

12. Bongino, Dan. *Life inside the bubble: why a top-ranked secret service agent walked away from it all.* Washington, D.C.: WND Books, 2013.

13. Venker, Marty, and George Rush. *Confessions of an ex-Secret Service agent.* New York: D.I. Fine, 1988.

14. Byrne, Gary J., and Grant M. Schmidt. *Crisis of character: a White House Secret Service officer discloses his firsthand experience with Hillary, Bill, and how they operate.* New York: Center Street, 2017.

15. Crabtree, Susan. "Secret Service removes agent who didn't want to take 'a bullet' for Trump." *Washington Examiner.* March 19, 2017.

16. Partnership For Public Service. "Overall Rankings." Best Places to Work in the Federal Government. 2016.

17. "Entertainers who have joked about harming Trump." *Fox News.* June 23, 2017.

18. Bowers, Becky. "In Context: Ted Nugent saying if Obama wins, 'I will either be dead or in jail'." PolitiFact. April 19, 2012.

19. "Kathy Griffin's Trump Beheading Photo Fetches Huge Price." TMZ. September 14, 2017.

20. Concha, Joe. "Former Mueller deputy on Trump: 'Government is going to kill this guy'." *The Hill.* August 11, 2017.

21. Bobic, Igor. "'Trump Is Treason!': Protester Throws Russian Flags At President." *The Huffington Post*. October 24, 2017.

22. Kutner, Max. "Alexandria shooting: Did anti-Trump rhetoric inspire James Hodgkinson?" *Newsweek*. June 14, 2017.

23. "Who we are." American Bridge PAC. https://americanbridgepac.org/about/

24. Lorber, Janie. "American Bridge 21st Century Super PAC Is Hub of Left." *Roll Call*. February 12, 2012.

25. Piaker, Zachary. "American Bridge 21st Century." FactCheck.org. June 27, 2014.

26. Estepa, Jessica. "Secret Service spends $13,500 on golf cart rentals for President Trump's Bedminster trip." *USA Today*. August 08, 2017.

27. Rein, Lisa. "Secret Service says it will run out of money to protect Trump and his family Sept. 30." *Washington Post*, August 21, 2017.

28. Alesci, Cristina, and Curt Devine. "Secret Service paid Mar-a-Lago at least $63,000, documents show." *CNN Money*. October 12, 2017.

29. Estepa, Jessica. "Secret Service spent $7,100 renting luxury portable toilets for Trump's Bedminster trip." *USA Today*. August 25, 2017.

30. Johnson, Kevin. "Exclusive: Secret Service depletes funds to pay agents because of Trump's frequent travel, large family." *USA Today*. August 22, 2017.

31. Maté, Aaron. "Russiagate Is More Fiction Than Fact." *The Nation*. October 06, 2017.

32. Sperry, Paul. "Sketchy firm behind Trump dossier is stalling investigators." *New York Post*. June 26, 2017.

33. Borger, Julian. "Louise Mensch: the former British MP who scooped US media on Trump's Russian ties." *The Guardian*. February 17, 2017.

34. Dinan, Stephen. "San Juan mayor accuses Trump of 'genocide' after hurricane." *The Washington Times*. October 12, 2017.

35. "North Carolina councilwoman compares Trump to Hitler." WTVD-TV. October 23, 2017.

36. Johnson, Kevin. "Secret Service: Trump faces same number of threats as Obama." *USA Today*. June 02, 2017.

37. "Several threats made against Trump per day: Secret Service director." *CBS News*. June 01, 2017.

38. Haggin, Joseph, Thomas Perrelli, Danielle Gray, and Mark Filip. "United States Secret Service Protective Mission Panel (USSSPMP)." Department of Homeland Security. December 15, 14.

39. Westwood, Sarah. "Trump announces new Secret Service director." *Washington Examiner*. April 25, 2017.

40. Ali, Yashar. "Secret Service agents under investigation for taking photos of Donald Trump's sleeping grandson." *Mother Jones.* June 23, 2017

9. Make The Secret Service Great Again

1. Trump, Donald. *Great again: how to fix our crippled America.* New York: Threshold Editions, 2016.

2. Bolden, Abraham. *The echo from Dealey Plaza: the true story of the first African American on the White House Secret Service detail and his quest for justice after the assassination of JFK.* New York: Three Rivers Press, 2008.

3. "Former agent reveals who 'ruined' the Secret Service." *WND.* September 10, 2017.

4. Baker, Sue Ann. *Behind the shades: a female secret service agents true story.* Roseburg, OR: WWP Publishing, 2015.

5. Bongino, Dan. *Protecting the president: an insiders account of the troubled Secret Service in an era of evolving threats.* Washington, DC: WND Books, 2017.

6. Goldstein, Bonnie. "Racist Secret Service E-Mails." *Slate* Magazine. May 12, 2008.

7. Johnston, David. "E-Mail Shows Racial Jokes by Secret Service Supervisors." *The New York Times.* May 09, 2008.

8. Chaffetz, Jason E., and Elijah E. Cummings. "House Committee on Oversight and Government Reform Report U.S. Secret Service: An Agency in Crisis." Committee on Oversight and Government Reform. December 9, 2015.

9. Rein, Lisa. "Secret Service says it will run out of money to protect Trump and his family Sept. 30." *Washington Post,* August 21, 2017.

10. Kurson, Ken. "Former Agent: The Secret Service Is In Collapse." *Observer.* October 12, 2014.

11. Emmett, Dan. "Alcohol isn't the Secret Service's problem. Lousy leadership is." *The Washington Post.* March 28, 2

12. Sun, Chhun, and Seth Bodine. "Colorado Springs motorcycle officer injured in crash while escorting VP Mike Pence's motorcade." Colorado Springs Gazette. June 24, 2017.

13. Partnership For Public Service. "Overall Rankings." Best Places to Work in the Federal Government. 2016.

14. Written testimony of USSS Director Randolph Alles for a House Committee on Homeland Security, Subcommittee on Transportation and Protective Security hearing titled "How Can the United States Secret Service Evolve to Meet the Challenges Ahead?" Department of Homeland Security. June 8, 2017.

ACKNOWLEDGMENTS.

I will repeat what I said in *Crisis of Character*: "'All gave some, but some gave all.' This book would not be possible without others whose memory and example of heroism and sacrifice to country continues to inspire."

A special thank-you to my cowriter, Grant Schmidt of Flim Films LLC, and to Remi Frieze, Grant's fiancée, for keeping us on track with the very tight deadline on such a timely book. Thank you to the writing team and our agents, without whom this book would not have been possible.

Of course, this book also felt so necessary for all the former colleagues who thanked me for writing *Crisis of Character* and whispering to me "Damn, Gary, I forgot all about those times! It's as if I blocked them out." I felt that if I didn't write this book, all our history, the good and the bad, would be blocked out and then doomed to repeat itself.

Thank you to our agent, Javelin Group, and our publisher, Center Street, for taking on yet another difficult project and for believing in free speech, not just through your words, but your actions, in allowing others to speak their truth. It is a value we need more and more each day.

ABOUT THE AUTHORS.

GARY J. BYRNE served in federal law enforcement for nearly thirty years in the US Air Force Security Police, in the uniformed division of the Secret Service, and most recently as a federal air marshal.

In his first book, the *New York Times* best-selling *Crisis of Character*, he shared his experiences as the first Secret Service employee compelled to testify in a criminal case against a sitting US president.

GRANT M. SCHMIDT, a Temple University graduate, is an entrepreneur and writer in the Philadelphia area.